JULIAN BARNES

Letters from London

Julian Barnes was born in Leicester, England, in 1946, was educated at Oxford University, and now lives in London. He is the author of seven novels—*Metroland, Before She Met Me, Flaubert's Parrot, Staring at the Sun, A History of the World in 10½ Chapters, Talking It Over,* and *The Porcupine.*

INTERNATIONAL

JULIAN BARNES

Letters
from
London

VINTAGE **I**NTERNATIONAL

Vintage Books

A Division of Random House, Inc. ■ New York

A Vintage International Original, July 1995
FIRST EDITION

Grateful acknowledgment is made to the following for permission
to reprint previously published material:
EMI Music Publishing: Excerpt from "Taxman," words and music by George Harrison,
copyright © 1966 by Northern Songs. All rights controlled and administered by EMI
Blackwood Music Inc., under license from ATV Music (BMI). All rights reserved.
International copyright secured. Reprinted by permission of EMI Music Publishing.
Farrar, Straus & Giroux, Inc.: Excerpt from "Bridge for the Living" from *Collected Poems*
by Philip Larkin, copyright © 1988, 1989 by the Estate of Philip Larkin; excerpts from
Mrs. Thatcher's Minister by Alan Clark, copyright © 1993 by Alan Clark. Reprinted by
permission of Farrar, Straus & Giroux, Inc. *HarperCollins Publishers:* Selected excerpts
from *The Downing Street Years* by Margaret Thatcher. Copyright © 1993 by Margaret
Thatcher. Reprinted by permission of HarperCollins Publishers, Inc.

Library of Congress Cataloging-in-Publication Data
Barnes, Julian.
Letters from London / by Julian Barnes.
p. cm.
"A Vintage original"–T.p. verso.
ISBN 0-679-76161-6
1. London (England)–Social life and customs–20th century.
I. Title
DA688.B28   1995
942.1'2082–dc20   95-3172
CIP

BOOK DESIGN BY CATHRYN S. AISON

Manufactured in the United States of America
10 9 8 7 6 5 4 3 2 1

to Jay and Helen

Contents

Preface: On Author

*A*s a child, I was a brief devotee of *I-Spy* books, those spotters' guides for the short-trousered. Each covered a single subject—butterflies, London statues, wheeled transport—and you were encouraged with a reward system: ten points for a red admiral, thirty for a rare Edward VIII pillar-box, and so on. You then filled in the precise location of each spotted item (not that anyone would have thought of cheating) and sent the completed book up to Big Chief I-Spy at the Wigwam, News Chronicle, Bouverie Street. This improbable fellow—who was, I trust, a deep suburbanite—posted you back a scout's feather as proof of your ocular zealotry.

I never gained a feather: either I failed to track down enough items or some detail of club membership prevented me from making a start on my headdress. But I remember a couple of chaperoned trips from Acton W.3. into the center of London during which, sharpened pencil aloft, I tried to bulk out my meager logging of such things as horse-drawn provisions vans or commissionaires' epaulets. This sort of enforced looking is, I realize, comparatively rare in our lives: on the whole, we seek out the things we are already interested in. Our habits of inspection and our view of the world are reconfirmed each time we concentrate our vision or avert our eye.

So when Bob Gottlieb, editor of *The New Yorker*, invited me late in 1989 to be the magazine's London correspondent, I had various predictable if contradictory reactions. This could be a very nice job; this could be a life sentence; this could be well paid; this could be the novelist's classic trap. However, beyond these pleadings, I heard the most persuasive argument of all for taking the job: this will make you look. I-Spy London, here we come, I thought; I-Spy England.

I was, in effect, to be a foreign correspondent in my own country. This brought with it a technical challenge I'd not encountered before in journalism. My readership would be sophisticated and would understand every single word I used, but the situations and events I was describing might seem as culturally strange to them as those of ancient Rome. Of course, there are many Anglophile Americans: those are the ones we in Britain tend to meet. But non-Americans should never forget that every country in the world is more interested in America than America is in it: this is the normal loading of the international equation of power and money. As a visitor to the States you can work a very inexpensive piece of magic: buy a newspaper and see your own country disappear. Ten years ago I found myself in Fort Worth watching the opening ceremony of the Los Angeles Olympics on television. During the march-past of contestants the ABC subtitles explained the location of each country and its size in domestic terms: thus Bhutan was in Central Asia and was "approx. ½ Indiana." However, it was not just Bhutan. Someone judged that the American viewer also needed enlightening about Belgium ("in NW Europe"), Bangladesh ("approx. Wisconsin"), and, saddeningly, about Britain. I was advised to rethink my own country as "size of Oregon."

So it was a useful discipline not to take even the most obvious sentence for granted. "The next general election, which will take place in either May or October . . ." Hang on, an American heckler in my skull would go, how come you don't know? Oh, you mean elections aren't held regularly? And the government chooses the election date itself? You're *kidding*. Who ever thought *that* was a good idea?

And so on. This sense of forcedly reexamining the supposedly familiar was at its strongest when I was working on Lloyd's of London, one of those typically British institutions which you half-assume you understand simply because you are British and live in Britain (size of Oregon). I don't think my eggshell preconceptions withstood the slightest tap of evidence. And if I, as a dispassionate outsider, was surprised by what appeared to be the case, imagine the surprise of a blithely ignorant Lloyd's Name suddenly bankrupted several times over, let alone the further and extreme surprise of an American investor. No wonder many American Names are currently refusing to pay their bills.

My predecessor as London correspondent, the novelist Mollie Panter-Downes, began filing in 1939 and held the job for nearly half a century. Brendan Gill wrote that, during the war, "To us and our readers, she was as much the embodiment of the gallant English spirit as Churchill himself." My own first (and last) five years were less world-historic than hers, but they had their instructive moments, some dramatic (like the fall of Mrs. Thatcher), some farcical (like the nonfall of Norman Lamont). I didn't, of course, set myself up as the embodiment of anything, let alone as a parallel spirit to either of the Prime Ministers I wrote under, and I doubt American readers viewed me as such. I'm also wary of zeitgeist journalism and decade summarizing. Was there, in the first half of the nineties, a tiredness and repetition to public life, a sense of things unraveling? It seemed to be the case. And if so, there are pleasures as well as despondencies to be had: Flaubert said that his favorite historical periods were those which were ending, because this meant that something new was being born. Unless most observers are mistaken—that journalistic formulation which tends to mean "I think"—the current fourth term of Conservative rule will be the last for a while. The final piece in this collection looks at the "something new" which might ensue.

WRITING FOR *The New Yorker* means, famously, being edited by *The New Yorker*: an immensely civilized, attentive, and beneficial process which tends to drive you crazy. It begins with the department known,

not always affectionately, as the "style police." These are the stern pu-
ritans who look at one of your sentences and instead of seeing, as you
do, a joyful fusion of truth, beauty, rhythm, and wit, discover only a
doltish wreckage of capsized grammar. Silently, they do their best to
protect you from yourself. You emit muted gargles of protest and attempt to restore your original text. A new set of proofs arrives, and
occasionally you will have been graciously permitted a single laxity;
but if so, you will also find that a further grammatical delinquency has
been corrected. The fact that you never get to talk to the style police,
while they retain the power of intervention in your text at any time,
makes them seem the more menacing. I used to imagine them sitting
in their office with nightsticks and manacles dangling from the walls,
swapping satirical and unforgiving opinions of *New Yorker* writers.
"Guess how many infinitives that Limey's split *this* time?" Actually,
they are less unbending than I make them sound, and even acknowledge how useful it may be to occasionally split an infinitive. My own
particular weakness is a refusal to learn the difference between *which*
and *that*. I know there's some rule, to do with individuality versus category or something, but I have my own rule, which goes like this (or
should it be "that goes like this"?—don't ask me): if you've already got
a *that* doing business in the vicinity, use *which* instead. I don't think I
ever converted the style police to this working principle.

The editor who gently interposed himself between me and the
style police was Charles McGrath. I worked closely with him for five
years, under the overall sovereignty first of Bob Gottlieb and then of
Tina Brown. It's customary at this point in the preface to a collection
of journalism to praise your editor's tact, savvy, unwavering helpful-
ness, and so on, and it's equally customary at this point for the preface reader to let rip a monster yawn. So instead I'll tell you a story
about Mr. McGrath's editing. About halfway through my stint, we
were on our third or fourth extended conversation about a particular
piece; it had been through a couple of sets of galleys and was now in
page proof. By this stage any writer knows the article almost by
heart: you are as fed up with it as you are familiar, you long for it to
be put to bed, but you civilly attend to what you hope will be the last

few queries. It was at this point that Chip picked on an adjective I'd used, one of those words like, say, *crepuscular* or *inspissated,* which don't form part of your core vocabulary but which you reach for from time to time. "You've used *crepuscular* before," said Chip. "I don't think so," I replied. "Yes, I think you have," he said. "I'm fairly sure I haven't," I replied, beginning to feel a little irritated—hell, I knew this piece inside out. "I'm pretty sure you have," Chip responded—and I could hear his tone hardening too, as if he was really going to dig in on this one. "Well," I said rather snappily, "which galley did I use it on then?" "Oh," said Chip, "I don't mean *this piece.* No, it was a couple of pieces back. I'll look it up." He did. I'd used the word some nine months previously. I naturally excised it now. And *that,* if anyone wants to know, is editing.

After your article has been clipped and styled (not always a gentle process: sometimes the whole poodle is thrown back at you), it is delivered to *The New Yorker*'s fact-checking department. The operatives here are young, unsleeping, scrupulously polite, and astoundingly pertinacious. They bug you to hell and then they save your ass. They are also suspicious of generalization and rhetorical exaggeration and would prefer that last sentence to read: "They bug you a quarter of the way to hell and on 17.34 percent of occasions they save your ass." Making a statement on oath before a judge is as nothing compared with making a statement before a *New Yorker* fact checker. They don't mind who they call in their lust for verification. They check with you, with your informants, with their computerized information system, with objective authorities; they check to your face and they check behind your back. When I interviewed Tony Blair at the House of Commons, I was impressed by the elegant door hinges of the Shadow Cabinet room. My Pevsner guide told me they were attributable to Pugin, or rather, "Augustus W. N. Pugin." Pevsner states: "He designed, it can safely be said, all the details in metal, stained glass, tiles, etc., down to door-furniture, ink-stands, coat-hangers, and so on." Half-wondering if the department of verification would swallow the clause "It can safely be said," I ascribed the hinges to "Augustus Pugin" in my copy and awaited the fact checker's call on this and related topics. "Could we leave out 'Augustus' so as not to confuse him with his father?" was the first shot. Sure, no problem: I'd only put "Augustus Pugin" because I fancied American style prefers "John Milton" to "Milton" (the truth also is that I didn't know Pugin had a father, let alone that my suppressing the initials would cause genealogical havoc). Then I waited for the next question. It didn't come. Semisatirically, and with my Pevsner open at the page before me, I asked, "You are *happy* that the hinges are by Pugin?" "Oh yes," came the reply, "I checked with the V and A."

In my five years I only knew the fact checkers defeated once. In a piece on the redesign of British coins, I referred to members of the Royal Mint Advisory Committee walking past a Landseer on their way to work at Buckingham Palace. The call from New York came through. "I'm having a little trouble with the Landseer." "What sort of trouble?" "I need to find out whether it's still hanging where it was hanging on the date your informant walked past it." "Well, I suppose you could always ring up Buckingham Palace." "Oh, I've talked to the Palace. No, the problem is, they refuse to confirm or deny whether such a painting is even *in* the Palace."

I used to rather enjoy it when the heat went off me and onto my informants. Apart from anything else, fact checking turns up comic disparities between how you describe people and how they see themselves. There was the Lloyd's Name who didn't want it said that he lived "off Ladbroke Grove" but rather "in Holland Park" (well, he was trying to sell his house at the time). There was the other Lloyd's Name who wanted the tainted words "second home" altered to "cottage." And there was the political observer who jibbed at the label "veteran" and pleaded with the fact checker that "seasoned" would be a more appropriate adjective.

But always, in the end, the fact checkers come back to you, the writer. And it was here that I discovered, after several years of filing, two of the most powerful words of *New Yorker*ese: the words *on author*. If, for example, the fact checkers are trying to confirm that dream about hamsters which your grandfather had on the night Hitler invaded Poland—a dream never written down but conveyed personally to you on the old boy's knee, a dream of which, since your grandfather's death, you are the sole repository—and if the fact checkers, having had all your grandfather's living associates up against a wall and having scoured dictionaries of the unconscious without success, finally admit they are stumped, then you murmur soothingly down the transatlantic phone, "I think you can put that on author." Those magical words are then scribbled in the margin of the proofs, words absolving *The New Yorker* and laying the final literary responsibility on you, the writer. Of course, you must utter the phrase in the right tone, implying that you are just as frustrated by the unverifiability as is the checker; and you must not use it too often, lest you be suspected of frivolity, of winging it with the truth. But once pronounced, the words have a quietly papal authority.

This preface has, faute de mieux, been fact-checked by me (and, yes, I can confirm that the United Kingdom's landmass is very close to that of Oregon), while the Letters from London have benefited from the deft editorial process I have just described. But it goes without saying that all of what follows is, in a phrase I shall regret not being able to use anymore, on author.

—*Julian Barnes*
NOVEMBER 1994

Letters from London

M P T V

*T*he best show in town" opened last November, with the unusual promise from backers that it would definitely run for eight months. The latest Lloyd Webber, or the speedy return of Dustin Hoffman after his triumphant Shylock? Not a bit of it: the new entertainment promised us was the televised proceedings of the House of Commons. And, in the finest traditions of showbiz, the high claim made for this live matinee show (Mondays through Fridays) came from one of its principal actors: Sir Bernard Weatherill, Speaker of the House, a Tory MP elected into benign impartiality by his office. The sixty-nine-year-old Sir Bernard, scion of a tailoring business that once presented jodhpurs to the Queen, now stands before the TV cameras as well as before the unruly House in buckle shoes, black stockings, bridal-length black gown, and full, clavicle-tickling wig. Bizarrely, he has landed himself the double job of Parliamentary disciplinarian and TV warm-up man. The barker outside the fairground boxing booth turns up inside as referee.

The British Parliament, which in the eighteenth century tried to jail those who sought to log its activities with precision, had doggedly resisted the claims of television since they were first debated back in the sixties. Coverage of the House of Lords was permitted a few years ago, though it can't be said that this golden-age soap opera has pulled in many viewers: everyone in the Upper House is formidably polite (some with the civility of Morpheus) and makes a show of attending to the graybeards opposite. This has not been the stuff of drama or ratings; on the other hand, it did point up the anomaly whereby the business of the Upper House was available to the citizen in normal televisual reality, while that of the Lower was represented on the nine-o'clock news by colored drawings backed by a radio tape.

There were, of course, the usual arguments beforehand. Television would detract from the dignity of the House; MPs would play up to the camera; the solemn process of government would fall victim to the TV ambitions of bit-parters. To outsiders, this seemed back to front, since the evidence of radio showed how undignified the House was already. The proceedings sounded to the mere voter's ear less like wise debate than beer-garden babble, with speakers struggling to make themselves heard over the interruptions of gargling shire-voiced Tories and raucous vox-pop Labourites. The Mother of Parliaments— which is how the British are encouraged to think of their legislature— came across more like a fat sow rolling on her farrow. Skeptics also wondered if the cameras were not being kept out of the club by members who didn't want the trouble of smartening up their act. The predominantly male chamber has for decades exhibited a shabbiness unmatched by any other profession except that of Oxford don: the place has been a market stall of ill-fitting suits, a museum of short socks, a vender's tray of matching tie-'n'-hanx sets, a flour bomb of dandruff. And, just as it remains spectacularly easy for an Oxford don to become famous as a local "character" (wear secondhand clothes, ride a motorbike, sit in the same chair in the same pub every evening), so in the House a career of facetious insult got a man labeled a wit, while the mildest self-indulgence in dress turned you into a dandy. Perhaps this is what they were afraid of letting us see.

Naturally, given the years of suspicion that preceded the introduction of the cameras, and the extra suspicion that the staid have of the flamboyant, strict rules were laid down about where the camera's snout could wander. General, wide-angle establishing shots of the House are permitted, but thereafter the director must (for the trial period, at least) follow a set of guidelines designed, according to your point of view, (a) to emphasize the solemnity of the proceedings or (b) to drain events of all possible drama. Thus, the camera must remain on a speaking MP for the duration of his or her speech; cutaways to other Members–reaction shots–are permitted only if an MP is specifically referred to in the course of the speech; coverage of the press or public galleries is not allowed, nor are pans across the benches; finally, in cases of disorder the camera must either settle for a picture of the Speaker calling the House to order or else revert to a wide shot that does not include a sighting of the fracas. As a set of rules to discourage showmanship and eye-catching bad behavior, it no doubt has its logic; but it reminds the impartial viewer of the stern guidelines that once governed burlesque revue at the old Windmill Theatre. Showgirls were permitted to be naked so long as they didn't move; if anything wobbled, it was against the law.

Not surprisingly, MPs have already begun to exploit the restrictions imposed upon the camera. If reaction shots depend upon the naming of an MP, then the speechifier may be tempted to casually throw in the name of a Member on the opposite benches who is ostentatiously not paying attention. And if the camera is otherwise to be held loyally on the speechifier, then it must also be held on the small cluster of people (members of the same party) beside and behind him or her. This leads to a technique known as "doughnutting," whereby those surrounding the speaker behave as if they had not heard such a riveting speech since Henry V addressed his troops before Agincourt. Doughnutting presents a problem for the smaller parties, and in the beginning the Liberal Democrats were seen to surge en masse (the masse being no more than half a dozen) into the Chamber as soon as one of their number was about to make a televised speech. "Doughnutting!" cried the other parties. Not at all, explained the Liberal Democrats; it's just that when one of us makes a speech, all the others like to listen. . . . There is also the ploy of "negative," or "poisoned," doughnutting. This occurs when a dissident member of a party is attacking his own front bench; in such circumstances, loyalists surrounding the dissident might yawn, scratch, fidget, shake their heads in vigorous negativity, and generally make with the body language.

The launch of "MPTV," as it is known, comes at a point when Mrs. Thatcher has been Prime Minister for ten years and the leader of her party for fifteen; by the time she takes the Conservatives into the next election (in 1991 or, at the latest, 1992), there will be first-time voters who since their earliest years of sentience will have known no other Tory leader (and hence no other Tory tradition—for instance, the liberal Conservatism of the previous leader, Edward Heath). The opposition parties—which effectively means only Labour, the others having retreated once more to rump status—have known a decade of schism, bickering, and impotence. But now, for the first time in years, the Labour Party is ahead—well ahead—in the opinion polls. And if the political ice packs are breaking up in Eastern Europe, why not at home? Seen from the Opposition benches, Mrs. Thatcher is an outcast among her fellow EEC leaders, cannot boast the cuddly relationship with Bush that she had with Reagan, is incapable of flexible response to the speedy unraveling of Eastern Europe, and remains as dogmatic and doctrinaire in her eleventh year of office as she was in her first. On MPTV, the Labour leader, Neil Kinnock, likes to begin his questions, "Is not the Prime Minister *totally isolated* in her position on . . ." Again and again, Labourites seek to present the Prime Minister as out of touch even with her allies—a leader surrounded by gibbering yes-men who conceal from her the realities of the world.

Isolation, however, is a matter of viewpoint. There was a bubble of excitement at the end of last year when, for the first time in her fifteen years, Mrs. Thatcher was challenged as the leader of the Conservatives. There is a provision in the Party's rules for an annual objection, but this was the first time anyone had wanted—or dared—to stand against her. Sir Anthony Meyer, an elderly, wettish backbencher with no obvious political future, put himself forward: he was the sacrificial rabbit, the twittering canary thrust into the coal mine to test the noxious air, or–to submit to the correct animal cliché–the stalking-horse. He wasn't expected to win; what would be interesting was the manner in which he lost. If he raised, say, 80 votes (out of a possible 374), then the great she-elephant would be seen to be wounded. If he raised enough to force a second ballot, then the real candidates would emerge: lone predators driven crazy with hunger after chewing long grass on the back benches; carnivorous front-bench pack leaders waiting for the first stumble.

The ballot showed that wherever else Mrs. Thatcher may be isolated, it isn't within the Conservative Party. She received 314 votes, Sir Anthony 33; there were 24 spoiled ballot papers and 3 nonvotes. These last two items require some explanation. It may seem odd to outsiders that 7.2 percent of a party supposedly versed in and proud of the ways of democracy should prove unable to answer a simple question as to which of two individuals it prefers to see leading its party. Not the sort of behavior to set a good example to the electorate at large. Why should an MP spoil a ballot paper? Does it mean what it means when a voter does so in a general election: the anarchic addition of an extra name on the paper, a harebrained attempt to vote for more than one candidate, a scrawled obscenity? Apparently, it's not so different. The most plausible explanation to be advanced for the spoiled ballot papers was that the Tory MPs in question didn't want to support Mrs. Thatcher but didn't want to confess their treason, either: by voting for both candidates (and thus invalidating their franchise), they could return to their constituencies and assure their more right-wing supporters that of course they had voted for Maggie, while all the time keeping their consciences warm.

The Labour Party, trying to look on the bright side, asserted that this result was exactly what it had wanted: the Prime Minister had been hurt but was still in residence. There is a certain plausibility in the Labour Party's view that Mrs. Thatcher is the Tory Party's greatest handicap (as well as in the Tories' view that she is their greatest strength), but the sight of Labourites congratulating themselves that the Prime Minister will now definitely lead the Conservatives into the next election isn't altogether convincing. Whom would you rather line up against in an Olympic final—a triple gold medalist whose practice times have recently been a bit disappointing or a novice substitute brought in at the last minute?

Labour has naturally greeted MPTV as an opportunity for public demonstration of what it had long felt certain of but had failed to get across at a general election: that the Prime Minister is a pigheaded extremist who has been systematically ruining the country for a decade. The time to make that demonstration is during an institution known as Prime Minister's Question Time, which takes place at three-fifteen every Tuesday and Thursday. This is a moment in the process of government which Parliamentarians boast of: no such equivalent, they point out, occurs in the American system. The Prime Minister is obliged to appear twice a week before the Commons and answer questions for a quarter of an hour from Members on both sides of the House about her duties and the policies of her Government. This, they say, is the moment when a Prime Minister is potentially most vulnerable, when Mrs. Thatcher, reliant only on her briefing notes and her wits to handle anything that is thrown at her, may be "bowled out" by the Opposition. The Speaker acts as referee and game-show host, calling on Members seemingly at random (he usually alternates between sides of the House) while reserving up to three questions for Neil Kinnock, and one for the leader of the Liberal Democrats. This is a moment—both sacred and vital—in the democratic life of the country which at last was to be fully witnessed by the voting public.

Such, at any rate, was the theory. The reality, now disclosed twice weekly live, is a bit less crisp and vibrant. For a start, there is tradition to be obeyed. Thus, each segment of interrogation is preceded by a nominal, not to say fatuous, question—about, for instance, what the Prime Minister is going to do that evening. In reply, she explains that she intends to dine with the Zambian Ambassador, then resumes her seat while the MP asks his "real" question. When the Speaker moves the House on to the next topic, the same opening question will be asked, whereupon the Prime Minister will rise, say, "I refer the Honorable Gentleman to the reply I gave some moments ago," and resume her place again to listen to the proper query. There is a lot of standing up and sitting down during Prime Minister's Question Time. When the first question on a topic has been dealt with, MPs will seek to "catch the Speaker's eye" in order to ask a supplementary question. This involves leaping vigorously to the feet, looking hopefully in the direction of the Chair, and then relapsing onto the green leather benches, all except for the solitary Member who, by some brief and seemingly arbitrary justice, has been smiled upon by the Speaker. With approximately half the House rising and falling in this manner every thirty seconds or so, the effect is of a ragged yet persistent Mexican wave.

This cumbersome method of seeking to extract information from and/or humiliate the Prime Minister is further weighed down by the knowledge that, apart from the Leader of the Opposition, no Member can come back at the PM if her answer is deemed unsatisfactory. The Tories, in any case, tend to ask their leader predictable, even toadying, questions, by which she is rarely stretched. At one of the first televised Question Times, for instance, the Conservative backbencher Dame Janet Fookes asked the Prime Minister, "Will my Right Honorable Friend take a little time today to reflect on . . . her own outstanding achievement as Britain's first woman Prime Minister?"–whereupon Mrs. Thatcher willingly did just that. The exchange was more appropriate to the dying years of Ceauşescu's Romania than to a Parliament that prides itself on plain speaking. The Labour Party, on the other hand, finds itself torn between (a) turning a question into a speech and (b) trying to bowl her out by asking something she might be unprepared for. Giles Radice, MP for North Durham since 1973 and a senior Labour backbencher, explains that the best way to do this is to invite her to reflect on the merits of something in which she is known to see no merit. "Would the Prime Minister tell the House what are the positive arguments for joining the Exchange Rate Mechanism?" might embarrass a Prime Minister who cannot think of any positive arguments, while annoying pro-Europe Tories, who disagree with her. Radice suggests that the Prime Minister is bowled out in this way about once a fortnight.

Whether or not the viewing public will notice that the Prime

Minister has been dismissed is another matter. Television is not about what happens but about what is seen to happen. An image consultant who approached MPs before curtain-up estimated that their viewer impact depended on the following factors: 55 percent on how they looked, 38 percent on their voice and body language, and 7 percent on what they actually said. Although the House scoffed jollily when these figures were laid before it, MPs have nonetheless been taking backstage advice about suits (medium gray is recommended), shirts (nothing stripy), and ties (nothing too flash, nothing too dark). Whatever the long-term advantages of MPTV to the electorate, there's no doubt that the first beneficiaries have been the dry cleaners and tie salesmen in the Westminster area. Balder Members of Parliament were even offered a free issue of *papier poudré* to diminish excess glare on the glistening pate; but cranial cover jobs seemingly have yet to find favor.

So far, MPTV has proved a modest, uncontentious success, even if Prime Minister's Question Time is unlikely to offer a ratings challenge to *The Oprah Winfrey Show,* against which it is set. Nor has the fear of bad behavior come to anything (though it has yet to be tested by a Cabinet crisis or the run-up to a general election). Conservatives occasionally bellow "This is London, not Bucharest!" at the Labour benches, and Her Majesty's Loyal Opposition responds with cries of "Sleaze government! Sleaze government!" But these are no more than routine diplomatic niceties. The main focus of interest in the opening months has been on the front-bench exchanges between Mrs. Thatcher and Mr. Kinnock. When coverage began, the Labour Party had more to gain than the Tories did: for a start, television would show the Opposition properly at work (instead of merely debating in a studio); the two party leaders, each standing at his (or her) own dispatch box and backed by his (or her) own team, would be displayed with some sort of useful parity; and Mrs. Thatcher might prove vulnerable when she was unable to control the rules of engagement in advance.

Yet it may be that the Prime Minister has benefited more than the Opposition. The longer her reign has gone on, the juicier have become the rumors. She's quite mad, people will assure you: paranoid; a megalomaniac; actually, it's hormone-replacement therapy that's done it—makes her think she can go on forever. When it became known last year that the Prime Minister every so often visits a nonmedical practitioner in West London and receives tiny electric shocks while sitting in a bath of warm water, this less than Churchillian behavior struck even some of her supporters as a bit quaint. But such whispers probably worked to her advantage: she only had to appear half normal on Prime Minister's Question Time to seem reassuringly in control.

In fact, everyone agrees that she has cannily altered her act for the TV camera. "We thought it would reveal Mrs. Thatcher as shrill and authoritarian," Giles Radice laments. "But she's avoided that problem. She's totally changed her style. She used to roar like a lion, now she coos like a dove." David Dimbleby, about the only political interviewer on British television who doesn't approach the Prime Minister on all fours while loosening the collar to allow easier entry of the stiletto heel between the neck vertebrae, recalls, "She used to stand with her hands on her hips and bawl at the Opposition like a fishwife." Now she has "completely changed her tone." But even in this modified version, softened for television, her act remains a compelling one, as forceful as it is eccentric. She stands rather stiffly at the dispatch box, with swept-back hair, firm features, and an increasingly generous embonpoint thrusting at her tailored suit of Tory blue or emerald green; there, butting into the spray and storm of Her Majesty's Loyal Opposition, she resembles the figurehead on the prow of some antique sailing ship, emblematic as much as decorative. She now sports a large pair of spectacles, which she often holds by the sidepiece while reading an answer, before whipping them off to give the Labour benches a basilisk stare. She has never been a great debater or a great emoter, but she remains a great presence. Just as in Jarry's play *Ubu Roi* a single performer is sometimes called upon to represent The Entire Russian Army, Mrs. Thatcher seems aware that she is acting The Entire Conservative Party. And it is part of this role and condition that occasionally one has to peer over the parapet and listen to the distant catcalls of those misfortunates who for some

peculiar reason have banded themselves into parties that are not conservative.

At Prime Minister's Question Time the day after the first Vietnamese boat people in Hong Kong were sent back to Hanoi during the
middle of the night, Mr. Kinnock launched a two-question attack that
deliberately sought comparison with the forcible repatriation by the
British in 1945 of Cossacks who then went to their deaths at the hands
of Stalin. Was it not the case, Mr. Kinnock asked, that the Prime
Minister in the present instance was the only person who couldn't
say she was "just obeying orders" in the matter of repatriating the
Vietnamese—for the very reason that she herself was "the one giving
the orders"? Cheeky stuff, but The Entire Conservative Party did not
deign to rise even to this implied smear of "war crimes." "The Right
Honorable Gentleman's remarks," she replied majestically, "are feeble
and nonsense." *Feeble and nonsense:* neither the lack of subtlety nor the
lack of grammar will probably do her any harm with the electorate. If
the House of Commons, with its incessant background noise, its
schoolboy rowdiness, its dominant maleness, and its low level of re-
partee, often resembles nothing so much as the canteen in a minor
public school, then Mrs. Thatcher is cast as Matron. She is the one who
supervises the dinners and hands out the cod-liver oil; when Kinnock
Minor accuses her of the worst crimes under the sun, she merely
frowns slightly, as if he were making yet another complaint about the
quality of her custard. For she has seen generations of boys come and
go, some well groomed and courteous, others rough and uppity, and
she knows that all of them, in the long run, will look back fondly on
her legendary strictness. She is also familiar with the work of Mr.
Hilaire Belloc, and knows that others, too, remember the couplet

> And always keep a hold of Nurse
> For fear of finding something worse.

IT WAS FITTING that MPTV started up at the same time that London's more traditional theaters gave themselves over to the winter
pantomime season. Both these venerable entertainment genres attract

sentimental homage; both regularly fall back on the oldest of plots, while intermittently updating their personnel; both are prone to infantilism. But, whereas the Mother of Parliaments can to some extent boast of its exportability, the pantomime remains stubbornly local. The British have managed to export some surprising things—cricket, marmalade, the humor of Benny Hill—but they have never succeeded in unloading the New Year pantomime on anyone else.

The panto has its historical roots in the harlequinade and was cross-fertilized by the Victorian music hall. In essence, it consists of a fairy tale—the story of Cinderella, Mother Goose, Aladdin, Dick Whittington—that, while drawing on a traditional narrative line, is constantly updated by topical references, often of a satirical nature. Its central modes are farce and melodrama, with large openings for the miraculous and the sentimental; it aims itself simultaneously at small children, who follow its twists with an awesome directness of response, and at their accompanying parents, who are wooed by coarse double entendres supposedly above the heads of their offspring. It includes two elements with powerful appeal to the British: cross-dressing (the principal boy is always played by a girl, and the Pantomime Dame by a middle-aged man) and comic animals (who aren't played by themselves, either). It retains, if in an attenuated form, a worldview in which Britannia rules the waves and foreigners are a humorous supporting act. Finally, it boasts a promiscuous permeability to modern culture, so that at any moment the stage is likely to be invaded by some two-minute television cult that the parents have barely caught on to. Darth Vader outfits jostle with TV magicians, old Empire racism with Green jokes, and all is resolved with much audience participation and a join-in-or-die singsong. Perhaps, on reflection, it isn't too surprising that the panto hasn't caught on in other countries.

It has always been a ramshackle, catchall, demotic genre. Parents returning to their first panto since they themselves were kids are apt to bemoan the debasement of this popular old British art form, but the truth is that it has always been debased—that's to say, various, eclectic, vulgar, referential, and topical. Whether one panto is actually "better" than any other is almost impossible for an adult eye to judge. Perhaps more to the point is that the pantomime is usually a child's first introduction to the theater, and that the allure of the tiered darkness, velvet curtains, and interval ice cream seems undiminished and undiminishable. Amazingly, the pantomime doesn't put kids off the theater for life.

This year, the pantos have ranged even more widely than usual. There have been modern pantos, retro pantos, Green pantos, even (perhaps not surprising, given the strand of sexual ambiguity in the genre) a lesbian panto (*The Snow Queen: A Fairy Tale for Christmas*). In terms of personnel, the genre has always drawn on a wide mix of performers: superannuated pop stars, TV comedians, young hopefuls, middle-ranking faces who were once young hopefuls, end-of-the-pier old-stagers brought out of semiretirement to "tread the boards" annually for a six-week run and bore the new young hopefuls about the romance of greasepaint, plus a raggle-taggle of outsiders who are celebrated enough in their own fields to make the transition to theater despite an alarming lack of thespian aptitude. This last category reflects the nature of modern fame, and is itself a form of cross-dressing: if you are acclaimed in one area, then you are accepted as a valued guest in another where you have no natural business. For instance, this year there were three television newsreaders appearing in panto, in London, Stevenage, and Torquay. Russell Grant, a spherical TV astrologer made famous by breakfast TV, fun sweaters, and a hospitable campiness, starred in *Robinson Crusoe* in Cardiff. Eddie Kidd, a motorbike stuntman who has leapt over dozens of London buses and broken almost as many limbs in the process, was in *Dick Whittington* at Deptford. But the real novelties this season were the pugilistic pantos. In Reading, you could see Barry McGuigan, the former featherweight world champion, make his theatrical debut in *Snow White*–while Snow White herself, with an ironical deftness rare to panto, was played by one of the nation's best-loved topless models, Linda Lusardi. In London, the hottest ticket, *Aladdin*, also featured a boxer, the former British heavyweight titleholder Frank Bruno.

Bruno, the first black champion here, is very large, very civil and very popular. He is an excellent example of the traditional British veneration for the good loser–the "plucky little Belgium" syndrome in the national psyche. For many decades, the country has not had a boxer capable of winning the world heavyweight title, but the manner in which local champions are dispatched by American titleholders is always carefully scrutinized. Henry Cooper once put Cassius Clay (as he then was) on the canvas with a left hook, and for buttoning The Lip, if briefly, Cooper has remained a national hero ever since, advertising Brut toiletries and appearing in countless TV game shows and pro-celebrity golf tournaments. Bruno is the most personable champ since Cooper, and the manner of his inevitable defeat last year by Mike Tyson endeared him to the nation with a solidity that only a charge of child molestation could conceivably budge. He stayed upright for several rounds, hit Tyson with one punch that we are practically sure almost hurt the American champion, and didn't disgrace the flag. Plucky big Frank! His salability as a TV commodity was greatly enhanced; he landed a six-week run in *Aladdin* at the Dominion Theatre, Tottenham Court Road; and in the New Year Honours List he was awarded an MBE by the Queen.

At the Dominion, Bruno plays the Genie of the Lamp, whose main task is to materialize whenever Aladdin rubs the magic lamp and seeks assistance. Bruno was never exactly twinkle-toed in the ring, and his Genie is a less than impish conception. When he is required to dance, he watches his feet lest they do something wrong; when he is required to spar, he watches his hands lest they forget themselves and do something right. He is dogged, wooden, and touchingly word-perfect, pushing out the words in the same way he pushed out the left jabs–schooled rather than natural. But this awkwardness makes him, if anything, even more popular with the audience, and as he stands there, in a costume half out of the boxing ring and half out of *Dynasty* (ankle boots and whopping shoulders), the former heavyweight champion doesn't look particularly incongruous.

Aladdin, the tale of the younger son of a Chinese laundrywoman and his love for the Emperor's daughter, turns out to have an appropriately yuppie message for our times: all you have to do is rub a magic lamp (make the right deal, buy the clever futures) and you'll get your heart's desire of goods, services, and love. It also has one archetypally Freudian moment, when the virginal boy Aladdin (played by a virginally pretty girl in very short skirts) is being tempted by the wicked Abanazer to visit the Dark Cave, where all the Secret Treasure is stored. "Shall I go in, children?" this innocent yet desirable boy-girl juve lead winsomely asks of his/her prepubescent audience. "Nooo!" they bellow back, most pleadingly. But in she goes, into the Dark Cave of the Secret Treasure, and wise old heads in the audience nod knowingly.

Mainly, however, the show consists of a series of quick-change acts designed to juggle the disparate interests of the audience: distract the kids, placate the mums, titillate the dads. Characters arrive by motorbike or fly past unsteadily on wires; a "Chinese" chorus line (a strange concept anyway, given the presumed prudery of that nation) flashes its satin knickers; a TV magician with no perceptible plot function pops up to do a series of tricks, then yields to Dooby Duck and His Friends, a collection of foot-high string-puppet animals who dance to disco music—an act somewhat lost on a grown-up stage. Nor should we forget the Chinese Policemen, fearsome enforcers of the Emperor's commands. In this version, they are played by the Roly Polys, a variety act consisting of half a dozen fat ladies aged roughly between thirty and fifty, who pander to the idea that female corpulence is intrinsically risible. Naturally plumpish, they are padded and costumed into grossness, and, in one of the stranger bits of transnational transvestism, play the Chinese Policemen as Victorian bobbies. They sing and dance in an approximate way—no doubt part of their charm—and as their porky contribution to the wedding feast for Aladdin and his Princess the Roly Polys troop on to perform "Anything Goes." In panto, truly it does.

STILL, FOR GROTESQUE comedy with which to ring in the nineties the professional stage had to yield, and not for the first time, to the House of Commons. When MPTV began, newspapers ran features on "The MPs to Watch," but none of them picked out the clown who was to enliven the New Year with a good old-fashioned upstaging extracurricular-sex court case. Ron Brown, Labour MP for Edinburgh Leith, is a forty-nine-year-old bouffant-haired left-winger ritually described as a "maverick"—that term which Parliamentary commentators reserve for those who are potty but interesting, loopy but semilovable, and seriously unfit for higher office. There are more such characters nowadays on the Labour benches than on the Conservative ones. Labour cherishes them for their colorfulness, their smack of nonconformity, their ability to discomfit, and their reminder that the Labour Party is, after all, a broad church. The Tories also cherish these loose cannons of the Opposition for their ability to embarrass their own leadership, for their regular and pungent proof that the whole Labour Party is deeply irresponsible.

Ron Brown was elected to Parliament in 1979. Two years later, he was banned from the Commons for five days after calling a Tory MP a liar; more recently, he was banned again, after seizing the Mace during a debate and denting it. (His repair bill came to almost twelve hundred pounds.) When he was arrested in Glasgow while protesting against a visit to the city by Mrs. Thatcher, it apparently took the police some time to become convinced that he could possibly be an MP as he claimed. (Fine: fifty pounds.) But his two most tabloid-stirring exploits hitherto had been a mission to Colonel Qaddafi, in Libya, and an all-expenses-paid visit to the Soviet-backed government in Afghanistan: photos of the MP posing beside a Soviet tank were much enjoyed by the Tories, and caused him to be satirically known in the House for a while as Brown of Kandahar. Such trips were enthusiastically denounced at the time, though recent events have confirmed that the problem of finding friends in a changing political world isn't confined to mavericks. In 1978, for instance, President Ceauşescu and his wife came on a state visit to Britain at a time when Romania was seen as the dissident in the Soviet bloc. My enemy's enemy is my friend, and Ceauşescu was awarded an honorary knighthood by the Queen. (This comparatively rare honor is given to much-favored nonnatives: recipients have included Bob Geldof, Ronald Reagan, Caspar Weinberger, and Magnus Magnusson, the

Icelandic TV star.) But then, after Gorbachev, Romania changed its status from Plucky Bulwark Against Soviet Imperialism to Filthy Little Balkan Dictatorship. (It was always both, of course, but countries rarely attain a complex, dual labeling in the eyes of others.) And in the brief hiatus between Ceauşescu's fall and his execution, the Queen managed to strip the Romanian leader of his embarrassing knighthood.

Ron Brown, as his recent legal entanglement disclosed, is a flouter of even more traditions than had been supposed. Over the last thirty years or so, it has become almost a Parliamentary rule that disgrace visits the two main parties in different ways. Tories are busted for sex, and Labourites are busted for graft. This doesn't mean that Labour MPs are tight-buttoned spouses and Tories financially impeccable, but merely that they are discreet—or wily—in different areas of life. With Ron Brown, though, it was sex, and the erotic angle ensured that the imbroglio which came to court in Lewes, Sussex, became known as the Case of Nonna's Knickers.

For three years, Mr. Brown had his life well worked out. He kept his wife and his constituency in Scotland, his mistress and his Commons seat in England. Nonna Longden, the woman in the case, even managed to accompany him as his "secretary" on the visit to Colonel Qaddafi. There was the occasional hiccup—like a report in the tabloid press that Ron and Nonna had had sex in a shower within the precincts of the House of Commons—but nothing too unusual, nothing that wasn't deniable. When the couple broke up, however, Mrs. Longden took a new lover—one Dermot Redmond, a carpet salesman in a tweed deerstalker—who happened to have a criminal record as a con man, and things got livelier. One day, Brown visited Nonna's apartment near Hastings, and here versions of what ensued differ. According to the prosecution, the MP, in a state of inebriation and jealousy, went berserk, and smashed all the windows in the flat with a bottle of Liebfraumilch; when the quailing Nonna summoned Dermot the carpet salesman for assistance, the MP stole a tape recorder, two pairs of knickers, a photograph of Mrs. Longden, a gold bar brooch, and a pair of china earrings, then decamped. According to the defense, Mr. Brown was merely having a quiet drink with Mrs. Longden when the carpet salesman erupted into the household, and it was *his* jealous rage that caused all the damage to the apartment. Moreover, the MP had no intention of permanently depriving Nonna of her valuables; he had taken them merely as bargaining counters against the return of some "politically sensitive" tapes in her possession—over which, incidentally, she was trying to blackmail him for twenty thousand pounds. As for the two pairs of knickers, it was Mrs. Longden herself who, ironically, had wrapped them round the tape recorder, and that explained their presence in the MP's pocket when he was arrested by police at the local railway station.

The Case of Nonna's Knickers enlivened the Crown Court at Lewes (and the surrounding Tory constituency) for a week. The bottle of Liebfraumilch, with a plume of grass waving from its neck, was displayed to the jury; so were the two pairs of knickers (one white and one black, for the record). Mrs. Ron Brown sat in court all week "silently supporting her husband"—or perhaps silently cursing his very name. Mr. Brown himself declined to take the witness stand, a decision from which nothing may be legally inferred but from which observers usually choose to infer plenty—in the present case, the probable view of the MP's lawyers that if their client were allowed to get up on his hind legs he would make a spectacular ass of himself and be eaten alive by the prosecution. The jury was faced with two separate charges and two wildly differing accounts of reality. Sagely, it split the difference: the MP was found not guilty of theft but guilty of criminal damage. (Fine: £1,000. Compensation: £628. Contribution to prosecution costs: £2,500.) Judge John Gower, QC, said, "I'm almost afraid to mention the words *ladies' knickers,* because they have assumed a significance out of all proportion to their rightful place in this case." Mrs. Ron Brown said, "My marriage is as good today as twenty-seven years ago," and declared herself unsurprised by her husband's behavior, "knowing men and having lived with one for twenty-seven years." Ron Brown himself, on being asked whether he was considering resignation, said, "No, why should I?"

Why should he? It's well known that a drunk-driving conviction does not diminish a judge's authority in the courts, though quite what degree of criminality is acceptable among those who construct and administer Britain's laws has never been officially laid down. In the present instance, the wise heads who weigh such matters tended to agree—theoretically, at least—with Mr. Brown. Had he been convicted of theft, he would have had to resign, but conviction for the lesser offense of wielding a bottle of Liebfraumilch in such a way as to commit *damage passionel* did not in itself diminish an MP's ability to represent his constituents and adorn his party. However, there is the manner as well as the matter of conviction to consider, and here Mr. Brown yet again did not behave in the accepted way. An MP emerging from court in his position is expected to say that the experience has been a deeply chastening one, that he has sworn off booze and mistresses for life and will humbly serve his constituents in whatever capacity they determine, be it only stamp licker and envelope sealer. Mr. Brown, however, was in triumphalist mood. What did he think of the verdict? "It's a moral victory," he bullishly declared. The gentlemen of Fleet Street, who had done well out of the story, presented the MP with a bottle of champagne. Mr. Brown shook it vigorously and showered the contents all over himself and Mrs. Brown. In this celebratory pose did the guilty MP bedeck the front pages next morning.

You are allowed to be a maverick; you are allowed even to be a minor criminal. But as an MP you are not allowed to be a cringe-making clown and a relentless embarrassment. You are not expected to load the gun and press it into the opponent's hands. Sir Anthony Meyer has just discovered this: having impudently challenged Mrs. Thatcher for the leadership, he has now been "deselected" (the current political euphemism for "sacked") by his constituency party, and will be put out to grass at the next election. And, on the other side of the House, Mr. Brown finds that his local party has denounced him, Neil Kinnock is after his blood, and nobody wants to hear his pathetic plea that the celebratory champagne was, in fact, mere sparkling wine. His chances of representing Edinburgh Leith at the next election are officially estimated at zero. However, given the nature of notoriety, there will always be a place for Ron Brown. The Rector of Stiffkey, who in a famous prewar morals case was dispossessed of his benefice, ended his days exhibiting himself in a lion's cage. (The resident lion, drawing on distant Roman memories, finally ate the Christian.) Mr. Brown might not have to go to such lengths as this; but he could do worse than start auditioning right now for the part of Mother Goose.

March 1990

Ron Brown was deselected by the Edinburgh Leith Labour Party. He fought the 1992 election there on an independent Labour ticket, without success. Mrs. Thatcher's impermanence was less predictable.

■ 2 ■

Fake!

We're back in London again," Mallarmé wrote to his friend Henri Cazalis in 1863, "the country of the fake Rubens paintings." The poet's judgment doubtless indicates a wider Gallic prejudice of the time, but it's no mere catty hyperbole. A casual tramp through the average stately home will take you past walls hung with pictures still confidently identified as being by Raphael, Rubens, El Greco, Rembrandt, Caravaggio, and other masters. Were most of them entered at auction, they would suffer the gentle torture of politely vilifying qualification—"school of," "style of," or the humiliating deletion of the painter's Christian name to denote uncertainty. It's not that the British are more naive or more aesthetically dim than other races; it's simply that fakery follows wherever money leads (the Japanese taste for Impressionists and for the work of Bernard Buffet is doubtless inspiring contemporary forgers, while in Buenos Aires, for some reason, the favorite fakee is Guido Reni), and Britain has for many centuries run a financial surplus. Besides, an artist rarely produces at exactly the rate the market requires; spare capacity or spare cash is the usual condition. Sometimes this results in the artist breaking his back or his talent to accommodate the patron. Thus Canaletto was known to the Venetians as "the painter the English spoiled" (and it does seem unfair that for all his fecundity there is scarcely a Canaletto to be seen in his native city). More usually, the gap between creative output and market demand is met by a merry band of fakers. Gazing at the rows of bumped and blackened Old Masters that still adorn the Big House, with their crazy-paving glaze and shameless attribution, one is tempted to imagine the circumstances of these questionable purchases some two or more centuries ago. It makes a little Italian genre scene, a picturesque morality. The svelte young milord posts into town on the second leg of his Grand Tour, accompanied only by a wise old tutor and a bag of doubloons; he expresses ardent interest in the local artists, and perhaps the more famous ones from the larger cities; and before Milord has dusted off his hat the word has gone out to old Luigi round the corner to put a little extra age on that veritable masterpiece he bodged together the week before last.

So London is the natural home for an exhibition on this subject. "Fake? The Art of Deception" at the British Museum is a most enticing show, and various to the point of being higgledy-piggledy: it takes in painting and sculpture, books and manuscripts, furniture, jewelry, pottery, stamps, coins, newspapers, cutlery, and torture instruments; it covers every civilization whose artifacts have attracted collectors and, therefore, fakers. It also serves as a wry example of curatorial economy, or how to make a silk purse out of a sow's ear. For where does this disgraced Dürer drawing, this dubious vellum miniature of Columbus landing in America, this dud "seventeenth-century" Turkish carpet come from? Why, from the British Museum, the British Library, the Victoria and Albert Museum. What was shamefully consigned to the deepest vaults is now back on display, and the conned experts of yesteryear blush—or perhaps chuckle—from their graves.

As you wander round this Aladdin's cave of bogus objects, you also encounter a wide spread of the baser human motives: the lust to deceive, to make money unlawfully, to swindle the faithful (as with the Turin Shroud), to destabilize the enemy's currency, to undermine the democratic process (the "Zinoviev Letter" of 1924, which stirred up the classic Red Scare in Britain), to foment anti-Semitism (the Protocols of the Elders of Zion). But overall the show leaves one uplifted rather than depressed–exhilarated by human inventiveness, charmed by these guerrilla attacks on the authority of the cognoscenti, amused, and even reassured, by the gullibility of our species. Who could resist, for instance, the case of the little-known Canadian furbearing trout? Belief in this exceptional fish seems to have first arisen in the seventeenth century, when a Scotsman wrote home about the abundance of "furried animals and fish" in Canada, was asked to provide a specimen, and duly did so. Fakes, in order to last more than a summer, must insert themselves into an appropriate crevice of probability and want: the Abominable Snowman, whose impressive tracks were almost certainly fabricated by a disgruntled British mountaineer, hits an exact nerve of phantasmagoric need in us. So did the bewhiskered trout: we imagine the deep and icy Canadian waters, and it suddenly seems plausible to us that survival is reserved only for those specimens which adapt–for instance, by sprouting fur. This fishy canard has tenaciously endured, been kept alive in recent years by an Ontario entrepreneur. About twenty years ago, an inquirer brought one of his products–white rabbit fur neatly attached to a brown trout–to the Royal Scottish Museum. The museum recognized the hoax and so didn't retain the object. But news of the "find" got out, and public demand was such that the museum was obliged to re-create the furbearing trout. And this hallucinatory hybrid–a rare double fake, in fact, being a fake of a fake–now takes its rightful place in the British Museum show alongside a caseful of other questionable items of zoology: a unicorn's horn, a griffin's claw, a couple of mermen (dried monkey atop a fishtail), and the famous "Vegetable Lamb of Tartary."

There are various sinister examples of "hostile fakes." During the Second World War, for example, the Germans produced an excellent set of standard British postage stamps with two minute and subversive emendations: the crown above King George VI's head was topped off by a Star of David, and the *D* of the pence sign was constructed from a hammer and sickle. (It seems from this distance an improbable insult to claim that the impeccably British monarch consorted with both Jews and Communists, but totalitarian abuse delights in the portmanteau mode: Shostakovich in his memoirs recalls Zhdanov's berating of the poet Akhmatova as "both a slut and a nun.") In the main, however, there is frequently a kind of tender complicity between faker and victim: I want you to believe that such-and-such is the case, says the faker; you want to believe it, too, and in order to cement that belief you, for your part, will give me a great deal of money, and I, for my part, will laugh behind your back. The deal is done. And public opinion, which likes to see the humiliation of the expert, usually gets over its first shudder of moral disapproval and ends up gleefully on the side of the faker. The best-known British art forger of postwar years, for instance, was a man named Tom Keating. Born in 1917, he had hopes of a regular career as an artist—or, at least, as an art teacher—but when thwarted began to diversify, first into art "restoration" at the shadier end of the market and then into straight forgery. He claimed to have produced a couple of thousand "Sexton Blakes"—as he referred, in Cockney rhyming slang, to his fakes—over a period of twenty years, specializing in the work of Samuel Palmer. He was finally unmasked in 1976 by the art-market correspondent of *The Times*. Keating then made a general confession at a press conference, claiming (with some justification) that he had begun forging as a protest against the exploitation of artists by dealers, and adding that he had in any case frequently given away his sly simulacra. He was arrested the following year, but the case never came to court: all charges were dropped because of Keating's poor health. Thereafter, his popularity rose no end: his "Sextons" changed hands at respectable prices, he gave a series of television lectures on the painting techniques of the great masters, and after his death, in 1984, a sale of his work fetched £274,000—seven times the auctioneers' estimate.

Keating's case offers a paradigm, and the fact that his forgeries often aren't much good increases his lovability: not only is the art market fooled, but it's fooled even by bad stuff. Similarly, we admire the chutzpah of the two potters who produced "Bernard Leach" pots (with convincing seals) good enough to fool the major auction houses, and we admire them the more for doing so from the obscurity of the pottery class at Fetherstone Prison, Wolverhampton. We applaud the medieval fakes of Billy and Charley, a pair of Victorian mud larks who perceived that instead of combing the Thames foreshore in search of antiquities it was quicker to invent their own. (At their trial, in the early 1860s, the scholar Charles Roach Smith argued for the authenticity of the "finds" on the ground that no forger would have produced anything so preposterous.) Even when we ourselves are the potential victims, we cannot always find it in us to get unalloyedly furious. That bogus Lacoste shirt, the bottle of "Johnnie Hawker" Scotch whiskey, the repro Vuitton luggage, the imitation Lego kits: of course we are being cheated (and so is the original manufacturer), but there is also something that makes us ask, Why do I value the maker's name so much? Is not my need for authenticity a bit absurd? If Johnnie Hawker makes me just as drunk as Johnnie Walker, why should I feel myself hard done by?

The British Museum show concludes with a handy section on the detection of fakes. Here there is, happily, still room for the scholar's intuition—the young Kenneth Clark first rumbled a "Botticelli" Madonna by pointing out that she had the face of a twenties screen goddess—but increasingly it is a matter of science: microscopy, ultraviolet and X-radiography, dendrochronology, thermoluminescence. And here again one often ends up more than a little on the forger's side. He (and it is always "he," for the profession is not as yet an equal-opportunity employer) has done his best, and the world has been fooled—indeed, the world has come to love and venerate his artifact—when along comes a white-coated spoilsport who blows the gaff. A particularly appealing case is that of the Agincourt spur, which for many years lived a quietly respectable life in the Victoria and Albert Museum's arms-and-armor collection. It consists of a genuine fifteenth-century spur round and through which the gnarled root of a tree has grown; a gilt-copper plaque set into the wood asserts that the item was picked up on the battlefield of Agincourt. And how evocative it seems to be: one imagines the loose spur falling from a knight's charger as Henry V's archers put the French to flight; it lies there disregarded until a sapling grows through it and lifts it back into human view, whereupon, centuries after the battle, a passing military-souvenir hunter . . . But none of this, alas, is likely. Dendrologists have gone to work and established that the wooden element in this resonant knickknack is almost certainly spruce. And one of the things about spruce is that it happens not to grow in the Pas de Calais. Another ingenious bodger (the more ingenious, since he used a spur that was genuinely fifteenth century) has finally received his comeuppance.

PICTURESQUE FAKERY, of course, doesn't stop at the museum's exit or the art collector's back door: it is embedded in many aspects of British life, just as that stub of spruce is wound into the Agincourt spur. The British are good at tradition; they're also good at the invention of tradition (from plowman's lunch to the clan tartan). And like any other nation, they aren't too keen on having those invented traditions exposed as bogus: they react like the boggling Harry of *When Harry Met Sally* in the face of a faked public orgasm. If we can't believe *that*, what can we believe? And since individual identity depends in part upon national identity, what happens when those symbolic props to national identity turn out to be no more authentic or probable than a furbearing trout? What happens if the Queen turns out to be a foreigner (which to some extent she is, the royal House of Windsor having been the House of Saxe-Coburg-Gotha until a diplomatic name change in 1917), or if we can't rely upon the British Christmas (which to some extent we can't, it being largely a Victorian invention)? Even the British Crown jewels are not above suspicion: a forthcoming report commissioned by the Lord Chamberlain's Office reveals, for instance, that the Black Prince's Ruby, which tourists admire at the Tower of London, had little connection with the Black Prince and is, in any case, a spinel of inferior quality. This need for authenticity, this lust for integrity, applies equally to the commercial world—or, rather, to how the commercial world is perceived by those outside it. When I was a child in the early fifties, I was much attached to my local Woolworth's. I liked its variety of goods, its cheapness, its user-friendly shelves (which facilitated a few illegal additions to my stamp collection); most of all, I liked its reliable fascia, "F. W. WOOL-WORTH & CO." Wherever in England you went, there in the High Street would be that gilt lettering on a burgundy background–F. W. Woolworth & Co., part of the very fabric of England. One day, when I was ten or so, I was informed that Woolworth's was an American business. Of course, I declined to believe it. I would have had to redefine Englishness (beyond my childish capacity) if I had believed that.

This sense of puzzlement and vague betrayal has been more widely felt during one of the longest and most Byzantine commercial sagas of recent times: the sale of the most famous shop in England, Harrods. For as long as Mrs. Thatcher has been in power, there has been a continuing and less than dignified scuffle for ownership of this Knightsbridge store. In fact, Harrods was only one of more than a hundred shops owned by the parent group and purchasee, the House of Fraser, but such was and is its enduring power as a British symbol that for prospective owners and the gawping public alike the battle has been about "who owns Harrods." The British middle classes may be able to afford to shop there only during the biannual sale (when some of the goods are bought in, and are therefore not authentically Harrodian), but this increases rather than diminishes the mystique. Even those who have never stepped inside its doors proudly quote the supposed reply of the Harrods assistant faced with a fantastical inquiry: "The impossible takes a little longer, sir." And this extra symbolic glitter naturally makes the institution alluring to outside plunderers. In the old imperial days, the British looted the treasure houses of their dominions (sometimes in the nicest possible way, of course, but sometimes not); now that the British are less dominant, their own prizes are up for grabs. It's perhaps no surprise that the two main aspirants to ownership of Harrods over the last ten years have been what the City of London considers underprivileged outsiders; that's to say, foreigners who have made, rather than inherited, their wealth.

The first of them is Roland "Tiny" Rowland, the German-born chief executive of the international trading company Lonrho, whose many possessions include the *Observer* Sunday newspaper, edited by Donald "Tiny" Trelford. (The rather British difference between the two Tinys should be explained: Tiny Rowland is called Tiny because he is very tall, Tiny Trelford because he is–well, tiny.) Rowland has attempted on three occasions to buy the House of Fraser group, his most publicized failure coming in 1981, when the Monopolies and Mergers Commission, a government regulatory agency, turned down his bid on the ground that Lonrho ownership would cause "at least a very real and substantial risk that the efficiency of Fraser would deteriorate seriously." This rejection did not come completely out of the blue, for Rowland was already a member of the extremely select clique of major capitalists who have managed to offend against even the constitutionally lax rules of capitalism and been publicly rebuked for it. In 1973, in the House of Commons, the Conservative Prime Minister Edward Heath described Rowland's business practices as "the unpleasant and unacceptable face of capitalism," a tag that has stuck ever since, and merited the unepigrammatic former Prime Minister his sole entry in *The Oxford Dictionary of Quotations*. The only other tycoon of similar standing to have been so stigmatized in Britain over the last quarter of a century was the newspaper magnate (and publisher of Ceauşescu, Zhivkov, Husák, and Kádár) Robert Maxwell, who was described in 1971 by a Department of Trade and Industry inquiry as being "not in our opinion a person who can be relied upon to exercise proper stewardship of a publicly quoted company." Needless to say, Mr. Maxwell has continued to run an increasing number of publicly quoted companies, while Mr. Rowland's face, unacceptable as it may have been to liberal Conservatism, has grown plumper with the ingestion of more and more enterprises.

The second claimant for the liver-spotted hand of Harrods was Mohamed Al-Fayed, an Egyptian businessman about whom not much was known when he first emerged except that he appeared to have large amounts of cash and his checks never bounced. He began, in the mid-1950s, as a protégé of the distinguished arms dealer Adnan Khashoggi, to whose sister he was married, and he prospered as a middleman. With his brothers, Ali and Salah, he developed interests in banking, construction, oil, and property. He bought the Paris Ritz, took a second, Finnish wife, and lived the normal life of the superrich:

homes in Paris and London, an estate in Surrey, a castle in Scotland, a villa in Gstaad, yachts in the South of France, armor-plated Mercedeses, bodyguards, and so on. But it was a fairly private life compared with that of Khashoggi, and was even marked by occasional benefactions. He gave financial support to the ultra-British film *Chariots of Fire,* and at the invitation of the mayor of Paris, Jacques Chirac, undertook the refurbishment of the Duke and Duchess of Windsor's house in the Bois de Boulogne. (Some said that, failing to understand the Windsors' renegade status, he hoped the job would ingratiate him with the Royal Family.)

By the end of 1984, Rowland was still hanging around the church like a much-rebuffed bridegroom, hoping that a ban imposed by the Department of Trade and Industry on Lonrho's making a bid for Harrods would be lifted. But he had retained 29.9 percent of the House of Fraser's shares and now agreed to sell them to Mohamed Al-Fayed (who had himself served on the board of Lonrho back in the seventies). Rowland offered the stock at three hundred pence a share, or fifty pence above the market price, on condition that he was paid in cash within forty-eight hours. Al-Fayed replied that Rowland could have the money within twenty-four hours. It must have seemed a sound enough deal to Rowland: first, he turned a decent profit, and, second, everyone knew that Al-Fayed did not have nearly enough money to mount a full-scale bid for the House of Fraser. If the DTI subsequently rescinded its ban on Lonrho, Rowland could always buy back the 29.9 percent. It was at this point, however, that someone shuffled the script. Rowland sold to Al-Fayed on November 2, 1984. On March 4, 1985, to everyone's surprise and to Rowland's fury, Al-Fayed bid for all the remaining shares of the House of Fraser, and the company's board, eager to escape the Unacceptable Face of Capitalism, swiftly accepted.

Two immediate questions were raised. Where on earth did the extra money—£450 million in cash, at a low estimate—come from? And would Al-Fayed be allowed to get away with the purchase without scrutiny from the Monopolies and Mergers Commission? Whereupon the story broadens politically and brings in the richest man in the world: the Sultan of Brunei. The Sultan had come to the attention of the British government and public a year and a half earlier: in August 1983, he had withdrawn the Brunei Reserve Fund, worth $5.7 billion, from the Crown Agents in Britain, to the noticeable detriment of sterling. In 1985, the following events occurred, some or all of which may be connected. In January, the Sultan of Brunei bought London's Dorchester Hotel—a deal fronted by Mohamed Al-Fayed, using a power of attorney to draw funds on the Sultan's behalf. On March 4, Mohamed Al-Fayed and his brothers were suddenly revealed to be much richer than anyone thought they had a right to be. On March 14, the Minister for Trade and Industry, Norman Tebbit, announced that he would not be referring the Al-Fayed bid for Harrods to the Monopolies and Mergers Commission; he also released Lonrho from the ban on its making a bid—by which time, of course, it was mockingly too late, as the Al-Fayeds had already acquired the 51 percent of the company's shares they needed. Later in the year, as the sterling crisis deepened, with the pound falling to $1.04 and a continuing miners' strike threatening to make things even worse, the Sultan of Brunei transferred £5 billion pounds into sterling to help prop up the British currency. Whereupon the pound sat up in bed and took a little soup, staggering back to $1.08.

The brothers Al-Fayed now owned Harrods, but Lonrho kicked up such a fuss that a Department of Trade and Industry inquiry was ordered into the circumstances of the takeover. In 1988, its report was presented to the new Trade Minister, Lord Young, but a delay of publication was immediately imposed on the ground that criminal investigations into the takeover were being conducted by the Fraud Squad. The chief executive of Lonrho continued to fume, and the following year, when the report had still not been published, Tiny Rowland (or one of his adjutants) slipped Tiny Trelford (or one of his adjutants) a bootleg copy of the report, which Trelford published as a special, unprecedented midweek edition of the Sunday *Observer.* It was injuncted shortly after it hit the streets, but Rowland, who by then seemed to be the only person in the country still interested in the ownership of Harrods, had managed to keep the story running.

Finally, this March, five years after the government gave the Al-Fayed brothers the nod, a 752-page report—by a High Court judge and an accountant—was published, and everyone got excited all over again. *The Times* ran the front-page headline "LYING FAYEDS" KEEP HARRODS over a large photograph of Mohamed Al-Fayed, straw-boatered and white-coated, slicing up a salami in the Harrods food department. The DTI inspectors declared that the brothers, both before and after their bid for the House of Fraser, had "dishonestly represented" their origins, wealth, business interests, and resources to the Secretary of State, the Office of Fair Trading, the press, the House of Fraser board, the company's shareholders, and even to their own financial advisers. The "catalog of lies" makes interesting reading, not least for its great variety of category: some of the lies seem to be calculated deceptions; others seem to the outsider like normal business practice; still others do no more than comically reflect the quaint British snobbery of those who compiled the report. The Al-Fayeds, the inspectors concluded, had inflated their income, had exaggerated the start-up wealth they possessed when they left Egypt, and had failed to come clean about the origins of their mysterious cash injection. They claimed to have had a fleet of ships that survived Nasser's nationalization, whereas in fact they had owned only two 1,600-ton cargo ferries at the time. In 1964, Mohamed had spent seven months in Haiti, where he posed as a Kuwaiti sheikh, obtained two valuable government concessions, and decamped after cheating Papa Doc out of $100,000 (which some might consider merited a medal for public service as much as a rebuke). The brothers' father had not, as they maintained, been close friends with the Sultan of Brunei. The yacht *Dodi,* which they claimed had always been in the family, was not acquired until 1962. And so on. Nor were their standards of veracity any better when it came to their personal lives and background. They did not, as they had said and allowed to be repeated, come from an old-established Egyptian family who had been shipowners and industrialists for more than a hundred years; on the contrary, they came from "respectable but humble origins" and were "the sons of teachers." They had supplied false birth certificates, lowering their ages by between four and ten years. They had "improved" their name from Fayed to Al-Fayed. Finally, their claim to have been subjected in childhood to the benign influence of British nannies was rejected as false.

Backbench Conservative MPs reacted to the report with pop-eyed rage. Don't let the crooks get away with it! Take the shop away from them! Damn Gippo parvenus—first you let them into the club and then it turns out they didn't even have proper nannies! Such was the tenor of their remarks. Sir Edward du Cann, a former chairman of the powerful Tory backbench pressure group the 1922 Committee, demanded that Harrods be stripped of its four royal warrants (the public sign that the store supplies members of the Royal Family), adding, "I think the Fayeds should be forced to leave the country." However, since Sir Edward is currently the chairman of Lonrho, his remarks may not have been entirely objective. In contrast with all this backbench clamor, the Conservative Cabinet has throughout the affair shown an extraordinary, almost heroic consistency. Despite the fiercest pressures, it has tenaciously stuck to the holy principle of laissez-faire and has most actively remained passive. The first Trade Secretary to be involved, Norman Tebbit, declined to refer the Al-Fayed bid to the Monopolies Commission. The second, Lord Young, followed this lead and also declined to publish the DTI report. Sir Patrick Mayhew, the Attorney General, declined to prosecute. The third Trade Minister involved, Nicholas Ridley, did even better. Naturally, he declined to refer the matter to the Monopolies Commission. Naturally, he declined to disqualify the brothers from being company directors, as he could have done. But he far outstripped his predecessors in Nelsonic nonnoticing and lizardlike somnolence. His entire statement to the Commons on the Harrods affair and the inspectors' epic report lasted a mere two minutes, and ended, "No other matters require action from me." The nearest he came to any judgment on the whole business was to say, "Anyone who reads the report can decide for themselves what they think of the conduct of those involved."

So what are we to decide? Tory MPs cry bounder and rogue. Labour MPs cry fraud and cover-up (plus bounder and rogue). The

Sultan of Brunei, who declined to cooperate with the inquiry, continues to deny that any of his money was involved in the purchase. (The
inspectors' theory runs as follows: the Fayeds used their association
with the Sultan, and their possession of wide powers of attorney, to
raise money on their own account. This would explain the sudden,
huge influx of funds, and also why the Sultan has severed contact
with his former representatives.) The Fayed brothers, having lost
their "Al-" throughout the British press, continue to own Harrods,
even if it is now smearily nicknamed Harrabs in some quarters. Mohamed Fayed, who never had a British nanny, continues to slice up
salami in the food hall whenever there is a photo opportunity. Harrods itself has gone from being a publicly owned company to being a
family business whose parent organization in Liechtenstein is beyond
British scrutiny and British law. And the Conservative Government, if
we are to believe some Labour analysts, has discovered a new way of
rescuing the currency when it bumps against the seabed. What does
it cost? Just the occasional national monument. Harrods and the
Dorchester this time, Windsor Castle the next.

As for Tiny Rowland, he continues, as he has done all through
the affair, to dispatch bizarre and hectoring circular letters to Members of Parliament and other opinion formers. They are printed on
fine paper and sturdily bound like an investment prospectus; inside,
they mix ferocious denunciations of the Fayeds with lofty calls to
arms. In their obsessiveness they are, in a way, love letters to Harrods.
The latest, a sixteen-pager (of March 27), typically entitled "Practise
to Deceive," catalogs the recent high crimes and misdemeanors of the
Fayeds—roughly, bleeding Harrods dry and cooking the books—but
also comes up with a novel line of attack. Rowland analyzes statements that the brothers made to the DTI inspectors about their
periods of residence in Britain (which do make very contradictory
reading) and concludes that, whatever they may have claimed officially for tax purposes, they are and have been resident in Britain for
many years. This, Rowland points out, makes them taxable in this
country. "There is one regulatory body still to act," he writes, and
bursts into capitals with the new threat: "THE INLAND REVENUE." The

Fayeds, he calculates, have over the years evaded "hundreds of millions" of pounds in income tax. Worse—though much better, of course, for Rowland—if, as they claim, they purchased the House of Fraser with their own money, "then their funds are the taxable funds of United Kingdom residents, bringing the outstanding Tax payable to one billion pounds. That is the position today." One billion pounds: as precise as that. It seems unlikely, however, that the Revenue will heed this public-spirited tip-off, and Rowland himself clearly doubts it. "All is silent," he laments on the final page of his letter. "No dogs bark. It is because the Fayed affair was put in motion by the Prime Minister, Mrs. Thatcher." At which point paranoia begins to fizz and crackle in the air like static. "Is it not laughable," he inquires of the MPs he is addressing, "that the Prime Minister of Britain should have been so naive as to seek advice from the Indian 'holy man' who introduced Fayed to the Sultan of Brunei; should have obeyed his instructions to part her hair, to wear a red dress, and to tie an Indian amulet above her left elbow to assist his supernatural pondering; should spend many hours closeted with him and his mystic tantric little balls of paper—and then tell the House of Commons that the Fayed decisions have nothing to do with her?"

What is the color of money? Amid the empurpled Tory rage, it's hard to make out whether the Fayeds' main offense is to have been (a) deceitful, (b) parvenu, or (c) Egyptian. Probably all three. Had the Sultan of Brunei come out and said *he* wanted to buy Harrods, we probably wouldn't have minded; but then not only did he have topnotch British nannies, but he also went to Sandhurst. (Though behind the snobbery a central point remains: if the money used to buy Harrods was not unequivocally owned by the Fayeds, then debt financing would have to take priority over capital investment, and the stability of the company might be affected.) In general, the Conservative Government has taken a relaxed view of foreign companies buying up parts of Britain. (Stop press: the American food giant CPC International has just bought three staples of the British kiddie's pigout—Ambrosia creamed rice; Bovril, an umber spread made from ground-up ox; and Marmite, a vegetarian equivalent of take-no-hostages pungency.) As for the Labour Party, though instinctively protectionist, it, too, knows when to take a practical stance on foreign ownership. For instance, I live in the London Borough of Camden. Like many other Labour councils squeezed by a Tory central government over the last decade, Camden at one point succumbed to a bit of creative accounting. In a striking (or perhaps batty) financial coup, it sold all the parking meters in the borough to a French bank and then leased them back. The council benefited by a capital sum, though quite what was in it for the French bank was a mystery to us locals. It also became a strange experience to park your car and reflect that the meter you were feeding belonged to the French. You felt as if you ought to insert a five-franc piece instead of fifty pence. And it has to be said that Gallic ownership has made no difference to the efficiency of these stubbornly temperamental machines.

IT'S NOT JUST the parking meters, the creamed rice, and Harrods. These days, we don't even own *The Times*. First, it was bought by a Canadian, Roy Thomson; and now it belongs to Rupert Murdoch, an Australian who couldn't even be relied upon to stay Australian but turned into an American, no doubt for the best of business reasons. At least the editor has remained traditionally British, and the new one, appointed in mid-March, couldn't be more so. Simon Jenkins is Murdoch's fourth editor in a decade, a period during which the newspaper's finances have remained healthy but its personality has endured a running state of trauma. *The Times*, of course, has always attracted labels and expectations like no other newspaper: from "the Thunderer" of Victorian days to "the newspaper of record," "the noticeboard of the Establishment," "the Top People's Paper," and so on. There is, naturally, a rival view as well: *The Times* is the paper that sought to appease Hitler in the late thirties, and a decade later kissed its hand to Stalin. "The Sycophants' Gazette," it was called recently by the columnist Edward Pearce. "In truth," wrote Pearce, "the old *Times* was a rotten paper, incapable of being judged objectively since it was not sustained by objective merits but [by] levitating two feet off the ground by divine will, like St Joseph of Copertino."

Still, even this Josephine trickery serves to mark *The Times* out from other journals, suggesting some cherished ideal of what it might be or perhaps once was. This notion has been under attack now for some time—internally, thanks to an editorial and marketing course of such zigzaggery that you would have thought the paper was trying to shake readers off rather than attract them, and externally by the rise of one particular rival. From the beginning of modern history, there were only three "quality" dailies in Britain. On the left, the *Guardian*; on the right, *The Times*; a bit farther to the right, the *Daily Telegraph*. That was all there was, and that, conventional wisdom claimed, was all there was room for. Change happened only when newspapers died; they didn't get born anymore. However, this lethargic cartel was broken in 1986 by the arrival of *The Independent*, a fresh-faced, tycoon-free, unaligned, upmarket, new-technology daily. Old Fleet Street hands tended to discount its chances: Anthony Howard, the former editor of both *The New Statesman* and *The Listener*, and deputy at the time to Tiny Trelford at the *Observer*, widely predicted that the paper would fail, and that its editor would be out within six months. Undeterred, the paper has flourished and is steadily beginning to overhaul its established rivals: the last set of audited circulation figures showed the *Guardian* at 433,530, *The Times* at 431,811, and *The Independent* at 415,609. Mr. Howard himself, a rueful smile on his face, now writes a weekly column for *The Independent*.

It's not just circulation, either. *The Independent* has shaken up newspaper design, with much bolder use of photographs (a move the *Guardian* has followed); it put strong foreign correspondents in place at a time when news values were generally becoming more Anglo-centric, and ran the first stirrings in Eastern Europe on its front page before its rivals did; it teasingly produced a color supplement largely in black-and-white, and offered broad, vivacious obituaries, which contrasted sharply with the turgid necrologies of Sir Tufton Bufton and his ilk to be found in *The Times*. While being "independent," the new paper has swiftly built up its own establishment, which alarmingly overlaps with that of the old *Times*. A small but pertinent distress signal blew when Graham Greene, inveterate writer of letters to

The Times and genial provocateur, started addressing his envelopes to *The Independent* instead. In one of his earliest statements after taking office, Simon Jenkins, asked to say which of his immediate rivals he was targeting, named them all, but added, "There is only one paper which, five years ago, put its tanks on our lawn and that is *The Independent.*" This is indeed the case, though it has to be said that the tanks went in with hardly a shot being fired, while the front fence hadn't been mended for years.

And when you get inside this famous stately home you find that the walls are peeling, the linen-fold paneling has been ripped out, and most of the (probably genuine) Old Masters have been sold off. Visitors are still happy to pay the entrance charge, but many leave shaking their heads at the way the old place has been run down. All of which makes the appointment of Simon Jenkins thoroughly appropriate not just in fact but also in metaphor. He first made his name in the early seventies as a journalist campaigning to save bits of London from the property developers and helped found an organization called Save Britain's Heritage. Now he has been handed the biggest heritage-saving job of his career.

Jenkins, who is forty-six, is a cultivated and charming man, dapper in appearance, scrupulously polite yet intellectually steely; very English, while also being married to the American actress Gayle Hunnicutt. He is a writing editor, with an excellent track record: as campaigner; as editor, at thirty-three, of the *London Evening Standard*; and then as political editor of *The Economist* for seven years. Until recently he was a columnist on the *Sunday Times,* while also occupying himself with the sort of great-and-good roles (on the board of British Rail) which normally come later in life. He had resigned from the *Sunday Times* and was just about to join *The Independent* when headhunted by *The Times*. Ironically, he now has to go into daily battle with the paper he nearly joined, convincing himself that it isn't really as good as he thought, scouting for weaknesses, and giving added credence to any whispers of financial instability.

But does *The Times* still have any symbolic value? Is it still "the newspaper of record"? (And does that phrase, in any case, mean much? Surely all newspapers aspire to be newspapers of record; the phrase is as redundant as "investigative journalist.") Rather to his surprise, Jenkins says, he finds that the *Times* legend retains its force. "There's something about British newspaper readers," he says. "They want there to be a *Times* even if they don't read it. It's like wanting the Royal Family to be there, or a rural station to be kept open even if they don't use it." Much goodwill remains, though of a rigorous kind: *The Times* doesn't just have readers; it has fingernail monitors. If a journalist puts "Lady Miranda Spofforth" instead of "Miranda, Lady Spofforth" (or vice versa), stern letters flow from rectory and dower house. After Lord Rothschild's death recently, *The Times* obituary muddled up his succession, and the rebukes came in like thrown fish knives.

When Jenkins is asked to locate his politics, he describes himself as an "enthusiastic Thatcherite," applauding her "iconoclasm" and finding her economic policies "wholly salutary." (Asked about the Rowland-Fayed squabble, he murmurs, "A plague on the whole bloody business," and judges Minister Ridley's nonintervention "quite right.") In other respects, he has reservations about Mrs. Thatcher–"I feel much more worrying is her appeal to basic instincts on social questions"–and on education Jenkins says he is "quite left-wing." (This, by the way, is the British *quite,* meaning "fairly," rather than the American *quite,* meaning "very.") He is also sophisticated or canny enough to know the dangers of a newspaper being seen as a political camp follower. Cautiously declining to criticize his predecessors, he notes that "*The Times* has been too closely identified with the present incumbent of Downing Street"–a polite way of saying that for some years it has wagged its tail off, rolled delightedly on its back, and brought Mrs. Thatcher her slippers in the evening.

Jenkins's first influence has been to calm down the strident–some would say vulgar–design of the paper: smaller headlines, no stories in bold, no double rules, less boxing of items, and a "light basement" (i.e., a nonpolitical, human-interest story) on the news pages. There is still a long way to go in terms of substance: he needs to win back some of the good writers *The Times* has lost over the years, or, preferably, to discover their successors; he needs better feature coverage, friskier arts pages, solider news; he needs to reimpose accuracy and authority. He also knows that there is an inevitable time lag between such things being established and their being spotted and relied upon by readers: for some time, dinner parties will continue to feature that impaling moment for Mr. Jenkins when the agreeable neighbor to his right congratulates him on his appointment and adds smilingly, "But of course I read *The Independent.*" Before his job is finished, he will need to delete a few bylines, and there can be little security in knowing that so far each of Murdoch's four editors seems to have been chosen for virtues that exactly contradict those of his immediate predecessor. Hearteningly, though, Jenkins is the first *Times* editor in recent years to be appointed with an evident brief to take the newspaper back upmarket. The office from which he seeks to do this is a small, windowless hutch in London's docklands—"the submarine captain's cabin," he calls it—whose walls are covered with ancestral portraits of previous editors. History breathes down his neck, and there is no contemporary view: skeptics might find these surroundings singularly appropriate for an editor of *The Times.* But for the moment even political and journalistic opponents are wishing Simon Jenkins well. You don't have to believe in feudalism to want the local castle to be in good repair.

June 1990

Simon Jenkins lasted until 1992; The Times *and* The Independent *are currently involved in a price-cutting war—not so much tanks on lawns as thumbs in eyes. Tiny Rowland and Mohamed Al-Fayed shook hands in the food hall of Harrods in October 1993; their reconciliation was brokered by Bassam Abu Sharif of the Palestine Liberation Organization. The Inland Revenue has so far declined to take up Mr. Rowland's invitation to investigate Mr. Al-Fayed.*

■ 3 ■

Mrs. Thatcher Discovers It's a Funny Old World

*I*n May 1979, when Margaret Thatcher formed her first Cabinet, she and her ministers sat for the traditional school photo. Twenty-four men, plus one central woman, lined up beneath the dewdrop chandelier, Axminster at their feet, Gainsborough behind them. Twenty-four men trying, variously, to exude gravitas, to look youthfully dynamic, to dissemble serious surprise at being there in the first place. Ten of the two dozen are faced with the first real problem of political office: what to do with your hands when sitting in the front row of an official photograph. Folding your arms, like Keith Joseph, looks a defensive, prim, keep-off gesture. Clasping your hands over your capacious stomach, like Lord Hailsham, looks the boast of a gourmandizer. Grasping the left wrist with the right hand, and allowing the left hand to dangle on the thigh, like Lord Carrington, seems indecisive, semiwet. Half-cupping both hands in front of the groin, like James Prior, is frankly inadvisable. Alternatively, as three of the ten newly appointed front-rank ministers do, you can deposit the hands, with fingers spread, firmly upon the thigh just above the knee. This pose looks crisply businesslike: here we are, ready for action, keen to clear up the mess left by the last government. So that is one problem solved. The second problem is what to do with the face: that intended smile of quiet confidence might translate as unctuous self-satisfaction, while the plan to appear weighty yet full of vigor often misfires into an expression of high anxiety. Perhaps the best solution is to be as straightforward as possible, and just look very cheerful.

One man who has found the correct lines on both face and hands sits two places to Mrs. Thatcher's left: a bespectacled figure, gray-haired but youthful, beaming but thrustful—in essence, jolly happy. So he should be: he has managed the conversion from liberal Conservatism to Thatcherism without angst, he was a key figure in drafting the election manifesto, and he has just been appointed Chancellor of the Exchequer. His name is Sir Geoffrey Howe, and for the next eleven years he is to remain the most loyal, the least disliked, and the most uncharismatic of leading Tory ministers. He is to spend four years as Chancellor, six as Foreign Secretary, one and a quarter as Deputy Prime Minister. His loyalty and tenacity can be judged by the fact that when he finally resigned, on November 1, 1990, he was the last but one of the original twenty-five Axminster squatters to depart: only Mrs. Thatcher herself remained of that team. Sir Geoffrey's longevity might not have surprised observers in 1979. What would have surprised them is that within a month of his departure, and as a direct consequence of it, Mrs. Thatcher herself, who had in the meantime won two more general elections and still enjoyed a majority of support within the Parliamentary Party, would be hustled into suburban exile, thus bringing to an end the longest premiership since the second Earl of Liverpool's unappealing stint of power from 1812 to 1827.

For much of last year, there was a tangy smell to British political life, though whether it was just the whiff of well-hung game—a mature government becoming more mature—wasn't clear. Certainly it was a year of deaths and resignations, though at first many of them had a comic slant. In June, for instance, the Social Democratic Party, after a decade of oscillating fortunes, finally went into liquidation. Founded in 1981 to wide media acclaim, the SDP in its early years looked to have revived the center of British politics and established a three-party system. But it was undone successively by the Falklands War (which solidified Tory support), by the voting system (proportional representation would have greatly helped the cause), by its own factionalism, and by a revived, middle-ground Labour Party. The SDP laid itself out and tucked the shroud around its own starved frame after a humiliating by-election in the Lancashire town of Bootle. In late 1981 and early 1982, the SDP had actually held an opinion-poll lead over both the Conservatives and Labour. Eight years later, at Bootle, their candidate was not treated seriously by the electorate; worse, he was not even treated as a joke. The representative of Screaming Lord Sutch's Monster Raving Loony Cavern Rock Party—which comes into existence only at by-elections, in order to publicize an aging rock star—received 418 votes, out of 35,477. The SDP polled a dismal 155.

Some of the resignations were distinctly comic, too. Take the case of Patrick Nicholls, a forty-one-year-old Junior Environment Minister, solicitor, and keen Thatcherite, whose more or less invisible career ended, after three years, in a moment of spectacular self-combustion. As minister responsible for health and safety at work, Nicholls campaigned against alcohol abuse. In March, he told an Alcohol Concern conference, "Quite simply, alcohol and work do not mix," pointing to the deleterious effects on health, family well-being, and company profits. In October, Mr. Nicholls was himself at work, and most publicly so, at the Conservative Party Conference in Bournemouth. On Wednesday, October 10, he sat on the platform listening to—or, at least, present at—the Home Secretary's warnings about drunken driving. That same evening, Mr. Nicholls went out to dinner with friends. Prudently, he had arranged with a local taxi firm for a cab to pick up the revelers at ten-fifteen and take them to Portsmouth. The agreed charge was to be £47.00. Imprudently, Mr. Nicholls and his party lingered at the restaurant until after midnight, at which point, the taxi driver informed them, the cost of transportation had gone up to £62.50. More imprudently, the Minister turned this offer down, thus depriving the cabbie of his hoped-for profit.

Most imprudently of all, he then asked the fellow to drive him as far as a car park, where he collected his own vehicle. Now, Bournemouth during a Conservative Party Conference must be one of the most densely policed areas of the country, and it is believed that the taxi driver, in understandable pique, denounced the Junior Minister to the local constabulary. Mr. Nicholls's career vanished as a flashing blue light pursued him out of the darkness. It was the update of a cautionary tale by Hilaire Belloc:

> Lord Finchley tried to mend the Electric Light
> Himself. It struck him dead: And serve him right!
> It is the business of the wealthy man
> To give employment to the artisan.

The more important resignation was that of the Secretary of State for Trade and Industry, Mr. Nicholas Ridley. At first, it too seemed largely a comic business, though it was here that one of the year's most powerful, if latent, political themes began to emerge: Europe. Most Cabinet ministers (and Mrs. Thatcher managed to chomp her way through fifty-six of them, in fifteen major reshuffles) resign or get sacked for disagreeing with the Prime Minister or her advisers. Mr. Ridley managed the rare and ingenious trick of being obliged to resign because he agreed all too thoroughly with the Prime Minister. His only mistake was to express in public opinions that Mrs. Thatcher could permit herself to endorse only in private. Ridley was, however, no damp-eared aspirant trying to fawn upon his leader; he was a trusted friend and political soul mate. Oddly, the old bruiser was valued equally on both sides of the House: Mrs. Thatcher saw in him someone unquestioningly devoted to the ideals of the market, while the Opposition treasured him for being just the sort of Tory they needed—not only a viscount's second son but one who every so often was given to making huge and exploitable gaffes. His devotion to the power of the market was evidenced during his spell as a minister at the Foreign Office, when he tackled the problems of decolonization in a novel way. He reportedly offered the Prime Minister of the Turks and Caicos Islands £12 million to go independent (the huffy reply came that they wanted £40 million and would revolt if bought off for less), while in 1980, two years before the Falklands War, he proposed that the continuing problem of these southerly islands be solved by transferring them to Argentina and then leasing them back–a suggestion that caused patriotic uproar in the Commons. Mr. Ridley's gaffes provoked almost as much of a stir as his politics. As Secretary of State for the Environment, he denounced country dwellers who were in favor of land development as long as it didn't happen near them– what he called the NIMBY factor. A little bit of journalistic digging later, and it emerged that Mr. Ridley himself had objected when a local farmer tried to build in a field backing onto his eighteenth-century Gloucestershire rectory. Even more embarrassing was his remark a few days after a cross-Channel ferry (named, ironically, the *Herald of Free Enterprise*) sank off Zeebrugge with the loss of 193 lives. Ridley made a joke about a fellow-minister going full steam ahead: "Though he is a pilot of the bill, I hasten to add he has not got his front doors open." He confessed the comment to be "inappropriate, inopportune, insensitive," and was permitted to survive. So he was never low-profile, and with a less understanding PM he might well have departed earlier. He entertained the right–for instance, by calling the Greens "pseudo Marxists"–and he infuriated the left with his dismissive, patrician air and his art of taking laissez-faire–as during the Harrods saga–to the point of inertia. Even his chain smoking (a reported four packs of Silk Cut per day) seemed designed to infuriate. When he arrived at the Department of Trade and Industry and said that in the long run his policy was to abolish the place, Labour dubbed him the minister with "no in-tray, no out-tray, only an ash-tray."

But this Grand Guignol figure, officially licensed to scare the lefties, finally overstepped. He gave an interview to the right-wing weekly *The Spectator* (no danger there, surely); the editor asked him a few questions, and Ridley said what he thought. About European monetary union: "This is all a German racket designed to take over the whole of Europe. It has to be thwarted." About the European

Commissioners: "Seventeen unelected reject politicians." About the French: "Behaving like poodles to the Germans." About the Germans: "Uppity." About the Irish: "Ireland gets six per cent of their gross domestic product [from the Community, by way of subsidy]. . . . When's Ireland going to stand up to the Germans?" On Helmut Kohl: "I'm not sure I wouldn't rather have the [air-raid] shelters and the chance to fight back than simply being taken over by economics. He'll soon be coming here and trying to say this is what we should do on the banking front and this is what our taxes should be. I mean, he'll soon be trying to take over everything." On Britain, Germany, the EC, the European Commissioners, and the question of national sovereignty: "I'm not against giving up sovereignty in principle, but not to this lot. You might just as well give it to Adolf Hitler, frankly."

Now, it is a well-established convention of British politics that you are allowed to mock the Irish and are positively encouraged to vilify the French (who understand the rules of the game, and react to being called poodles with the most urbane of shrugs), but Germany is another matter. So first there was the official denial, and then the resignation. This being Ridley, however, the "official denial" didn't relate to the words allegedly spoken but to the level of alcohol in the blood at the time. Count Otto Lambsdorff, the leader of the German Liberal Party, declared that the Trade Secretary "was either drunk . . . or he could not stomach England's World Cup defeat at the hands of the Germans." But Ridley was not known for his interest in soccer, so the initial conclusion, drawn even by some of his Conservative colleagues, was that he must have been plastered. Not so: the editor of *The Spectator* assured the world that during their lunch together Ridley had imbibed only "the smallest glass of wine." This left unanswered one interesting question: if insulting the Germans while sober is a matter for resignation, is insulting the Germans while drunk a greater or a lesser offense? Would Ridley have survived if it could have been proved that he was sozzled out of his skull? But, no, he was sober, and soon jobless. Tracked down in Budapest on the day *The Spectator* came out, Ridley commented, "This time I've really gone and done it." He had: two days later, Mrs. Thatcher was tenderly accepting his resignation.

Of course, Mr. Ridley's words were not just a contextless outburst occasioned by, say, the sight of a dachshund or a corked bottle of German wine from which he had taken only "the smallest glass." If Mrs. Thatcher officially dissociated herself from his views and his language, her suspicions about economic and monetary union— and her fear that it might lead to a Europe dominated by a powerful, enlarged Germany—were well known. Ridley's interview, however miscalculated, was part of a long wrangle within the Conservative Party and, more particularly, within the Cabinet. The old argument—which in the sixties and seventies had split both Tories and Labour, leading to bizarre coalitions of Tory right and Labour left—was whether or not to join Europe. The new argument is about what sort of Europeans the British want to be: reluctant, carping, tail-end-Charlie Europeans or bright-eyed, opportunity-grabbing, here-comes-the-sun Europeans. Where do we define ourselves on the spectrum from insularity to federalism, from aloofness to camaraderie? These are not, of course, the sorts of questions that profoundly stir the soul of the average voter; and it was all the stranger to see them dividing the most traditionally united of British political parties, the Conservatives. It was, perhaps, a measure of the extent to which the Party had changed under Mrs. Thatcher from one of pragmatism and fudge to one of ideology and dogma that this should have happened.

It was the question of Europe again, and Sir Geoffrey Howe's resignation over it, that brought an astonishingly swift leadership crisis—the first serious one in fifteen years—and the equally swift departure of Mrs. Thatcher. She had, it is true, been unpopular in the opinion polls for some time, and Sir Geoffrey was Deputy Leader of the Party and Leader of the House. But Mrs. Thatcher had toughed her way out of unpopularity before, and Sir Geoffrey's titles should not be overestimated: Deputy Leader is more akin to Emeritus Professor than to Vice President, while the Leadership of the House is usually given to an amiable but efficient old buffer whose political time has passed, as it seemingly had for Sir Geoffrey when Mrs. Thatcher humiliatingly sacked him as Foreign Secretary seventeen months previously. He was and is, as they say, "well liked" and "greatly respected," which means that he is a cautious career politician who has never raised either his voice or the temperature of the room; who in forty years of professional oratory has never threatened the dictionary of quotations; whose honesty has never been questioned and whose loyalty has never been doubted; whose survival has depended on a basic competence, a general inability to give or take offense, and a skill at blending effortlessly with the wallpaper.

If politics were a fairy tale–and sometimes it is–and Mrs. Thatcher were the Wicked Witch, then Sir Geoffrey would be the elderly Bunny Rabbit who every morning loyally fixed her porridge and fetched her shaving water. One day, despite his years of service, the Wicked Witch viciously cut off his ears and whiskers, but still Old Geoff hung about the Gingerbread Cottage, because even though she'd cut off his ears and whiskers, she had given him a nice present of a secondhand waistcoat at the same time, and Geoff thought he looked quite smart in it. Slowly, however, he began to realize that an old waistcoat didn't quite make up for the loss of his ears and whiskers, and so after sulking for a year and a half he just lolloped off into the forest. Whereupon–and this is the peculiar part of the story– all the other animals, who had admitted that the Witch had a perfect right to cut off his ears and whiskers if she thought it necessary, were up in arms about Old Geoff's hurt feelings, stormed the Gingerbread Cottage, and flung the Wicked Witch onto the dung heap. Then everybody looked for a moral.

More precisely, what happened was this. In late October, there was a two-day summit in Rome of European Community leaders, at which it was decided that January 1994 would mark the start of the next stage of economic and monetary union; beyond that, a single European currency would be established "in a reasonable time"– which might mean 1998 or 2000, depending on economic performance. Afterward, Mrs. Thatcher in an outburst of acrimony and pique openly dissociated herself from the communiqué: the agreement reached was "like cloud-cuckoo land"; sterling was "the most powerful expression of sovereignty you can have"; and "if anyone is suggesting that I would go to Parliament and suggest the abolition of the pound sterling–no!" This was, of course, roughly, if not exactly, what most, if not all, of the others were suggesting. St. Augustine's cry was "Give me chastity and continency but not yet"; Mrs. Thatcher's has been "Give me economic and monetary union but not yet." Some of those close to Mrs. Thatcher put it about that she had been bounced into an agreement by Continental knavery. However, the European leaders had become accustomed to the British Prime Minister's position as a one-woman awkward squad. As President Mitterrand suavely observed, "It is not for the slowest country to tell the others how quickly they should move to European union."

A new declaration of strident Euro-laggardliness, though no surprise to the eleven other EC leaders–or, for that matter, to the wider British public–was finally too much, however, for the Deputy Leader. Within a week, he had resigned, citing, among other reasons, "the mood" Mrs. Thatcher had struck in Rome. His resignation letter was that of a man weary of constantly papering over the cracks and of nudging his reluctant leader centimeter by centimeter along the road to Europe. "I shall, of course," he concluded, "maintain my support for your government." Mrs. Thatcher in her reply downplayed their differences on Europe–"not . . . nearly as great as you suggest"–and declared herself "most grateful for your assurance of continued support." The Labour leader, Neil Kinnock, a man noted more for verbal fluency than for verbal finesse, declared that "Mrs. Thatcher has been bitten by the man she treated as a doormat, and she deserves it."

The resignation of a senior minister usually comes in two parts: the act of demission, which may or may not be timed to embarrass the Government, and the subsequent resignation speech before the House of Commons. The latter occasions are comparatively solemn moments in the continuing adversarial rowdiness of Commons life: the minister will be listened to in decent silence, the Opposition quietly working out the plus factor for them (and nodding sympathetically when the ex-minister explains how beastly She has been to him), the Government reckoning the damage limitation that might be necessary. Sir Geoffrey came before the House on the afternoon of Tuesday, November 13, and perhaps the fact that in the twelve days since his resignation former Cabinet colleagues and others had queued up to explain to the media that his differences with the Prime Minister were more of style than of substance had toughened his resolve. For the speech he proceeded to give was very much not that of a man maintaining his promised support for a government. Those who witnessed it from the Government benches judged it a devastating blow to Mrs. Thatcher and a signal for a leadership race to start; the Opposition called for an immediate general election (though Oppositions tend to call for an immediate general election whenever a mouse runs out of the wainscot). Later that evening, outside the House of Commons, Tory knights of the shires blinked into the TV lights like endangered moths and declared that they had not heard a resignation speech with such oomph in twenty–nay, twenty-five–years. The Biting Doormat had taken a chunk out of the Lady of the House. Or, as Peter Rost, MP for Erewash, put it, "A dead sheep has turned out to be a Rottweiler in drag. It was the most dramatic performance I have experienced in twenty years."

Dramatic here has to be understood in the context of Sir Geoffrey Howe. He stood halfway down the Tory benches, next to his fellow-sufferer Nigel Lawson, ex-Chancellor and the previous year's Thatcher Euro-victim; he spoke quietly, hunched over his notes, occasionally letting go of them with one hand to saw the air vigorously to a depth of several millimeters. He looked and sounded as ovine as his reputation; in fact he was doing his best to bring down a Prime Minister. Were the differences between the two of them merely matters of style? "If some of my former colleagues are to be believed, I must be the first minister in history to resign because he was in full agreement with government policy." (Perhaps Sir Geoffrey was forgetting the case of Nicholas Ridley.) He had, he said, shared something like seven hundred Cabinet or Shadow Cabinet meetings with Mrs. Thatcher over the previous eighteen years, and spent some four hundred hours alongside her at more than thirty international summits.

Most of it had been a great privilege, and so on. But latterly things had changed. The Prime Minister, he said, "increasingly risks leading herself and others astray in matters of substance as well as style." On style, he mentioned the PM's habit of adding "background noise" and "personalized incredulity" to official statements, and cited what a British businessman working in Europe had written to him (with impeccable timing) the previous week. "People throughout Europe," complained the businessman, "see our Prime Minister's finger wagging, and hear her passionate No, No, No, much more clearly than the content of the carefully worded formal texts." As for substance, Howe portrayed the PM as deeply uncommitted to Europe, as one who "seems sometimes to look out upon a continent that is positively teeming with ill-intentioned people, scheming, in her words, to extinguish democracy, to 'dissolve our national identities,' to lead us 'through the back door into a federal Europe.'" Sir Geoffrey even quoted Winston Churchill against her—a matchlessly impudent move, since Mrs. Thatcher has herself copyrighted quoting from Churchill in recent years, the only exception granted being when a toadying MP desires to compare the two Premiers. Howe concluded by saying that in resigning, "I have done what I believe to be right for my party and my country," and he added, "The time has come for others to consider their own response to the tragic conflict of loyalties with which I have myself wrestled for perhaps too long." That *perhaps* was a classic moment of Howeish qualification (as in "I have perhaps married you" or "We are perhaps declaring war"), but the fact that in delivery and phraseology Sir Geoffrey remained throughout his speech almost parodically Howeish made—very well, *perhaps* made—its impact the greater.

Tory MPs taken aback by Sir Geoffrey's low-key vehemence couldn't believe that he was the author of such disloyalty, and some fingered the ex-Minister's wife, who was known to dislike Mrs. Thatcher's policies. "A speech it took Elspeth Howe ten minutes to write and Geoffrey ten years to deliver" was one verdict. But the question of authorship was not pursued, for Sir Geoffrey, like a one-sting bee that had done its business, now fell down behind the radiator, his distant buzz drowned by the whirr of an arriving hornet. The day after Howe spoke in the Commons, Michael Heseltine, a former Cabinet minister who had whirred at the Prime Minister from the back benches since his resignation in January 1986, announced that he would stand for the leadership. Unlike Sir Geoffrey, who in forty years of politics has been compared only to a dead sheep and a biting doormat, Heseltine has always been a high-profile politician, whose active, warrior stance (and slight absurdity) is reflected in his nickname: Tarzan. Like Mrs. Thatcher, he is a rich, well-groomed, fairly glamorous blond who makes the rank and file's heart beat faster; but, whereas Mrs. Thatcher is a millionaire only by marriage, Heseltine is one in his own right. His current fortune is put at approximately £65 million, which makes him the richest man in the House of Commons. It has also allowed him to fund what for nearly five years amounted to an undeclared campaign for the leadership. Now at last the challenge was in the open. "Tarzan vs. The Iron Lady"—it may sound like a novelty fight rather low down on a wrestling bill, but it engrossed the nation.

In 1952, while still an undergraduate at Oxford (where he was known, variously, as Michael Philistine, for his cultural interests, and Von Heseltine, for his Aryan looks), Heseltine scribbled a campaign plan for life on the back of an envelope. Presidency of the Oxford Union, the successful pursuit of a fortune, a seat in Parliament, a post in the Cabinet—all of these he noted and duly achieved. Finally, in his master plan from all those years ago, he had written against the nineties: "Downing Street." It's apposite, almost poignant, to note that in the 1979 Cabinet photograph Heseltine stands immediately behind Mrs. Thatcher's chair—perfectly placed to be the smiler with the knife. From the beginning, he was openly ambitious (the ambition is not a sin in British politics, the openness is); he cut a flamboyant figure at Tory conferences, like a Chippendale at a Tupperware party; as a minister, he was a diligent Thatcherite, selling off council houses and privatizing government ordnance factories; he seemed bright but not damagingly intelligent. As his old friend and fellow MP Julian Critchley has written, "Michael is surely no intellectual, but that is no handicap in the Tory Party." A greater handicap might have been that to the Conservative Old Guard he seemed a bit flash, something of a counter jumper. From middle-class Swansea, via property development and publishing, to a house in Belgravia, plus a four-hundred-acre country estate whose park gates had been recast to include the self-promoting initials *MRDH*–wasn't that taking social mobility a little damn far? William Whitelaw, former Deputy Prime Minister to Mrs. Thatcher and one of the bluff-squire contingent, dismissed Heseltine as "a man who combs his hair in public." But such sneers and snobberies from the aristocratic and squirearchical end of the Tory Party are inevitable, amounting mainly to an admission of a loss of power. The last two Conservative Prime Ministers have endured similar smirks: Edward Heath was widely known as the Grocer, Margaret Thatcher as the Grocer's Daughter (not because of her political succession but because her father ran a corner shop).

More pertinent than the charge of uppityness was the suggestion that Tarzan lived up to his nickname–that he swung unpredictably through the trees while letting rip with attention-grabbing howls. This reputation is based mainly on two incidents. In the first, back in 1976, he seized the mace during a debate in the House of Commons and waved it about in an indecorous fashion. In the second, ten years after the first, he stormed impetuously out of Mrs. Thatcher's Cabinet, consigning himself to the wilderness of the backbenches. Those were two things that everyone knew about Mr. Heseltine; but now that he was transformed from flamboyant outsider into postulant Premier they were held up to the light again, and this time showed a quite different aspect. Did he seize the mace and wave it Tarzanically around, threatening to brain the poor, quivering front-bench members of the then Labour Government with this blunt and glittering object? Was it a rash and vulgar act, which offended against the dignity of the House? Not at all, according to the corrected version: it was a subtle gesture, a piece of stage irony, one that at the time had brought cheers from those old Tory graybeards who later tut-tutted.

As for the resignation from Mrs. Thatcher's Cabinet, both its matter and its manner are worth examining. Resignation in politics is a bit like creative bankruptcy: if effected in the right way and at the right time, it can restore the fortunes, and even the reputation. Look, the electorate says, here we are dealing with a man of principle, someone who puts wider considerations above his pocket and his badge of office—we'll remember that later. But you have to choose the right issue. A resignation over the Munich agreement with Hitler gave a career-long mark of sanctity. A resignation over the Anglo-French invasion of Suez was equally dramatic, though trickier. (Charges of treachery were subsequently laid by the Tory right.) Unfortunately, most politicians never obtain the required coincidence of a national event, a question of principle, and a moment in their career when *reculer pour mieux sauter* is the best policy. Michael Heseltine resigned from Mrs. Thatcher's Cabinet over what is known as the Westland Helicopter Affair. Four years later, few can remember, and even fewer care about, the details of this imbroglio. Voters might recall the sale of a British helicopter company to an American firm; Heseltine, as Minister of Defence, wanting a European bid to be discussed; some paper shuffling and maneuvering by Mrs. Thatcher's minions; Heseltine storming out of the Cabinet; the business of some leaked papers; then another ministerial resignation. But the principle involved? Something to do with a defense asset staying in European hands, something to do with the way Cabinet government should operate, and much to do with the principle of the Prime Minister being a beastly old bossy-boots.

Most voters, however, would remember one thing about the event: that Mr. Heseltine had "stormed" out of No 10. The word was constantly applied. It was, after all, the verb of departure that fitted his image: he was Action Man, dynamic, Tarzanic. How else could he possibly depart? Over the past four years, everyone believed in the storming. But once Mr. Heseltine became a potential Prime Minister he began to deny in television interviews that *storm* was at all an appropriate word to describe his behavior that long-ago morning: no, he had merely expressed his inability any longer to serve, gathered up his papers, and left. Altogether more decorous and responsible, and more appropriate to one now seeking to return to No. 10 in a fuller capacity. And it has to be said that accounts given at the time by those present confirm the later, more sober version of events. Mr. Heseltine was overruled on a procedural matter and said quietly in response, "I cannot accept that decision. I must therefore leave this Cabinet." Then he left. But his colleagues were comically unsure of what he had intended. By "this Cabinet" did he mean "this particular meeting of the Cabinet" or did he mean "your Cabinet, which you, Madam, run in an unacceptable way"? Only when news filtered back from the street outside that Heseltine had confirmed his resignation could colleagues be sure of what they had just witnessed. And then what did they do? Douglas Hurd, Home Secretary at the time, recalled a few days later how amusingly British the whole scene had been. According to him, the Cabinet carried on almost as if nothing had happened. There was a discussion about Nigeria and, after a coffee break, a perfectly sensible roundtable debate on rates reform.

Rates reform: it is apposite that this was what the Cabinet went on to discuss, and, moreover, that their exchange appeared "perfectly sensible." For if they had scarcely been aware at the time of what Heseltine had done, neither did they predict what rates reform would lead to in the next few years: deep unpopularity of the Government, street fighting in central London, renewed perception of the Prime Minister as an unfeeling autocrat, dismay at constituency level, disaffection among the skilled-working-class and lower-middle-class voters the Tories need to carry in order to win a fourth election in a row—and then, to an Elmer Bernstein score, the thunderous return from out of the west, sun glinting in his golden locks, of none other than Michael Heseltine. And this time it would be accurate to say that when he returned to center stage he did indeed "storm" back.

The old rating system in Britain was the means by which citizens contributed to local government revenue. Each house or apartment was assigned by the local authority a "ratable value" based theoretically on the value of the place if anyone wanted to rent it. It was a rough-and-ready system, made more so by the long periods of time between the revaluation of properties for rating purposes (revaluations that were always unpopular), but it meant, more or less, that those who lived in large houses paid more toward the cost of local services than those who lived in small ones, and that the poor paid significantly less, or nothing at all. Every so often during the postwar period, there would be grumbles about the rates, but after other systems—such as a local sales tax or a local income tax—were examined, the existing method was concluded to be the least bad. What stirred the Tories into action in 1987 was three things. First, a series of run-ins between central Tory government and "high-spending" (as they were always dubbed) local Labour councils, which in Tory eyes needed bringing to heel. Second, fear that a forthcoming rates revaluation in England and Wales was likely to prove extremely unpopular. And, third, the simple fact that Thatcherism was a doctrine of radical reform, and after a while there weren't too many things left still in need of radical reform. Mrs. Thatcher took a strong personal interest in the abolition of the rates, and orders were orders. It goes almost without saying that one of the most enthusiastic proponents of the self-mutilating course the Tories now embarked on was Mr. Nicholas Ridley.

The new "community charge" to replace the rates was introduced in Scotland on April 1, 1989, and in England and Wales a year later. Based not on property value but on local citizenship, it was very easy to understand, and its justification went like this: since everyone living in the same area makes roughly the same use of the same amenities (roads, schools, hospitals, policing, refuse collection, libraries, street lighting, and so on), then everyone should pay roughly the same amount to support these services. Under the rating system, some £45 billion was raised from some 14 million electors. Millions paid nothing yet benefited from the services; how much fairer to spread the cost of these services more widely among the 34 million local electors. That was the logic; but importantly close to the surface of the reforming Tory mind lay the following social vignette: decent Tory voters in nasty Labour boroughs being squeezed for unfairly high rates and constantly outvoted by squalid nests of four-to-a-council-flat Labourites who were being featherbedded by rates rebates that acted as an open bribe to carry on voting Labour.

The community charge, as its name implied, was about democrati- cally equal fiscal responsibility within a given area. Opponents said that it was a poll tax, a straight per capita levy. Just as you can tell an Irishman's politics from the use of *Londonderry* as opposed to *Derry*, so the employment of *community charge* or *poll tax* translates immedi- ately into *pro* or *anti*. Within weeks of its introduction, only members of the Tory Cabinet and diehard loyalists were sticking to *community charge*.

In the summer of 1989, the Tory Reform Group had predicted, "It has all the makings of a disaster. The poll tax is fair only in the sense that the black death was fair." They were right: the tax was an immediate disaster. One trouble with very simple ideas is that what is wrong with them becomes swiftly apparent to even the dimmest op- ponent. In the present case, everyone could see what the tax implied: that two street sweepers living in a single room at the most fetid end of the Borough of Westminster would pay the same as a millionaire and his well-salaried wife living at No. 10 Downing Street. The earl in his castle (or Tarzan behind his monogrammed gates) would benefit by several hundred or several thousand pounds; massed farm laborers and their families would bear this cost. Mrs. Thatcher likes to offer patronizing economic homilies to her opponents, and a favorite, oft- repeated line goes "You don't make the poor richer by making the rich poorer." Here, though, was the starkest possible case of making the rich richer while at the same time, and by the same process, mak- ing the poor (and middle-incomed) poorer.

In the first year of the tax in Scotland, £158 million, or 16.3 per- cent of expected revenue, went uncollected. The next year, it got worse: by September 1990, almost halfway through the fiscal year, £769 million, or 73 percent of the tax, had still not been paid. At- tempts at arresting bank accounts and wages proved largely unsuc- cessful; in Strathclyde, 500,000 warrants had to be issued. Many refused to pay the second year's tax as a protest against subsidizing those who hadn't paid the first time round. In England and Wales, the poll tax was no less resented. On March 31, there was the biggest riot central London had seen in decades: a pitched battle in Trafalgar

Square, cars burned out in St. Martin's Lane, looting in the Charing Cross Road. Three hundred and thirty-nine people were arrested, and 144 needed hospital treatment. Trotskyist and anarchist groups were blamed for hijacking a peaceful demonstration; even so, that protest was itself massive, consisting of 200,000 people.

Complaints came from all political quarters, about both the nature of the tax and the blithe ineptitude of its implementation. The Government had estimated that nationally the average community-charge bill would be £278 (as opposed to the previous year's average rates of £274); it turned out to be £370. Nor could the Government blame those "high-spending" Labour councils; the Tory tax hit the Tory shires. Government estimates of tax levels in Chelmsford and Dover, for instance, were £180 and £150; the levels set by these Tory councils were, respectively, £397 and £298. In West Oxfordshire, eighteen Conservative councilors resigned en masse in protest against the community charge; when the leader of this group stood for re-election as an independent, he defeated the official Tory candidate by a margin of four to one.

The grumbles and the rumbles continued all year, as a stretched bureaucracy sought to administer an unwelcome tax. Demands sent out to those who had recently died seemed more shocking when the charge was per capita rather than merely on property. A group of soldiers on Salisbury Plain tried to refuse the charge, on the ground that they didn't use council services; magistrates ordered 389 of them to pay. On the Isle of Wight, there was a mass summons of 4,000 defaulters; the case collapsed in farce, because the reminders had been sent out by second-class post, thus not giving people enough time to pay. In the East London borough of Tower Hamlets, the Liberal Democrat council threatened to cut off refuse collection for those who failed to stump up. Elsewhere, bailiffs did a growing business. "Can't Pay—Won't Pay" was the protesters' slogan. By the end of October, six months after the introduction of the charge, one in seven of the 36 million poll-tax payers in England had paid nothing; a quarter of Londoners were not cooperating; the London borough of Haringey had nonpayment running at 42 percent. Nor could it even be argued that the tax was efficient to organize: collecting it cost twelve pounds per head, as against five pounds per head for the rates.

The most prominent Tory to campaign against the poll tax—or, at least, against the manner of its implementation—was Michael Heseltine. In May, writing in *The Times*, he linked it directly, if grandiloquently, to Tory chances at the next election: "In many of the marginal constituencies by which the tenure of power is determined, the community charge is perceived to have broken the Disraelian compact upon which Tory power rests," which translates as "Make it easy on the skilled workers or we're scuppered, mate." His three main suggestions were: that local authorities should be free to set whatever level of budget they chose, but that if they exceeded the Government's calculation by a certain percentage local elections must be called to give the budget a proper mandate; that politically damaging taxes—on students, student nurses, the elderly living at home, and the physically disabled—should be scrapped; and that better-off members of the community should pay more. The lumpy Newspeak for this last, un-Thatcherite concept is "banding upwards by income."

So the first round of the leadership election, a straight fight between Tarzan and The Iron Lady, was about Europe, the poll tax, the Conservative Party's chances of winning a fourth successive general election, the notion that the Cabinet should be properly consulted by the Prime Minister, and the notion that Mrs. Thatcher was barkingly out of control and handbagged anyone who uttered a squeak against her. The campaign lasted less than a week, but was nasty enough to gratify the most vampiric Opposition. The natural tactics for a sitting Prime Minister would have been to go about her business as normal, looking serene and efficient, while the impertinent pretender jumped up and down trying to draw attention to himself. In fact, the opposite took place—a clear sign of unease on the part of the Thatcher camp. True, the PM took herself off to Paris a couple of days before the vote, to attend the Conference on Security and Cooperation in Europe, but the reckless accusations were all coming from her side. These were mainly along the risible line that Mr. Heseltine, the richest man in the House of Commons, the counter-jumping squire, the committed privatizer, was secretly, deep down under that suspicious blond hair of his, some kind of crypto-socialist. Mrs. Thatcher attacked Heseltine from Paris, while at home her team wheeled out two of her favorite old bruisers, Norman Tebbit and the inescapable Nicholas Ridley, to do a bit of kneeing and gouging on their former Cabinet colleague. Ridley, ironically, was now seen as the official Thatcher spokesman on Europe, although this time he managed to avoid references to uppity Germans and the Poodles of Paris. The chief wicked things alleged against Heseltine were that in economic policy he would be "interventionist" and "corporatist," while over Europe he would be "federalist." It was rather too jargonized for true knee-in-the-groin stuff, but at least it allowed Heseltine to take the high, not to say Prime Ministerial, ground. When Mrs. Thatcher accused him of a mixture of "personal ambitions and private rancor," he could afford a statesmanlike smile, while the rest of us were left to wonder at the concept of "impersonal ambitions," from which presumably Mrs. Thatcher had been suffering when she ousted the sitting Tory leader Edward Heath in 1975.

The Labour Party, which knows all about political masochism and ruling oneself out of power by internal strife, sat back with rare pleasure as the Tory Party drew the ceremonial sword across its own belly. Tory MPs of an older vintage must have looked back with fondness to the pre-1965 days, when a "magic circle" decided such matters, and when after "the customary processes of consultation" a new leader simply "emerged." Postulant A would be told to dust off his morning suit for a visit to Buckingham Palace, and Postulant B instructed to walk out into the snow and not come back for some time. Now the whole system had gone open, messy, and uncontrollably democratic. Worse, it had snarled itself up with some quite unnecessary sophistications. To win on the first ballot, a candidate needs to obtain an overall majority but also 15 percent more of the votes cast than his or her opponent. Thus, in the present case, if there were no abstentions, Mrs. Thatcher could defeat Mr. Heseltine by fifty or so votes in a straight fight and yet be driven to a second ballot. At a second ballot, other candidates might come in, complicating things further and splitting the vote. The 15 percent factor is discarded in this second round, but if no candidate has an overall majority the contest might still be deadlocked, and thus go into a third round. Worse, there are no provisions for candidates to drop out between the second and third rounds, and if no clear majority is obtained at the third time of asking, then a transferable-vote system operates until white smoke finally dribbles from the chimney.

The first ballot approached with the Tories in extraordinary disarray. Nobody knew quite how the voting system worked. Nobody knew who might or might not declare himself in a second ballot. Those who wanted neither Heseltine nor Thatcher would have to decide whether to abstain, and perhaps hand Thatcher a first-ballot victory, or to vote for Heseltine, and possibly give him such a head of steam that their own second-ballot candidate would have no chance. Conservative MPs faced more than tactical problems, too. Should they be loyal to the past, to a Prime Minister who had won three successive elections, or be practical about saving their own skins at the next general election? Polls published over the crucial weekend of the first-round campaign showed that while a Thatcher-led Party trailed Labour by fifteen points, a switch to Heseltine would transform the deficit into a one-point lead. Yet even if the troubled MP persuaded himself into that juicy position where personal, party, and national interests appeared to be the same, there were other, rogue factors. A cross section of the Party at this time would have shown a layer-cake effect: the Cabinet publicly supporting Thatcher, the back benches deeply split, the hard-core constituency workers very pro-Thatcher, the soft core much less committed. If you were an MP in a marginal constituency, Mrs. Thatcher might win you one solid vote from the electorate, while Mr. Heseltine might win you one and a half shaky ones. How to make the calculation? And how to explain it to your Thatcherite Party workers? Mr. Cyril Townsend, MP for Bexleyheath since 1974, decided to vote for Heseltine, though he knew that support among his own grassroots organizers was running four to one in favor of Mrs. Thatcher. The chairman of the Bexleyheath Conservative Association took Townsend aside ten minutes before a meeting of the local executive committee and urged him to keep his mouth shut about his voting intentions. "His views," said the chairman, "went against those of the ward committees, ladies' clubs, luncheon and supper clubs, the businessmen, the local council, and all but one senior member of the executive." Mr. Townsend declined to keep his mouth shut; worse, he appealed over the heads of the luncheon and supper clubs, the ladies' clubs, and the businessmen. "I believe I have the support of the majority of people who voted for me," he declared as he endorsed Mr. Heseltine. The vice chairman of his own organization responded by demanding a new Parliamentary candidate: "I am asking [the chairman] to set the process in motion. Candidates will come forward and one of them will be Cyril Townsend. I hope he loses."

The first ballot was held on Tuesday, November 20, and the result was perfect for the Labour Party—what Tory managers had called "the nightmare scenario": Thatcher 204 votes, Heseltine 152, abstentions 16. So although the Prime Minister had won a straight race by 52 clear votes, she had failed by four to obtain the 15 percent over and above a clear majority which the rules demanded. (At this point, people started asking who had invented such a batty system. The answer turned out to be a former Conservative MP, Humphry Berkeley, back in 1964 at the request of the then Tory leader, Sir Alec Douglas-Home. Berkeley subsequently deserted the Tories for Labour, deserted Labour for the SDP, and deserted the SDP for Labour again. Such a career perhaps helps explain the tortuous rules he invented.) The result meant that Mrs. Thatcher was wounded, but not mortally; that Mr. Heseltine had shown himself a more serious contender than had been imagined; and that another grueling round of campaigning was to come. The former Tory Party chairman and loyal Thatcherite Cecil Parkinson immediately called the result "as bad as it could be for the Party as a whole."

Mrs. Thatcher promptly made it worse. Before the election, she had let it be known that she would fight to the last in defense of her Premiership, that victory by even the smallest margin was still victory. This was widely taken to be a rhetorical declaration: a bad result for Mrs. Thatcher and she would make way for a Thatcherite successor in the second round—whether a calmingly paternal figure like Douglas Hurd, her thriller-writing Foreign Secretary, or one of the next generation, like her Chancellor of the Exchequer, John Major. But what was a bad result for Mrs. Thatcher? The BBC's political editor, John Cole, estimated that 210 was the lowest acceptable vote, while 200 or under was "unacceptable." It was at 6:34 P.M. that the news came through that Mrs. Thatcher had received 204 votes. Clearly, the pundits agreed, this would mean an evening on the telephone—advice from "the men in suits," as senior Party figures are picturesquely termed. She would sleep on the result and announce her decision in the fullness of time. The BBC's chief Parliamentary correspondent, standing in front of the British Embassy residence in Paris, where Mrs. Thatcher was staying, assured viewers that nothing much was likely to happen for a while, and prepared to sign off. But Mrs. Thatcher is, as has been repeated many times, a "conviction politician," and one of her convictions has always been that she is the best person to lead the Conservative Party. At 6:36 P.M., just as the correspondent in Paris was about to return viewers to London, there was a scurry of activity over his right shoulder. Mrs. Thatcher, having thought over her predicament for a full ninety seconds, came roaring down the residence steps and fell upon the waiting journalists like a wolf on the fold. She had clearly won the first round; therefore, she would allow her name to go forward to the second ballot. Once more, the Prime Minister had plunged the nation into certainty. She had also killed off the possibility that Mr. Hurd or Mr. Major would come in as a compromise Thatcherite candidate on the second round. One of the more pathetic sights of the evening was that of Mr. Hurd later trooping out of the Embassy residence to record his continuing loyalty to his leader. It took him forty minutes to make this appearance, and it was one of the shorter declarations of obeisance on record, occupying a full twenty-three seconds.

Perhaps this exorbitant display of Thatcherian self-certainty, her conviction that she was still playing the role of The Entire Conservative Party, and her snubbingly public contempt for advice—even for the niceties of appearing to seek advice—stiffened the resistance of Cabinet ministers and the men in suits. (There is, naturally, some crossover between the two categories.) The next day, November 21, she returned to London, replaced her campaign manager, declared, "I fight on, I fight to win," and summoned her Cabinet one by one to listen to what seemed distinctly post hoc consultations. Most of her ministers said they would continue to support her in the second round of voting. Many added, however, that they thought she would lose; some expressed fear that she might be humiliated. At seven-thirty the next morning, this time having slept on it, Mrs. Thatcher told her private office that she had decided to resign. The Cabinet was summoned for nine o'clock, an hour earlier than usual, and shortly afterward the country heard that the longest Premiership since 1827 would be over within a week. Once again, Douglas Hurd was sent into a scuttle, for second-round nominations (accompanied by the names of proposer and seconder) had to be in by midday. The Chancellor, John Major, also scuttled, while Mrs. Thatcher set off to break the news officially to the Queen. The Prime Minister's widely reported comment on the fact that she could be deposed after winning three general elections, never losing a confidence motion in the House, and manifestly defeating her main challenger was couched with a homeliness appropriate to the tabloid headline it soon became: WHAT A FUNNY OLD WORLD IT IS. Kenneth Baker, the Tory Party chairman and a person of literary aspirations, reached stylistically somewhat higher, saying, "I do not believe we will see her like again"—though the resemblance between the departing leader and Hamlet's father was not immediately apparent. (Both poisoned by ambitious rivals?) Winston Churchill, MP, in the House of Commons that afternoon, called her "the greatest peacetime Prime Minister this country has ever had," carefully reserving the wider title for his own grandfather.

The second round of the election was fought in an overtly correct fashion, as if in deliberate defiance of the Thatcher manner. It was that curious thing, a healing battle. A small amount of mileage was made out of the candidates' social origins, though, this being the modern Conservative Party, it was along the lines of "prolier than thou." (Mr. Major, it turned out, had left school at sixteen and worked on a building site. This gave him the drop on Mr. Hurd, who had been burdened with a thorough education and a father who had been an MP before him. Hurd was driven by the handicap of privilege into some awkward son-of-the-soil reminiscences about planting potatoes as a boy.) No scandal was mooted, though the press enjoyed disinterring Mr. Hurd's out-of-print thrillers and quoting all the descriptions of breasts they could find in them. (The Hurd camp at once ascribed these passages to their boss's coauthor.) But the main sounds heard during the campaign were of eerie concord. Each candidate was eager to unite the Party; each claimed support from left, right, and center; each admired the other's achievements; each was keen on Europe—or, at least, keener than Mrs. Thatcher, whose negative image and opinions hung over the contest. Each was committed to a review of the poll tax, though here there was a slight difference, for once prettily mocked by Neil Kinnock: "When it comes to the poll tax, the choice is between Heseltine, who knows there is a problem and doesn't really know what to do about it; Major, who knows there is a problem and doesn't really want to do anything about it; and Hurd, who has only just found out there's a problem."

THE CONTEST WAS fought in a gentlemanly fashion—except, of course, by the Lady herself. What would Mrs. Thatcher do? Well, it was generally agreed that, having retired from the election, she would do her best to assist the search for Tory unity by not interfering too much, though she might perhaps allow it to be gently intuited which way she was going to vote. But allowing things to be gently intuited has never been Mrs. Thatcher's style. It soon became known that she would be voting for Major; and it was even suggested that if Heseltine won she would resign her seat in the House of Commons and force a by-election in her constituency of Finchley. (This was one of those "damaging but deniable" rumors, which came with the qualification that she might, of course, have been merely speaking in the heat of the moment.) The day before the second round, she was on the telephone actively arm-twisting for Major. And, being Mrs. Thatcher, of course, she went too far. Her farewell speech to Conservative Central Office, which, not surprisingly, was recorded by someone present and leaked to the press, contained praise for both President Bush and herself over the crisis in the Gulf: "He won't falter, and I shan't falter. It's just that I shan't be pulling the levers there. But I shall be a very good back-seat driver." Thatcher might have gone, but Thatcherism would continue, she was instructing the candidates. Anyone would have thought she had just read the *Encyclopædia Britannica* entry for the second Earl of Liverpool, whose length of Premiership she would never now exceed: "Lord Liverpool was destitute of wide sympathies and of true political insight, and his resignation of office was followed almost immediately by the complete and permanent reversal of his domestic policy." None of that for Mrs. Thatcher: the rebels might have pushed her out of the driver's seat and seized the wheel, but she had crawled along the running board and climbed back in behind them.

The second campaign was marked by slightly nervous, negative speculation. Sir Geoffrey Howe (now "the Assassin" to Tory loyalists) endorsed Heseltine, just as Mrs. Thatcher endorsed Major. How welcome was either kiss? Conservative MPs declared themselves "the most sophisticated electorate in the world," which meant mainly that some of them lied to the press, some to the men in suits, some to the three candidates, and most to their own constituency organizations. At the local level, the removal of Mrs. Thatcher was widely regarded as akin to treason, and a vote for Heseltine as an endorsement of murder. Would a sense of shame at the murky deed lead MPs to favor her nominee, Mr. Major? Was Heseltine too risky? Was Hurd, lauded as the "safe pair of hands," too fogeyish? Was Major, at forty-seven, too young? And not just young in experience: what if he lasted as long as She had done, and thus clogged up the normal processes of succession?

The three candidates had a long weekend to make their pitches: nominations had closed at midday on Thursday, the twenty-second, and voting opened on Tuesday, the twenty-seventh. Campaign managers looked under stones for hitherto disregarded MPs and tickled them behind the ears; senior Party figures came out with endorsements; constituency parties were consulted with trepidation. Mr. Heseltine had generously announced that as Prime Minister he would keep his rivals in the Cabinet in their present positions; the two others cannily made no promises to Mr. Heseltine. By the day of voting, it was clear that Mr. Heseltine's first-round surge was not continuing, that Mr. Hurd's wise-head, safe-hands appeal was limited, and that the only recognizable progress was being made by the least known, least experienced, least charismatic, and least characterizable figure of John Major. Over the weekend, the polls confirmed what they had said seven days earlier—that Mr. Heseltine would be capable of defeating Labour—but they menacingly added that Mr. Major would too, and by a greater margin. Such brief opinion samplings ought to be easily discountable, but if the earlier poll had given Mr. Heseltine extra credibility, perhaps this would do the same for Mr. Major. Every little helps, particularly in the uncertain, slightly mesmerized condition the Conservative Party found itself in. They had killed the Wicked Witch and flung her onto the dung heap, but they still believed in magic. They were long familiar with the hex of Hez; maybe the featureless fellow they knew little about had some special juju they were as yet unaware of?

On the final Tuesday morning, Mr. Major opened a Japanese bank in the City, Mr. Hurd had a photo session with Alexander Dubček at the Foreign Office, and poor Mr. Heseltine went off to his publishing company. The results came through at about half past six that evening. For once, all 372 Conservative MPs had managed to vote without spoiling even one ballot paper: 185 for Major, 131 for Heseltine, 56 for Hurd. Two kinds of gasp went up: one of surprise at the extent of Major's progress, and one of seething frustration at what the voting system had once again managed to achieve. If Mrs. Thatcher had been 4 votes short of accepted victory on the first ballot, Major was even closer: 2 short. So what did the rules, those blasted un-Conservative rules so many had fretted against, say now? They ordered a third ballot in two days' time, with both the trailing candidates instructed to soldier on whether they liked it or not. Whereupon two things happened. First, Heseltine and Hurd effectively conceded defeat by announcing that on the third ballot they would vote for Major; and shortly afterward the Tory back-bench 1922 Committee, which is in charge of running leadership elections, decided that the rule book they had been obliged to work with was a frightful piece of non-Tory hogwash. Transferable votes? Who ever heard of such a thing? There would be no third ballot, and that was that. Who were they to be dictated to by some chappie who in any case had deserted the Party for the pinkos?

So a second man from the East Anglian county town of Huntingdon had been selected to govern the country—the previous one being Oliver Cromwell. And the country was left puzzling briefly over a small mystery: how Mrs. Thatcher, supported by 204 Conservative MPs, was judged to have lost the Premiership, while Mr. Major, supported by only 185, was judged to have won it. Still, this was a time of freaks and records: the Tories, in deposing the longest-serving Prime Minister this century, had replaced her with the youngest Prime Minister this century. (The previous youngest was Lord Rosebery, who in 1894 had inherited power, as John Major did, from a formidable predecessor: Gladstone. Coincidentally, Rosebery was also a great admirer of Cromwell. Mr. Major would be advised not to hope for closer comparison with Rosebery's Premiership, which swiftly ran into trouble—Asquith said it was "ploughing the sands." Rosebery was out within sixteen months, defeated in the Commons on a vote over the supply and reserve of small-arms ammunition. Major himself has no more than eighteen months before he is obliged to call an election.)

The country also settled back to puzzle over a larger mystery: the nature of John Major, this man thrust so quickly into both the leadership and the Premiership, a man who in four days of campaigning achieved more than Michael Heseltine had done in five years of eating rubber-chicken dinners throughout the length of the country. What do we know about the sudden victor? He is, as his supporters told us perhaps too often during the election, "a man of the people."

His father, who was sixty-six when he begat John, was a music-hall and circus artiste, who with his first wife, Kitty Drum, had an act called Drum & Major; later, he set up in business manufacturing garden ornaments, including gnomes. John's schooling ended at sixteen; he worked as a navvy, spent nine months on the dole, and then applied to become a bus conductor. "There were three of us," he recalled when he was Chancellor of the Exchequer, "and there was an arithmetic test, then they tried us out with these machines to see how good we were, and I wasn't the best at that." (It is interesting to note how irrelevant academic qualifications have become to obtaining the highest office. The current leaders of the two main political parties have, between them, the combined achievement of a single pass degree, received at the second attempt, from the University of Wales. Is this bracingly meritocratic, dismally anti-intellectual, or just hazard?) Mr. Major, who had also dreamed of becoming a professional cricketer, joined an insurance company, then went into the Standard Chartered Bank. Local politics in South London led to national politics, a seat in Parliament in 1979, work in the Whips' Office, junior postings, an unhappy three months as Foreign Secretary, then a year at the Exchequer. He is said to be on the right of the Party in economics, on the left in social policy, central on Europe, and pretty much God knows where on the world outside. Everyone who has worked with him has described him—so far, at least—as decent, honest, able, and hardworking; the word *flair* is rarely mentioned. His first move in forming his Cabinet was shrewd enough: he appointed Michael Heseltine his Minister of the Environment, thus making the principal Tory critic of the poll tax responsible for sorting it out and saving the Government's neck. (Within days of Tarzan's return, an unemployed Lincolnshire builder became the first person to be jailed for refusing to pay the poll tax; with perfect appropriateness, the case happened in Grantham, a town famous mainly for being the birthplace of Margaret Thatcher.) Major's second move was less shrewd: having announced a Cabinet "of all the talents," he forgot to include a single woman.

Skeptics, of course, suggested that there was one there already:

Mrs. Thatcher's ghost would haunt No. 10, and her disembodied voice speak from the backseat of John Major's car. Certainly, and inevitably, in the frenzied second half of November 1990, his accession was eclipsed by her departure. How do politicians leave office? Broken in spirit? Sadder but wiser? Quietly proud? Anxious about the Verdict of History? Mrs. Thatcher, who after all had been dismissed from the highest public office by her own closest supporters and in full public view, left not just bullishly but in a mood of rampant self-congratulation. She took History by the lapels and slapped it around the face in case it was planning to give her less than her due. Speaking to Tory Party Central Office workers, she commented on how other European leaders were "quite grief-stricken" at her departure (which must be one of the drollest misconceptions of the last decade). Standing outside No. 10 Downing Street while the moving van headed for the South London suburb of Dulwich, she bade the public temporary farewell, reverting once more to the royal "we"—an increasing tendency in her latter years. "We are very happy," she said, "that we leave the United Kingdom in a very, very much better state than when we came here." It was breathtaking, quasi-regal, and also reminiscent of those discreet plaques in French water closets which beg you to leave the place on departure as clean as you would hope to find it on arrival.

She left, and all the main players could reflect that they had achieved something. Mr. Howe had gained the removal of Mrs. Thatcher; Mrs. Thatcher the succession she favored; Mr. Major the keys to No. 10; Mr. Heseltine a seat in the Cabinet and his own political rehabilitation. And Mr. Hurd? Even Mr. Hurd could joke that at least he'd got a good plot for a novel out of the previous fortnight's events. Other commentators reckoned the affair more than just the stuff of fiction. The word *tragedy* was frequently invoked, especially with reference to *Julius Caesar*, while the esteemed journalist Peter Jenkins, of *The Independent*, claimed to have observed a "tragic drama" rooted in Mrs. Thatcher's "Nietzschean will." But it's hardly likely that future tragedians scouring the twentieth century for material will fall delightedly upon the events of November 1990. Of course, they were richly exciting, and it is arguable that Mrs. Thatcher's inflexible sense of purpose and rightness, so much her strength when she was climbing to power and clamping herself there, became the weakness that helped her lose that power. But there was no great fall, as was demonstrated by the former Prime Minister's appearance in the Commons the very afternoon of her resignation. Here was no riven character; she was infrangible, buoyant, even jolly. And it's hard to talk of tragedy when the estimated price of the victim's memoirs is several million pounds and her husband has been rewarded with the hereditary title of baronet. So, at most, we had witnessed an absorbing drama, in which a democratically elected leader of the Conservative Party was democratically rejected by the same party, which decided that although she had won three general elections, her chances of winning a fourth were markedly slimmer than those of someone else.

And should we even be quite so certain of the pattern of events which apparently led so inescapably to this conclusion? When Mr. Heseltine walked out of the Cabinet in 1986, was it a decision of high principle or merely a resignation waiting to happen? When the Biting Doormat nipped the ankles of the Lady of the House, was it on a new matter of major importance, some unprecedented aspect of Thatcherian behavior, or just a weary sense that even downtrodden bristles can take only so much? And when the Conservative Party finally gave the Prime Minister too exiguous a majority for her own survival, were they censuring her style of leadership (which had brought them so much), or declaring that her stance on Europe was henceforth unacceptable, or worrying about the poll tax? It suits us to identify specific reasons, to play the game of if-only-she-hadn't-done-this, but perhaps what occurred was less close to Shakespeare and Nietzsche than it was to a marriage that runs out of steam and hits the divorce court. There the couple seek the reasons that explain their legal requests, and these reasons have to be couched in a way that the court understands: look how he knocked me about, see how she neglected the kids. But sometimes there are no reasons except that one partner doesn't want to live with the other anymore and doesn't see why he or she should. "Europe" was partly the cause of Mr. Heseltine's resignation, and of Sir Geoffrey Howe's resignation, and of Mrs. Thatcher's unacceptability. But one of the most perceptive, if least dramatic, views of her departure was offered by the Honorable William Walde-grave, whom Mrs. Thatcher had recently appointed Minister of Health. Did she have to go because of Europe? He replied, "Apart from two small groups, one of federalists, and one of anti-Europeans, it's very difficult to get the Conservative Party to argue over Europe. It was more a feeling that time passes, and eleven and a half years was enough." The divorce had its acrimonious moments, but the Conservative Party retains some gentlemanly instincts, and the couple will go on seeing quite a lot of each other despite the decree absolute. In fact, you could say they're getting on rather better now that they've divorced than they did in the last few years of their marriage.

January 1991

Bexleyheath Conservatives forgave Cyril Townsend, who retained his seat in the 1992 election.

▪ 4 ▪

Year of the Maze

I was once waiting for a plane at Heathrow, sitting in one of those bland pieces of space designed to turn the anxious into docile, processible units. Opposite me, an equally characterless passenger funnel began to disgorge arrivals from a Swissair flight. Some businessmen, a few tanned sporters of upmarket leisure wear, and then about two dozen inhabitants of the nineteenth century: a squire in noisy tweeds, a bishop in full fig, two lushly draped satiny ladies, a masher with velvet jacket and waxed mustaches, another gentleman of the cloth in black stockings. They moved with the assurance of the previous century, their carry-on luggage of finest Victorian leather. Silver-topped cane or three-decker novel to hand, they ignored both the twentieth-century surroundings and the twentieth-century disbelieving gaze. It felt like a moment of Carrollian hallucination. But reality's explanation proved both simpler and more interesting: here were members of the Sherlock Holmes Society of London returning from an outing to the Reichenbach Falls.

Nobody pointed, nobody mocked, no bustle was goosed. The British rather enjoy their reputation as a people poised between formality and eccentricity, and this applies not just to players but also to airport spectators: the fact that a whole bunch of these Victorian oddities existed confirmed their legitimacy. When playing the fool, there is safety in numbers. During Evelyn Waugh's time as an Oxford undergraduate in the twenties, there was a society called the Hysteron-Proteron Club. Its members, he recalled in *A Little Learning*, "put themselves to great discomfort by living a day in reverse, getting up in evening dress, drinking whisky, smoking cigars and playing cards, then at ten o'clock dining backwards starting with savouries and ending with soup." Today's less decadent undergraduates might instead join the Oxford Stunt Factory, whose members jump off suspension bridges while attached to large rubber bands, or roar down the Cresta Run in washing-up bowls while smoking a hookah.

A nation's larger character shows in its foreign policy, its formal architecture, its great writers. Curlicues of temperament are apparent farther away from the center. One typical indicator is garden design. In France, the continuing ferocity of bourgeois values can be observed even in up-country villages; nature there is mercilessly subdued, gravel laundered, bulbs regimented, hedges barbered, flowers submitted to rigid class distinction. The British tradition is more easygoing, treating nature more as chum than as victim; individuality and self-indulgence are allowed their say. At the suburban level, this might translate into a monkey puzzle tree in the front garden, a lean-to greenhouse at the back where an attempt is being made to grow the world's largest gooseberry, plus an ornamental pond in which plaster gnomes silently fish. At the grander level, this shows itself in the long tradition of the architectural folly: not just the sham ruin and shell grotto but the Gothic boathouse and castellated forge, the Moorish pagoda and Egyptian aviary, or the forty-foot-high stone pineapple at Dunmore Castle, in Stirlingshire. Another emanation of this spirit of planned fantasy is the garden maze, that curious form which lies at the conjunction of two English passions: the love of horticulture and the love of crossword puzzles. Rather to the surprise of even the relatively few people who have noticed, 1991 has been officially designated the Year of the Maze. Why 1991? Because this year the British, apart from melodiously huzzahing the bicentenary of Mozart's death like the rest of the world, have been able to celebrate pianissimo the tercentenary of the planting of the Hampton Court Maze.

On the ninth of June, 1662, the diarist and gardening expert John Evelyn visited Hampton Court, finding it "as noble and uniform a pile, and as capacious as any Gothic architecture can have made it." He praised the "incomparable furniture"; the Mantegnas; the "gallery of horns" (hunting trophies); the Queen's bed, which had cost eight thousand pounds; and the chapel roof, "excellently fretted and gilt." When he went outside, Evelyn, the translator of *The French Gardener* and soon-to-be author of the influential arboricultural treatise *Sylva*, was at first equally impressed: by the park, "now planted with sweet rows of lime trees," and by "the canal for water now nearly perfected." The "cradle-work of horn beam in the garden is, for the perplexed twining of the trees, very observable"—an adjective that, though certainly a term of praise, sounds rather cautious, like the word *collectible* as used by antique dealers to recommend items they consider vulgar but in which the moneyed amateur ignorantly delights. Evelyn concludes his description with the only moment of courtly doubt to ease from his pen. "All these gardens," he notes, "might be exceedingly improved, as being too narrow for such a palace."

Within Evelyn's lifetime, the gardens were indeed exceedingly improved, by George London and Henry Wise. Their plantings included the hedge maze, the most venerable of its kind extant in Britain and the world's most famous horticultural puzzle. Whether in fact we are right to celebrate its tercentenary this year is somewhat open to doubt: the gardens were laid out between 1689 and 1702, no precise planting record survives, and the birth year most commonly agreed on hitherto has been 1690. But we shouldn't be overfastidious when commerce and the tourist trade beckon. As Adrian Fisher, the country's leading maze designer, who for the last decade has been pushing for *any* year to be the Year of the Maze, explains, "an odd-dated year is best, because it avoids the Olympics, the World Cup, and things like that." Almost as usefully, 1991 makes a numerical palindrome, the sort of thing that appeals to mazophiles.

The Hampton Court Maze has had much to put up with in its first three hundred years. Early on, it had to fight off the attentions of

Capability Brown, who, as Royal Gardener, lived close by from 1764 to 1783 and had to be specifically instructed by the King not to interfere with it. In the following century, the maze had to endure sanctification in Jerome K. Jerome's jocose late Victorian banjo-'n'-boaters classic, *Three Men in a Boat*. And in modern times it has been required to survive the greedy descent of coach parties thronging to one of the most famous sites in England. The pathway has become asphalt, the plantings (originally hornbeam but now multispecied, with yew predominating) have to be protected in places by assegai railings, traffic throbs constantly on the road past the nearby Lion Gate, and the entrance fee has gone up from twopence in Jerome's time to £1.25. Despite all this, the maze retains a certain mystery, and the height of the hedges (about seven feet) even gives it a gentle menace. It is also a gratifyingly complicated maze. Harris, in *Three Men in a Boat*, confidently proclaims that all you have to do is keep taking the first turning to the right, and is punished by getting pompously lost. The correct, quick way to get to the center is to turn left on entering the maze, then right, right again, left, left, left, and left. The alternative, slow way is to use the "hand on wall" technique, which unfailingly—if ploddingly—cracks labyrinths of this type. Place your right (or left) hand on the right (or left) wall of green, and doggedly keep it there, in and out of dead ends, and you will finally get to the middle. There you will find two white horse chestnuts whose trunks bear a furious intaglio of victorious names. Cyril, Mad, Tito, Yin, Mig, and Iky, among others, have all conquered the complexities of this trapezoid puzzle, whose design, incidentally, was used for many of the earliest behaviorist experiments on rats. Then there is the problem of getting out. All you need to do is . . . but that would be telling. And don't expect any help from the man at the ticket kiosk, either. What does he do when people shout for help? "We don't take any notice." These are cruel times, still stained by the ideal of Thatcherite self-help. "In the old days there used to be someone on the viewing platform to guide people out at the end of the day. Now we just lock up and go away. They'll find the turnstile sooner or later."

Britain has the richest and most varied maze tradition in Europe, with splendid examples of the two main labyrinthine genres. Hampton Court is a classic hedge maze: such puzzles are usually found on private land, adornments to aristocratic territory (or, more recently, to country house hotels and theme parks); planting materials generally include yew, holly, hornbeam, and beech. The other type is the ground-level turf or stone labyrinth. Map reading here is no problem: a unicursal path leads inevitably, if circuitously, to a central goal. Such mazes are usually found on common land, at settlements with Norse origins, and were presumably constructed by the immigrants as a badge of their culture. Their original Scandinavian purposes were practical as well as symbolic: they were used either as a means of bringing good fortune to fishermen (nasty weather would be persuaded to rush in and get trapped) or as places to perform fertility and courtship rites, with a maid running complicatedly to the center pursued by her puffing swain.

The largest surviving turf-cut maze in the world is on the common at Saffron Walden in Essex: thirty-eight yards across, it looks from the air like a circular griddle pan with four jug ears, and the path that winds its serpentine way to the center is almost a mile long. The maze's date of origin is unknown, the earliest reference to its existence coming in 1699, when the Guild of the Holy Trinity paid fifteen shillings for it to be recut. (It has been recut six times since then, and in 1911 the path, previously chalk, was relaid in brick.) An eighteenth-century document describes the ancient running contests that still took place on it: "The Maze at Saffron Walden is the gathering place for the young men of the district, who have a system of rules connected with walking the maze, and wagers of gallons of beer are frequently won or lost. For a time it was used by the beaux and belles of the town, a young maiden standing in the centre, known as Home, while the boy tried to get her out in record time without stumbling."

Walking the Saffron Walden maze takes about fifteen minutes if you decide not to cheat, and since there are no forking paths the only anxiety aroused is about whether you might turn an ankle where the narrow brick path and the foot-wide turf corridors meet at uneven heights. It is a pleasantly mind-emptying activity—a sort of pedal mantra—and its uniformity of experience tempts you to reflect on how simple some of the Simple Pleasures of Times Past were. Finally, you reach the raised circular mound where an ash tree stood until it was burned down during the Guy Fawkes celebrations of 1823. Here intimations of twentieth-century superiority tend to evaporate as you examine the celebratory detritus left by contemporary smokers and dogs.

Nowadays, the curiosity of the tourist has largely replaced the atavism of the turf runner or the piety of the Christian pilgrim as motive for maze treading; but occasionally the old associations resurface. When the previous Archbishop of Canterbury, Robert Runcie, was enthroned in March 1980, he included in his address the following psychoanalytic detail: "I had a dream of a maze. There were some people very close to the center, but they could not find a way through. Just outside the maze others were standing. They were further away from the heart of the maze, but they would be there sooner than the party that fretted and fumed inside." Such a dream might be taken to offer surprising encouragement to those of us who loiter theologically outside the labyrinth; more directly, it inspired Lady Brunner, of Greys Court in the Thames Valley, to order the construction of an Archbishop's Maze. A neat brick-and-turf design, bedding easily into gardens that consist of a series of secret spaces each with its private character, it is both unicursal and multicursal, and bubbles with Christian symbolism (the seven days of Creation, the nine hours of Agony, the twelve Apostles). At its center, a Roman cross of gray Bath stone is laid within a Byzantine cross of blue Westmorland stone, proposing reconciliation between West and East, Catholic and Protestant, Roman and Orthodox (an ambition dear to the incoming Archbishop's heart). On a square stone pillar, four texts are carved, the most mazily appropriate being from St. Augustine: "We come to God not by navigation but by love." The Archbishop of Canterbury himself dedicated the maze a bare nineteen months after going public with his dream, and if its psychic origins seem perhaps a little back-to-front—the symbol inspiring the Christian thought, rather than the Christian thought embodying itself in the symbol—it shows that one strand of the maze tradition is still alive.

There is further evidence of this, if of a less Establishment kind. While mazes appeal to cerebral crossword-puzzle solvers, it's clear that they equally delight the spoon benders. Witness the large and respectful gathering at the Church of St. James Piccadilly in the fourth month of the Year of the Maze, to hear the words of the American labyrinthologist Sig Lonegren. Wren's church is elegant, rectilinear, and cool, arguing a rational relationship with God. Sig Lonegren, a resident of Vermont, is rumpled, curvilinear (potbellied, to be precise), and effusive, leaning perhaps toward the intuitive in intellectual matters. The evening began in the modern ecclesiastical manner–that's to say, one calculated to bemuse the outsider. First, we lit three candles–"one for Love, one for Truth, and one for something of the speaker's choosing." Sig had chosen Communication. Next, we had a democratic show of hands as to whether we should have two, five, or ten minutes' silent meditation. Being British, we chose the middle path on this one. Finally, we had an obligatory two minutes' conversation with a nearby stranger, and then we were away. Well, almost. There were just a few announcements, including the almost parodic one that there would be no food tonight, as "Inneka has gone to a business-network meeting."

Besides being a labyrinthologist, Sig Lonegren has been a big twig in the American Society of Dowsers; indeed, his first volume, *Spiritual Dowsing*, is still available. He has put in good time at Glastonbury, the center of English hippie-spiritual activity, and has the unnerving habit of referring to the Earth as "Mom"–as in "There's something about being right on Mom, right on the Earth, when you're dowsing." And his involvement with mazes? "For the past twenty years, I've been working with ancient tools that can help us with our intuition." So we were off into an evening of "sacred geometry," "nodes of power," numerology, Mom, the music of the labyrinth (wonkily executed on the recorder by Sig), Jungian-shadow talk, "what I like to call herstory," and the myth of Daedalus cozified for modern use. (Daedalus told Icarus not to fly too close to the sun. . . . "But do kids listen? Never.") Sig, promiscuously mixing his religions and civilizations as if sifting homemade muesli, worried briefly whether anyone might take offense when he modishly renamed the

Lord's Prayer "the Lord-and-Lady's Prayer." But who would take offense at anything in the modern Anglican Church? Only the shades of Wren's benefactors growled back from their beleaguered lair in the organ loft—whence they could see that Sig had laid out a red-yarn labyrinth in front of the altar area, so that we could all tread it after the lecture. Well, all but one. As Sig reached his closing theme of the evening, "How we can *use* the labyrinth today," the Candle of Communication blazed on unashamedly. That's enough awe, admiration, diversion—what about *use*? "The labyrinth is a problem-solving device," announced Sig. "It works great with kids." At which point, like a yellow-press reporter before a den of vice, your correspondent made an excuse and left.

In 1980, there were forty-two mazes in Britain. The present count stands at more than a hundred, with about twenty of them having been opened during the Year of the Maze. Over a third of those built in the past decade are the work of a firm called Minotaur Designs, whose chief executive is Adrian Fisher. A plumpish, ebullient forty-year-old Englishman, Fisher comes from the other side of the rainbow to Sig Lonegren. He lives in a large red-brick semi in St. Albans, his front door guarded by two garish knee-high gnomes, "so that we don't get too pompous about gardening ideas." Inside his front room are stacked rolls of vibrantly colored plastic matting, which make up into cart-away mazes. Formerly a management consultant with ITT, Fisher built his first maze in his father's garden. (It was made of holly, and "if you turned left right, left right, left right, you got to the middle; if you turned right left, right left, right left, you went one and a half times round the maze and still got to the middle.") He became a full-time maze designer in 1983. Since then, he has constructed hedge mazes, path mazes (including the Archbishop's at Greys Court), water mazes, pavement mazes in city centers, a Beatles maze in Liverpool with a diving Yellow Submarine, and even a mirror maze at Wookey Hole Caves in Somerset. Such items do not come cheap. A maze might start in the £20,000 to £50,000 bracket—a pair of Lion and Unicorn brick pavements for the pedestrian precinct in Worksop cost £35,000 each—and can rise to £250,000 or more. Fisher also designs bus-route maps and visitor plans for country houses; these will cost you less.

Minotaur Designs is the only maze-building firm in Europe, and probably in the world; Fisher has heard of no other, at any rate. Asked if the extraordinary resurgence of the British maze in the last ten years can be credited to him, he replies, "Yes, mainly." He sees maze design as "a thoroughly modern art form" and "a new way of treating landscape," and locates the appeal of the labyrinth in its being "a description of life." ("The choices you made in your twenties you're stuck with in your thirties.") He has noticed the way mazes seem to release the spirit of the child in most adults but becomes wary, not to say downright evasive, when asked if for him they have any transcendental element. "It's a bit hard when there are kids around," he finally concedes. He is happier talking about the business and design side of things. "My style," he explains, "is to find a market where no one's in, and exploit it." He thinks of a maze as "a marketing machine"; to give one a name is "a good marketing strategy." This is all sensible, if unmystical. But then even at the Archbishop's rampantly spiritual maze few visitors, on reaching the armillary sundial at the center, appear to reflect, as they are intended to, upon how they, frail mortals standing on a particular spot at a particular time, are rendered inconsequential by the eternal time and eternal space of the divine setup. Far from it: when I was there, the next maze solver along first checked his watch, and then lamented that sundials aren't adjustable for British summer time.

As Fisher appreciates, there is a bums-on-seats aspect to maze building nowadays. Rare is the landed viscount who desires an enigma in hornbeam for his own private puzzlement; he wants one because he needs to open his parkland to the charabanc crowd and a maze is an extra attraction, one that seems to fit historically without being vulgar, something more tony than a ghost train. It goes with the homemade jam, the garden center, and the leatherette bookmarks embossed with monumental brasses. So some of the country's oldest and most visited great houses have only recently become bemazed: Chatsworth in 1962, Longleat in 1978, Hatfield House in the 1980s, while Blenheim acquired the world's largest symbolic hedge maze in March of this year. Where the designer puts the maze that embellishes the grand house is a decision based as much on tourist throughput as on landscape aesthetics. Leeds Castle, in Kent, offers the tourist (as of 1988) a split-level extravaganza with surprise grotto and underground exit tunnel; Fisher explains that this maze is deliberately placed quite some distance from the castle, so that customers can be "spread around like Marmite."

What constitutes a good maze? According to Fisher, one that contributes positively to its setting, one that makes an enjoyable puzzle ("*Fun* is the word that gets lost"), and one that is designed with imagination, so as to make the experience unfold "like a Disney ride," leading, preferably, to "a sensational treat" at the end. Thus, a balance of time spent and trickery conquered, plus reward. And since Hampton Court's successors must appeal to the turnstile rather than to seigneurial solipsism, the attention span and problem-solving skills of the populace at large have to be taken into account. When asked what makes a bad maze, Fisher cites the one at Longleat (not built by him) with active disapproval. "It goes on for an hour and a half, and that's not funny. It doesn't vary its pace, and that's not funny. There's an utter contempt for the market." Or, at least, for the British market. Perhaps Longleat was aiming at Japanese customers. In the 1980s, there was a brief but intense maze craze in Japan, with more than two hundred built in five years. Elaborate, three-dimensional, and made of wood, they were also adjustable: the pattern could be altered from day to day and loyal customers regularly remystified. There would be a series of objectives to be reached, for each of which the visitor would be rewarded with a stamp on his or her entry card. Solving these Japanese mazes took many happy hours—a happiness not unconnected with competitive frenzy.

Fisher's design team has also been responsible for one of the boldest, most spectacular, and most contentious mazes built in modern times. Kentwell Hall, near Long Melford in Suffolk, is a distinguished Tudor manor house in mellowed red brick; its principal buildings form three tall sides of a square, with the fourth side opening onto a moat and the access bridge across it. The courtyard, once cobbled, had long since disappeared under layers of gravel when the present owners took charge. They decided against excavating the cobbles and preferred instead to pave the courtyard with toning brick. So far, so uncontroversial. But as the owner, Patrick Phillips, QC, explains to visitors, "we determined to make it something special." The something special turned out to be a huge pavement maze in the shape of a monster Tudor rose, seventy feet across, made from 25,000 bricks, about 17,000 of which had to be hand-cut. The bricks are of four colors—pinky red, brown, orange, and cream—and they took two men five months to lay. To install such a maze today would cost about £120,000. "We decided upon a Tudor motif because of the house's strong Tudor flavor and our own interest in the period," Phillips explains. "We also wished to celebrate the five-hundredth anniversary of the Tudor accession. We decided upon a maze puzzle because we thought it would be fun and would re-create in a modern idiom the Tudor fancy of a knot garden."

Did such an addition require planning permission from the local council? "We wrote to them," Adrian Fisher explains, "and said did we need permission for bricking the courtyard in an unusual manner, and they said don't even bother to waste our time by applying." There were some protests from the local civic society, which fell silent when the official opening of the courtyard included the announcement that the maze had won a Heritage in the Making Award from the British Tourist Authority. (The prizes were sponsored by a dairy company, the winners receiving a lump of cheese cast in bronze, with a bronze cheese knife alongside.) But was Fisher himself trepidatious about thrusting his design into an established manor house? He characterizes his attitude to Kentwell as "mildly reverential," and explains, "To be too timid would be pathetic." It's a bit like a mugging, he says: if the potential victim is too acquiescent, he is liable to suffer the more.

This is all very well, but who is the mugger and who the muggee? Some might judge Kentwell Hall victim rather than assailant. For if the pavement maze looks fairly contentious from ground level, it increases in forcefulness as the eye gets farther off the ground. The maze is certainly "very observable," as John Evelyn might have put it. From above, either you see toning brickwork and a harmonious symbolic design that extends the house's period flavor with a characterful modern flourish, or else you see something that resembles a vast–and vastly cute–target for a parachuting competition. And isn't there something fundamentally dubious, if very British, about the very concept of Heritage in the Making? It speaks of self-consciousness, of historical preening. Every nation naturally has its bucketload of guilt about the stuff that's been knocked down over the centuries (and mazes, which are swiftly obliterated by mere neglect, have been lost in large numbers). But do we assuage that guilt by pronouncing some wet-eared artifact an instant classic? Is it good for cultural items to be no sooner created than lacquered and preserved: cheese cast in bronze? Isn't it impertinent to second-guess history in this way? The courtyard maze at Kentwell Hall has forfeited its right to a real, actual, bruisable existence, a life in the present, because it has already been classified, with nosy authoritarianism, as the future's past.

September 1991

▪ 5 ▪

John Major Makes a Joke

At the Conservative Party Conference in early October, the Prime Minister made a joke. In truth, he made several, and they were hard to miss, because John Major has not yet mastered one of the refinements of public comedy, which is to smile after you make the hit rather than beforehand. But there was one particular jest that merits recall and annotation. The Labour Party had held its annual conference a week or so previously, and Mr. Major allowed himself the traditional accusation that the Opposition had been purloining some of his Government's ideas. He continued, "They don't even hide it when they steal some of my clothes. Did you see how many of them were wearing gray suits last week? Have they no shame?"

The first point to make is that Mr. Major's idea of a joke—or, more exactly, his speechwriters' idea of the sort of joke that is appropriate to Mr. Major—is very different from his predecessor's idea of a joke. Mrs. Thatcher, for most of her sovereignty, showed no public awareness of the existence of humor. A joke for her would be a sign of feebleness, an attempt at consensus politics, something uneconomic and possibly subversive, like a bottle of foreign mineral water on the table at a Downing Street banquet. Hefty sarcasm was about as far as she went in this field until almost the end of her Premiership, when there was a last-ditch attempt to project a new, caring, human Maggie in place of the Robocop figure previously running the show. So occasionally she relaxed into the sort of wordplay that would stun a rhino: attacking Jacques Delors, the president of the European Commission, she maintained her furious opposition to federalism, which included "federalism by the back Delors." Even in the joke she remained aggressive and dismissive. Whereas the quip Mr. Major delivered to the conference was modest, self-deprecating, and voter-friendly.

The second point to consider is the reference to the gray suit. Mr. Major had several problems when he took over in November of 1990, one of them being that hardly anyone knew who he was or what he was like. Down the Thatcher years, there had been a number of young aspirants unofficially tagged as Possible Successor. It was an arduous post, rather like being the court favorite of Catherine the Great, and those whose summer of favor ran out were left occupying a difficult—even risible—position. But Mr. Major had the good fortune to find himself the frolicker standing next to the sole remaining chair when the music happened to stop. As he settled onto the seat cushion molded firmly by the capacious derriere of another and found the arms a little higher than he'd imagined, he had an immediate tactical problem. Mrs. Thatcher had been removed because enough members of her party thought that her domineering dogmatism had become electorally counterproductive. On the other hand, Mr. Major had been the candidate of the outgoing leader and the die-hard Thatcherites. So he had to keep the BUSINESS AS USUAL sign up in the window while redecorating the place and updating the stock: instead of barbed wire and rifles, the family store would in future sell chocolate bars and liniment. And in terms of personal image—where, admittedly, there was less room for maneuver—Mr. Major also had a dilemma. If he tried to play the decisive, uncompromising leader, he could only come across as a pale substitute for his predecessor; if he took his time and went back to the antiquarian system of consultation, of being prepared to change his point of view when presented with a convincing argument, he would be accused of indecision. The new Prime Minister has had an occasional stab at audacious leadership–such as proposing a safe haven for the Kurds while others were still dozing–but the style didn't really suit. Instead, Mr. Major has broadly followed the honorable political line of not doing anything in particular unless it's otherwise inevitable, while nevertheless proclaiming that there is Still Much to Do. He is therefore frequently denounced by the Opposition as a ditherer.

He has also been denounced as dull, boring, and uncharismatic. But in certain political times (and in the context of your predecessor) these characteristics are not necessarily negative. Add to this that all sides agreed early on that Mr. Major was a decent, honest chap, the sort of bloke who liked to watch the cricket from a stripy deck chair while a steaming mug of tea warmed his groin. He didn't have anything threatening about him, like an academic record, a furtive interest in modern sculpture, or a tendency to use long words in his speeches. He was the sort of PM who, it was usefully allowed to leak out, would stop his official car and tuck into a humble meal at a humble motorway restaurant known by the resolutely uncharismatic name of Happy Eater. In other words, the natural process of political presentation and self-presentation was under way: limitations were made into normality, normality into virtue. And so when at his first Tory conference as leader–which could also prove his last, since an election must take place in the first six months of 1992–Mr. Major acknowledged his self-image as a fellow in a gray suit, he was acknowledging what could not be changed and was now declared to be what the country requires. Call me a dull dog if you wish, he seemed to be saying, but that is what I am: self-made, hardworking, unspectacular, trustworthy, the very spirit of middle England. Snobs may find Mr. Major suburban, but then snobs always have fewer votes than suburbanites. The Prime Minister has not yet, so far as is publicly known, visited the Toulouse-Lautrec show at the Hayward Gallery (he has until January 19), but were he to do so he might be pleased by one of the artist's most elegant and daring lithographs, *The Englishman at the Moulin Rouge* (1892). It shows a correctly dressed middle-aged man accosting two young women. The background is bright yellow and bright blue; the principal female figure has startlingly red hair and a dress of delicate green. Thrust into this surround of cheery color, the Englishman is depicted in monolithic gray. His suit, hat, tie, gloves, and stick are gray; his hair, mustache, face, and ears are gray. The tone washes ineradicably through him.

And the final point to make about Mr. Major's joke is that it contains some truth. We have now entered that final, wearisome stage before a general election when the contending parties are keenest to avoid mistakes, when image becomes more important than policy, and when the gap between Labour and Conservative in terms of promised programs tends to narrow. Hence the accusation of clothes stealing. For this year will see the Battle of the Men in Gray Suits. Long gone is the time of nobs in grouse-moor tweeds versus yobs in cloth caps; now everywhere you look is a seal beach of gray. The two parties are shuffling closer to one another, like gawky cadets on parade, each keeping eyes front and pretending that the other one is doing the moving. The rough aim for each of them in the next election is to present itself as an efficient, forward-looking organizer of a market economy who yet displays the correct degree of social concern. The Tories know that their decade-long fling with Thatcherite ideology must come to an end—that it is time to dig out from the attic the old mothbally uniform of pragmatism, and also make sure that not too many hospitals close down in the coming months. The Labour Party, having lost three elections on the trot and having seen the so-called socialist Eastern bloc collapse, has (according to your point of view) either junked most of its long-held principles or finally adjusted to the realities of the world. For instance, just when Gorbachev was making the world safer and serious disarmament was beginning, the British Labour Party reversed its nonnuclear policy and declared that it loved the bomb—or, at any rate, loved it a little bit, though naturally much less than the Tories did, and anyway it was a mistake to go naked into the conference chamber, while Labour would, of course, be more responsible, more caring bomb users than the Conservatives in the unfortunate event . . . And all because at election after election it had become painfully clear that the British voter didn't much care for a stance of principled emasculation. Similarly, the suave and harmonious enthusiasm for Europe currently displayed by the Labour Party contrasts ironically with the huffiness and fretful insularity of earlier years. But then Europe is where self-respecting men in suits congregate nowadays. In Europe, they wear power gray.

Britain has no fixed electoral term—only a five-year limit within which the Government must face the nation. So if you are elected with a small majority you might swiftly dash back to the voters for a more generous and useful endorsement, and if things are going badly you might hang on until the last possible minute. This flexibility gives the Government a tactical advantage; instead of the parties' gearing their efforts to a known month, there is much posturing on both sides about announcing the date. The spectacle often resembles the start of a playground fight where the two opponents dance around trying to look tough, one of them shouting, "Come on, I'm ready for you, let's see what you're made of, scaredy-cat," while the other strikes a nobler pose, ignoring the taunts and declaring, "*I'll* be the one to say when the fight begins." Such ritualistic behavior is intensified at the time of the party conferences. This autumn, there were authoritative leaks that the Prime Minister would definitely—well, almost definitely—go to the country before the end of the year, yes he would, almost certainly in November—that is, unless he changed his mind.

This will-he/won't-he atmosphere was heightened by the appearance in late September of the latest TV commercials from the two parties. If Major versus Neil Kinnock is the main scrap in the coming months, we shouldn't ignore a tasty little scuffle lower down the bill: that between Hugh (*Chariots of Fire*) Hudson, a supplier of Labour's TV advertising, and John (*Midnight Cowboy*) Schlesinger, brought in to beef up the Conservative effort. Given the near moribundity of the domestic film industry, which for the past decade has been told by the Government to stand on its own wheelchair, there is a cinematic as well as a political interest for the viewer. If it is not quite a head-to-head battle—Schlesinger has been brought in more as a troubleshooter, a last-minute rejigger, whereas Hudson was committed from the start—it promises slightly higher production values at least. Not that the first round of commercials exactly stays quivering in the memory. The Schlesinger film had sunrises and sunsets, a new-born baby, and Mozart's Twenty-first Piano Concerto: Tory Britain, we deduced, was peaceful and pastoral, energetic but also somehow elegiac. Hudson's Labour riposte was a toiling piece of agitprop, in which a couple of eager parents (Mr. and Mrs. Voter) went to the school for a report on their boy (the Conservative Party) from the headmaster (God, perhaps), only to be told, with plodding pre-dictability, "The Tories have come bottom of the class" and "Quite frankly, I wouldn't let them run the tuckshop."

In the Conservative commercial, the Prime Minister was seen in a brief sound bite speaking of "a nation at ease with itself." Such soporific complacency is, of course, traditional Tory policy: in 1957, Prime Minister Macmillan, echoing—or perhaps stealing—the 1952 Democratic Party slogan, assured voters that "most of our people have never had it so good." The Thatcher years were in many re-spects an aberration, for the idea that the British way of life needs a good kicking around comes hard to a Conservative; the corny image of the nation as a sleeping lion, with the emphasis on the sleeping, is much preferred. Eighteen months (the time from Mrs. Thatcher's de-parture to the latest possible election date) was not long for John Major to shake off this new, ahistoric image of the Tories as a radical, reforming party; and shaking off the image was much connected with shaking off Mrs. Thatcher—with persuading her to keep her mouth shut.

But Mrs. Thatcher has never been good at keeping her mouth shut—indeed, bawling out trade unionists, the unemployed, foreigners, and other miscreants has been part of her enduring appeal to the British public. Since her retirement as PM, she has had her memoirs to think about—the selling, that is, not yet the writing. There has also been the setting up of the Thatcher Foundation, a kind of interna-tional think tank, whose officially registered objectives are of nar-coleptic generality, and were much better summed up by the lady herself: the foundation's aim, she said, was to "perpetuate all the kinds of things I believe in." The project got off to an inauspicious start when the Charity Commissioners refused it tax-relieving status, on the ground that spreading Mrs. Thatcher's word could not by any stretch of the rules be considered a charitable activity; the foundation is also now registered, unpatriotically, in Switzerland, where it is much harder for journalists to discover which foreign billionaires are putting up the moola. The start-up target was £12 million per annum, and Mrs. Thatcher has spent a good part of the last year on the stump among the very rich: the Sultan of Brunei is said to have promised $5 million the other week. These trips naturally involve pleasant bits of flummery, like the acceptance of honorary degrees. She got one in November from Kuwait University (having been turned down for one a few years ago by Oxford: a unique snub to a Prime Minister). In her acceptance speech she revealed a hitherto unsuspected backer for her worldview. "Leafing through Tennyson's works, as I sometimes do in the early hours, looking for inspiration," she had found lines that encapsulated and foreshadowed the Thatcher philosophy:

> This main miracle, that thou art thou
> With power on thine own act, and on the world.

Tennyson's poem "The Two Greetings," a rather maundering celebration of the birth of a child, is in fact entirely devoid of any political subtext; but no doubt we should just be grateful when any verse sets off a ping on a politician's late-night sonar.

The traditional way of keeping an ex–Prime Minister busy–that's to say, out of harm's way–is to shunt him or her off to the House of Lords. It was always an irritation to Mrs. Thatcher's Parliamentary acolytes that her Tory predecessor, Edward Heath, resisted both the Lords and a tempting ambassadorship, preferring to stay in the Commons as a spikily disapproving remnant of an earlier, more liberal Conservatism. The shunting off of Mrs. Thatcher, if agreed on in theory, is proving no less tricky. The idea of a sweet transition to ermined dotage came unstuck when it emerged that Mrs. Thatcher did not have in mind what her immediate predecessors understood by retiring to the Lords. Apart from Heath, who stayed in the Commons without even the promotion of a knighthood, recent Premiers—Wilson, Callaghan, Home—have taken life peerages. Mrs. Thatcher let it be known that, far from accepting such a half-baked recognition of her services to the nation as a mere personal ennoblement for the rest of her days, she wanted the full hereditary works. WAY CLEARED FOR THATCHER TO BECOME COUNTESS OF FINCHLEY, said a front-page headline in *The Times* of October 3, and the whole potentially embarrassing issue of hereditary peers having a hand in democratic government came to the fore again. It's true that Harold Macmillan accepted an earldom, but he held out for more than twenty years after leaving the Premiership, and took the honor at the age of ninety only, it is said, out of boredom. Winston Churchill, a regular—indeed, fetishistic—figure of reference in Mrs. Thatcher's speeches, even turned down a dukedom. In her case, there is an extra element. The prospect of her son proceeding cozily from Mr. Mark to Sir Mark to the Earl of Finchley and thus becoming one of the nation's legislators is one to appall the meritocrat and delight only the satirist. Thatcher Junior's heavy-handedness has already put off several likely supporters of the Thatcher Foundation, including Charles Price, the former United States Ambassador to the Court of St. James's. His delicacy of approach was illustrated on a recent fund-raising tour of the Far East, when he offended one Hong Kong millionaire with the memorable instruction "It's time to pay up for Mumsie."

The fact that even the nature of Mrs. Thatcher's thank-you present from the Conservatives became an issue—one commentator remarked that the title Countess of Finchley was "the heraldic equivalent of a pair of furry dice bouncing around in the back of a state coach"—shows what a contentious figure she remains. Even a year after her departure from office, her capacity for provoking fission in her own party is unmatched. At the Tory conference, for instance, it was judged unsafe to let the lady address the delegates and the nation directly. But since it would have been overbrusque to suddenly declare her a nonperson, she was allowed a brief appearance in the conference hall—a vision bite, if not a sound bite. The ovation she received for her nonspeaking walk-on part lasted five minutes and was measured at 101.0 decibels. The keynote speech of John Major received applause of four minutes and twenty-eight seconds, reaching the lower decibel level of 97.5. (Lesser ministers garnered one to three minutes, with noise levels in the low 90s.) Interestingly, the only speaker to raise greater hysteria than the silent Mrs. Thatcher was one of the men who brought her down, Michael Heseltine; he got the clapometer up to 102.0.

Mr. Major's need and desire to show difference from the previous leadership declared themselves in the choreographing of his appearance. Low-key and feel-good in style as he is, he entered the hall from the rear, shaking hands with grassroots Tories on his way to the rostrum. After his speech—or, more exactly, after the subsequent patriotic singing of "Land of Hope and Glory" (and the 100-decibel, five-minute-and-fourteen-second ovation which *that* set off)—he returned to circulate below the salt. As for the speech itself, an indication of its New Tory Tone can be had from Mr. Major's reference to Churchill. For ten years, Mrs. Thatcher appeared to own the copyright on allusions to Winston, as she familiarly called him: only she could smoke the cigar and doff the gray homburg, because she, too, had fought the foreigners on the beaches, urged blood, sweat, toil, and so on. Mr. Major's Churchillian moment came when he was discussing government education policy. Churchill's praise of the RAF Fighter Command's performance in the Battle of Britain ("Never in the field of human conflict was so much owed by so many to so few") was tweaked by Major into a joke about his own thin scholastic record and the curiosity it has provoked among journalists: "Never has so much been written about so little." It was jauntily downbeat, unrhetorical, human.

But unrhetorical is what Mr. Major is, and what he is best advised to stay. Agreeable drabness of diction will offer fetching contrast not just with Mrs. Thatcher but also with his immediate opponent, Neil Kinnock, who, despite having curbed some of his orotund tendencies, is always likely to lapse back into Welsh windbaggery. The only moment of near-rhetoric in Mr. Major's text came when he embarked on that painful but necessary part of a keynote speech, My Vision of the Future (though My Vision of Next Week might have been more characteristic, and perhaps more voter-useful). He was hinting at a possible change in the inheritance tax: "I want," he declared, "to see wealth cascading down the generations." This seemed all wrong; in Mr. Major's world, nothing does or should *cascade*. Waterfalls are much too dramatic: a metaphor from irrigation or, better still, plumbing would have seemed apter. And though Britain under Mrs. Thatcher has been coarsened and desensitized about the notion of great, vulgar gouts of money, the Niagara splash of cascading wealth still has an unmerited—indeed, American—sound to it.

For the rest of his fifty-seven-minute speech, Mr. Major played safe, with bumbling banality and uncontentious hopefulness. "I should like to live in a world where opportunity is for everyone, where peace is truly universal and where freedom is secure," he declared, thereby distinguishing himself from few other politicians in the Western World except intransigent Brezhnevites and members of the Ku Klux Klan. Mr. Major wants a strong Britain, a secure defense, respect for the law, good education, lower inflation, a crackdown on crime, European partnership, a classless society, and a free health service for all. Mr. Major's "vision" of "freedom and opportunity" sounds—even if it does not quite mean—the same as everybody else's; it is as flat as a pavement, and this is its appeal. Received wisdom states that those who occupy the middle of the road in politics risk getting run down from both directions. But in Britain today all the political traffic keeps its snout firmly planted on the big white line; few see the appeal of the gutter, and the verges are being returned to cow parsley, the shrew, and the wren.

Mr. Major, both in public and in private life, has no vivid characteristics, no suspected vices, no dangerous passions. He is a satirist's nemesis. Attempts to call him Major Minor and other variants on Joseph Heller have largely petered out; old Major, the prize Middle White boar in *Animal Farm*, seems no help. One early interviewer, catching the Prime Minister in a relaxed moment when his pants had ridden down an inch or two, spotted that Mr. Major's shirt was tucked into his undershorts. Whether this sartorial inelegance is a matter of habit or was the momentary and venial maladroitness of a busy politician remains unverified, but it did give the country's most pugnacious satirical cartoonist—Steve Bell, of the *Guardian*—a welcome point of entry. He draws Mr. Major in his Lautrecian gray suit but with his undershorts—unstylishly pouchy Y-fronts, of course, not boxers—worn over his pants. Occasionally in the life of Bell's strip, the PM persuades his other ministers, as a demonstration of loyalty, to wear their undershorts publicly after the same fashion. It is a pleasant thrust, but such is Major's unconfrontational nature that the caricature no longer seems particularly fierce. This graphic reversal of over- and underwear has come to seem almost cozy: downbeat, unrhetorical, human—yes, all of that again.

It is to Mr. Major's advantage that very little cosmetic work has had to be done on him. Mrs. Thatcher fixed her voice, her hair, her clothes; George Bush called upon the valuable coaching skills of Roger Ailes. ("There you go again with that fucking hand!" he once berated the President. "You look like a fucking pansy!") All Mr. Major has to do is remember to tuck his shirt into the correct garment, and there he is—Prime Minister. When you see him in the flesh, what is extraordinary is that he looks exactly as you would imagine, neither taller nor shorter, drabber nor sprucer, jollier nor gloomier. In the short term, this ordinariness—or simplicity—will probably benefit Mr. Major. We seem, domestically, to be living in ordinary times at the moment. Our new Archbishop of Canterbury, George Carey, is a very ordinary man—one who on attaining office gave his first national press interview not to *The Times* or the *Daily Telegraph* but to *Reader's Digest*. Mr. Major's equivalent was to give a quite magnificently platitudinous interview this summer to *Hello!* magazine. This is a publication that specializes in not embarrassing celebrities, unless they have the wit to be embarrassed by glutinous fawning. Princess Di's brother was caught with his trousers down not long after his marriage, and ended up indecorously trading sexual insults across the press with his ex-girlfriend; *Hello!* was where the Viscount's rehabilitation could begin. *Hello!* (the exclamation mark in the title aptly reflects the magazine's tone of excited innocence) likes to look to the future, prefers tragedy to smut, and interviews from the kneeling position. So John and Norma Major, quizzed about the sort of things they liked to do on their holidays in Spain, were able to reply very much in the spirit of the journal. Thus John: "Well, first of all I get a bit more sleep than I'm used to. I've even been known to have a Spanish siesta! And a very good invention it is too." Asked to expatiate on the national characteristics of the locals, Mr. Major responded, "The Spanish are a very warm people. When I became Prime Minister I received a number of charming letters from Candeleda—even a sausage." *Hello!* avoided the potentially criminal aspect of this sunny avowal—the question of whether the gifted sausage was raw or cooked. If raw, its importation, even by a Prime Minister, would be in breach of Her Majesty's Customs and Excise regulations.

So Mr. Major's game plan from the Tory conference to the forthcoming election is one for which he seems by nature well suited: that of not doing anything rash. The Labour Party, despite appearing to demand a general election in the autumn, can remain privately content that it has been put off beyond the winter. The longer Mr. Major goes on, the greater the chance of some blissful foul-up. Labour can point to an encouraging tradition of recent British Prime Ministers being brought down by a tough "winter of discontent" (a phrase that has suffered a rare linguistic reversal: a metaphor in Shakespeare's original use, it has now been turned back into a realistic description). Both Heath and Callaghan fell after hibernal turmoil. On the other hand, the trade unions are now in a much weaker position than they were a decade ago. And the longer Mr. Major continues, the less he will look like a stopgap and the more like a genuine, sausage-eating Prime Minister.

But it all depends on the avoidance of trouble. Trouble with a *T,* and that usually stands for Thatcher. If the Tories damped her down at their conference, she burst spectacularly into flame again at the end of November. The occasion was a Commons debate in the run-up to the European Community summit at Maastricht, where the next stages of political and monetary union were to be decided. With the three main parties more agreed on the progress of integration than they are probably prepared to admit, the exchange could have been a comparatively peaceful affair, with just a few bits of fake warfare. Instead, the occasion marked the rancorous reentry into domestic politics of Mrs. Thatcher, first in the Commons debate and subsequently on television.

In the debate, she was very much her old self: imperious, finger wagging, basic—at one point even referring to "my Foreign Secretary," as if she were still running the show. She scornfully dismissed the idea of a single European currency, and brazenly suggested a national referendum on the matter if the three main parties all agreed on being Europe's lackeys. The Tory Cabinet sat through this blast in silent embarrassment, each member reflecting, perhaps, as her late-found Tennyson put it, that she had

> Gorgonized me from head to foot
> With a stony British stare.

But her performance in a television interview on prime-time news two days later was both more revealing and potentially more damaging. She seemed angrier and also more anguished, like a dowager who has handed over the running of her estate to the next generation only to see her favorite stretch of woodland being sold for timber and the lake drained to make room for a skateboarding arena. Her line was populist, sentimental, and fueled by national fantasy. "Have a little bit more faith in your own fellow countrymen," she instructed her interviewer at one point. "It was we who rolled back the frontiers of socialism, and we were the first country to do it." Viewers were reminded, "It was the chimes of Big Ben that rang out across Europe during the war. I do not want our powers taken away." She ended with another appeal to her totemic figure: "What ever happened to the British lion of whom Winston said it was his privilege to give the roar? And Winston said in 1953, 'We will be with Europe but not of it, and when they ask us why we take that view, we will say we dwell in our own land.' "

All very fine to point out the irony of Mrs. Thatcher's sudden conversion to the joys of the referendum; as Douglas Hurd, no doubt displeased at being labeled "her" Foreign Secretary, reminded the House of Commons, it was she who had argued most persuasively against the Euro-referendum proposed by Harold Wilson in 1975. And all very fine to doubt the impact of some thirty-eight-year-old phrasing ("Where do you stand on the hard ecu?" "Oh, I prefer to dwell in my own land"). The fact is that Mrs. Thatcher—whether from injured pride or true belief—looks to be suffering from a dangerous attack of idealism. When professional politicians start murmuring about "putting my country before my party," it is usually time to call for the padded van.

However, Mr. Major's performance at Maastricht in early December succeeded in pacifying the Europhobes of his party while pleasing the Europhiles. Mrs. Thatcher initially pronounced herself "absolutely thrilled" with the deal he brought back. The Prime Minister himself commented with enthusiastic homeliness that it had been "game, set, and match" to Britain; and since every other European head of state was busy celebrating a different victory in his own way, nobody minded this British claim to a sporting Agincourt. The Government's version of events was that there had been some pretty rough street fighting over there in Holland but that the PM had rolled up his sleeves and punched his weight. *Federal*—the dreaded *F* word, currently much more offensive to men in gray suits than the more colloquial *F* word—had been deleted from the treaty; Britain had won special dispensation on monetary union, and had also been allowed to opt out of the "social chapter" (a section covering workers' rights, such as a minimum wage and equal opportunity). To doubters, Mr. Major resembled a driver whose response to obtaining his license was to argue vigorously that he should only be permitted to drive his car in the slow lane, while Mr. Kinnock had much fun with the PM's lack of true Euro-commitment. "Opt-in, opt-out, shake it all about— it's obviously the hokeycokey clause," he taunted in the two-day

Commons debate over Maastricht. A week after the summit, Mrs. Thatcher herself began to seem rather less than "absolutely thrilled": she did not speak in the debate, and abstained from voting. Still, at least she did not utter or act against Mr. Major, and, since her power to influence his job prospects over the next few years is undoubtedly greater than that of either President Mitterrand or Chancellor Kohl, some would say that his political priorities at Maastricht had been correct.

So for the moment Mrs. Thatcher is shutting up, if in her own way. However, Mr. Major and his colleagues would be advised to insert a fallback or opt-out clause in their current election strategy. This would involve a series of pressing invitations to Mrs. Thatcher from foreign billionaires. Large sums of money would be promised to the Thatcher Foundation, in return for the acceptance of enforced hospitality. This would always take place in remote hill country, beyond the reach of fax and phone. And if this fails to work Mr. Major should perhaps take up a little late-night Tennyson himself. There he might discover the poem "Hands All Round" and the following advice:

> That man's the best Conservative
> Who lops the moulder'd branch away.

January 1992

Mrs. Thatcher became a life baroness; Mark Thatcher will inherit only his father's baronetcy, and thus presents no immediate threat to the House of Lords.

■ 6 ■

Vote Glenda!

On a dull and edgily damp Saturday afternoon in mid-March, that time of year when the presumptuous prunus blossom is about to be snubbed by winter's last revengeful frost, a world-famous, Oscar-winning actress rang my doorbell and introduced herself. She was miked up, and there was a TV crew on the pavement a dozen yards away, but this didn't interfere with our natural, if low-key, chat. Her voice was quiet and sounded tired, but I understood that the more challenging parts of her role lay ahead. Nor did she try to stun me with glamour: her face was devoid of makeup, her hair was wind-battered, and the scarlet trousers that glared from beneath her long brown coat added a homely rather than a dashing touch. She listened attentively to my views, asked for my assistance, and after a couple of minutes—but it seemed longer, much longer—she departed with a friendly smile. I realized as I watched her go that *l'esprit de l'escalier* also strikes those standing at the top of the steps. My best quips and questions had gone unvoiced. But when Glenda Jackson comes to call, as a Labour candidate soliciting your vote in the general election, you do tend to get a bit tongue-tied.

Such personal moments are to be treasured and remembered, because the 1992 general election was a dull affair, cagey, grouchy, and
grinding, its tone a down-market snarl. Every facet of life seemed
temporarily politicized—even the Grand National steeplechase was
won by a horse called Party Politics—while the party leaders dug up
extra reasons to impose themselves on us: both John Major and Neil
Kinnock managed to celebrate their birthdays during the four-week
election period, and Kinnock threw in the twenty-fifth anniversary of
his wedding to Glenys. Of course, the result of this election was always going to be fascinating, with Labour and the Conservatives
neck and neck in the polls throughout, giving the Liberal Democrats
a real chance to hold the balance of power; but the actual process of
getting to that result felt interminable. For the voter, it was like getting caught in some deeply unwelcome relationship, one with definite
sadomasochistic overtones, involving both addiction and revulsion,
endurable only because of the knowledge that it would certainly be
over within a month—over, that is, until the next time. So you gritted
your teeth and thought of England, amazed yet again at the driven
quest for power and domination that you had got yourself involved
with.

Electoral warfare traditionally begins with the dropping of propaganda leaflets. In the old days, party manifestos were brief statements of intent and hope, normally given away or sold for coppers;
over the years, though, they have grown to novella length, are priced
accordingly, and are, some would say, just as fictional in content.
Labour's booklet ("It's Time to Get Britain Working Again") was
the cheapest, and the only one not featuring the party leader's face
on its cover; instead, it showed the four flags of the United Kingdom, subliminally declaring, perhaps, an equal-but-separate message.
The Conservative manifesto ("The Best Future for Britain") showed a
bleached-blue, slightly out-of-focus John Major, smiling merrily, as if
personally illustrating his much-stated vision of "a nation at ease with
itself." The Liberal Democrat manifesto ("Changing Britain for Good")
was, as befits the smallest party, comfortably the largest in format, its
cover occupied by a pore-scouringly high-definition mug shot of

rugged Paddy Ashdown, not smiling at all (nothing to smile about given the mess Britain's in) but looking determined (there are tough decisions to be made) yet humane (and we shall make those decisions with compassion). Whether these booklets are intended to convert or are meant as pocket catechisms for canvassers, reminding them of this year's promises as opposed to last year's, is not clear; either way, they contain a target-'em-all scattershot of policies. The Conservatives promise to keep "the toughest anti-pornography laws in Western Europe" while teaching every child to swim by the age of eleven. Labour will insist on the fencing off of wasteland while banning the sale of replica guns and ensuring better treatment for animals in transit. The Liberal Democrats will plant more broad-leaved hardwoods, "protect those who fish sustainably, such as mackerel handliners," and introduce new efficiency standards for lightbulbs, fridges, and cookers.

Few candidates mentioned infant swimmers or broad-leaved hardwoods in their campaigns; but then equally few mentioned such graver matters as foreign policy, Northern Ireland (Britain's Croatia), or the European Community, these being subjects that, like the fate of Mr. Salman Rushdie, are regarded by the main parties as largely vote-losing—or, at any rate, not vote-attracting. The Liberal Democrats concentrated their campaign on the gubernatorial qualities of Mr. Paddy Ashdown, a policy of one penny on the basic rate of tax specifically to pay for improvements in education, and a demand to rejuvenate the voting system with proportional representation. Labour emphasized the health service and education, offering an alternative budget designed to make the fiscally advantaged pay more tax (raising the top rate from 40 percent to 50), while seeking to reassure everyone else that under Labour nine families out of ten would be better off. The Conservatives campaigned for the most part negatively, claiming that Labour's figures didn't add up, that a vote for the Liberal Democrats would let in Labour, and that the recession, which wasn't their fault anyway, was coming to an end, in which case it would be lunacy to exchange such a soberly responsible government for a high-tax, high-spend Labour alternative at this crucial moment in Britain's history. (Elections, it is worth noting, are always held at crucial moments in Britain's history. One of these days, a Prime Minister will have the guts to call an election with the cry "This is a comparatively unimportant time in our nation's history.")

A week before Election Day, I suggested to Oliver Letwin, Glenda Jackson's Tory opponent in Hampstead and Highgate, that the Conservative campaign had been uninspiring. He replied (after first wisely checking when this piece would run), "Oh, it's been no good at all. Nobody decided early on what they were trying to say in the campaign." When a party has been in power—and a fortiori when it has been in power for thirteen years—there are two ways of best approaching the electorate. One is to boast of what you have already achieved; the other is energetically to lay out your plans for the next five years. The Tories took a third route: that of trashing Labour's proposals (and, in the time left over, those of the Lib Dems as well). This may have been understandable, given the closeness of the polls, but it was tactically dumb. Letwin contrasted John Major's campaign with those of Mrs. Thatcher, in whose Policy Unit at No. 10 he had worked: she went into a campaign knowing exactly what she wanted to say, and said it again and again and again, unworried by repetitive strain injury, ensuring by this method that at least it was she who set the agenda.

One effect of the Tory campaign's uncertain focus and general negativity was automatically to dress Labour in a little brief authority. Not that Labour weren't so dressing themselves, even in the most literal way. For some time, Barbara Follett, wife of the novelist Ken, had been advising Labour MPs and Shadow Ministers on how to look their likeliest. The process had a certain comic aspect for longtime Labour watchers. In the old days, a Labour MP would be comfortingly shabby; the clothes would proclaim that the mind was on higher, more idealistic things. A baggy trouser out at the knee was proof of working-class solidarity, a leather elbow patch on a tweed jacket a badge of thrift and virtue. On special occasions, the MP would put on his least tattered suit and sport a red tie. The *point culminant* of Labour's sartorial dereliction came a few years ago when

Michael Foot, Neil Kinnock's predecessor, turned up for the Armistice Day wreath-laying ceremony at the Cenotaph wearing what was generally denounced as a duffel coat (though his description of the garment differed). From that moment, Labour politicians—except for rank ideologues—became smarter dressers, until the top brass now present themselves like cautious stockbrokers. The arrival of MPTV helped speed the makeover. Those midgray off-the-peg High Street suits, worn with crepe-soled brown suede shoes, have been replaced by well-tailored numbers of somber hue; ties have become much more bankerish, even unto those dark blue ones with little white spots; while the special-occasion red tie has been transformed, as in some minor Greek myth, into a red rose worn in the buttonhole. As a result, Labour came into the election looking as if they already were the Government. That they were also allowed to behave as such was another mistake on the Tories' part. The natural way for a sitting government to play the game is to act as if your side are statesmen (the masculine noun is appropriate, since there were no women in Mr. Major's Cabinet), while the opposition are mere politicians. The Tories incompetently managed to reverse these standings, and on TV commercials Mr. Kinnock referred relaxedly to "my Chancellor of the Exchequer" and "my Health Secretary," as if his team were merely waiting out the few necessary days before acquiring office.

Although a dirty campaign was widely predicted, for the most part the politicians contented themselves with insults and lies. Such restraint was wise, since each party was believed to have sexual dossiers on leading members of the other side, but the absence of erotic slurs might also have been caused by the surprise failure of an earlier mud strike. Three months before the election, when it already looked as if the Liberal Democrats might be a significant factor in the outcome, there was a break-in at the offices of Paddy Ashdown's solicitor. The safe there happened to contain the lawyer's working notes of a meeting with Mr. Ashdown in which the leader admitted an affair five years previously with his secretary. Details of the stolen notes naturally found their way to several London newspapers, and during a bit of will-they-won't-they and aren't-we-being-responsible,

Mr. Ashdown, perhaps unwisely, injuncted most of Fleet Street. Since these injunctions petered out at Hadrian's Wall, *The Scotsman* promptly published the story, whereupon the whole of Fleet Street gleefully piled in. *The Sun,* a right-wing tabloid that spends much time honing its headlines because there is little room for anything else on the front page, led with this well-pondered screamer: IT's PADDY PANTSDOWN!

What happened next was instructive, and allowed British connoisseurs of sex scandals to feel briefly superior to their American counterparts. Mr. Ashdown admitted that the affair had taken place; the secretary was discreet; Mrs. Ashdown, doorstepped by a TV team announcing that her husband had publicly admitted his infidelity, gave an impassive nod and replied, "Well, well, well," before disappearing into her house without further comment. Whereupon the most surprising thing in the history of British political sex scandals occurred: the next opinion poll to be taken recorded that Mr. Ashdown's personal rating had improved thirteen points. This effectively killed off the story and must have left other party leaders wondering if a little indiscreet dalliance mightn't be necessary for the good of the cause.

Of course, it didn't all end quite as neatly as this. There was an embarrassing coda when the April issue of *Good Housekeeping* carried interviews with the wives of the three main party leaders. Given the magazine's lead time, these had to have been conducted before the Ashdown story broke. Jane Ashdown here referred to herself self-deprecatingly as "a scruffy cow" and as "just an also-ran, a wife." What provoked a greater wince, though, was her guileless loyalty to Paddy: "People have accused him of having affairs and he was outraged, terribly hurt. He doesn't flirt but he likes the company of women. He is totally unaware when they are flirting with him."

Furthermore, the nation quickly discovered that the No Damage (or even Enhanced Rating) rule suggested by the Ashdown saga has very limited application. The infidelity must be old and terminated, all parties must behave well, and the central figure must be a man. (If the party leader in question had been a woman, imagine the hypocrisy and aggression of newspaper response.) And it goes without saying that the man must be heterosexual. As if to sternly point the limits on an MP's permitted behavior, a new case broke in March, just before the election was called. The Conservative MP for Hexham in Northumberland, a thirty-nine-year-old bachelor (right-wing, anti-abortion, antismoking, teetotaler), was arrested with another man near Hampstead Heath; they were in a car parked in a street known to the gay community, who frequent a certain area of the Heath, as Gobblers' Gulch. The MP was cautioned, as is normal with first of-fenders, but not charged; and though police cautions are not a matter of public record, this one unsurprisingly leaked out. M.P.'S GAY SEX SHAME, *The Sun* compassionately headlined it; and within forty-eight hours Hexham Tories were looking for a new candidate. Fleet Street, having sniffed further around Hexham, then put pressure on the young Liberal Democrat contender to admit *his* homosexuality. He obligingly did so, while declaring, "I just want to win on the issues." He lost, of course, either on the issues or not, polling four thousand fewer votes than the Liberal had done in 1987, while the (presumably nonhomosexual) Conservative rompingly increased the Tory major-ity in the seat by more than five thousand.

NO SUCH MATTERS disturbed the campaign in the constituency of Hampstead and Highgate. Despite the occasional healthy insult—like a rousing cry of "Neanderthal"—the fight was clean. At first glance, the seat must have looked a pushover for Labour. They had a celebrity candidate; the Tory majority at the last election had been a mere 2,221, making it number twenty-four in the list of key marginals Labour needed to win; national polls were showing a healthy swing to Labour; the sitting Tory MP was retiring, so no personal vote was involved; and Glenda Jackson's young opponent was one of those re-sponsible for inventing the community charge or poll tax, the most reviled tax imposed on the country in decades, if not centuries. What could possibly go wrong for Labour?

Several things. For a start, despite its reputation as a hatchery of pinko intellectuals, the constituency has only once, in its eighty-plus years, returned a Labour candidate, and that only for a period of four years after kicking out a spectacular dud of a Tory minister. In addition, it normally swings no more than about half the national average: Conservatives and Labour have solidly entrenched pockets of support. And there were two more recent factors that might also weigh against Labour. The first is that Hampstead and Highgate lies within the London Borough of Camden, which twenty or so years ago was held up as a model of committed and sympathetic municipal socialism but is now widely denounced as inept, spendthrift, bankrupt, idle, corrupt, and deaf. Camden did the Labour Party candidate no good by putting up council-housing rents an average of eleven pounds per week shortly before the election, and its very existence and reputation gave the Conservative Oliver Letwin an easy line of attack in his election pamphlet: "Look at our own government in miniature, Camden Council. The Labour Party has been in control of Camden for years. No doubt, when the Labour leaders set out to run and plan our lives they genuinely thought that they would improve matters. The result, as you will know only too well, is dismal and dingy.... The same thing happened when British governments tried to apply the Camden treatment on a national scale. Under the postwar 'moderate' Labour Party, plans and bureaucracies flourished. But the results were little short of catastrophic. Britain became known as the sick man of Europe." Note, incidentally, the sleight of hand in the allegation that Labour governments followed "the Camden treatment," as if the borough had been an antique nest of William Morris spinners and dyers who inspired the whole Party, the source of original collectivist sin; whereas in fact Camden was merely effecting, with embellishments, central Labour policy.

The second extra factor was one little mentioned locally. Even party workers weren't very interested in discussing it, as they fought for a vital vote here, a tactical switch in the next street, and so on, doughtily adding up a hundred or so shifts or stabilities in each ward, leading to a successful assault on, or defense of, that alluring figure of 2,221. But if you examined the electoral register you discovered a figure that could prove more significant than the result of all the loyal efforts of any number of diligent party workers. In 1987, at the time of the previous general election, there were 63,301 people registered to vote in the constituency; in 1992, the figure was down to 58,203. Camden has always had a transient population, but here was a demographic decline of 8 percent in five years. What could account for it? People moving out of the borough to avoid being ruled by Camden Council? General apathy about the political process? Perhaps. But the most plausible explanation was that quite a large number of people had declined to put themselves on the electoral register for a simple reason: fear, or disapproval, or hatred, of the poll tax. Technically, the electoral register has no connection with the list used to collect the poll tax, but few believe this. If you aren't registered to vote, then they can't pursue you for the poll tax—that is the received wisdom. Which left us with the possibility of one of the ripest political ironies: that of Mr. Letwin retaining Hampstead and Highgate for the Conservatives thanks to the absence of a key number of Labour sympathizers who had deprived themselves of the vote in order to avoid paying the tax which he helped devise.

Letwin is thirty-five, went to Eton and Cambridge, worked in the Downing Street Policy Unit under Mrs. Thatcher, and now heads the privatization-and-utilities team at Rothschild; Glenda Jackson is fifty-five, worked as a shop assistant in Boots the Chemist for two years, went to the Royal Academy of Dramatic Art, won two Oscars, and was awarded the CBE in 1978. Letwin puts on a brave face at having drawn such a celebrated opponent: "They are very sophisticated voters here," he replies as often as the question is put, "and they will not be sidetracked by glamour—either Glenda's or mine." Labour naturally makes the most of the frenzied press interest, and the results of photo opportunities stud the national dailies: Glenda serving tea at a community center, Glenda with her best foot forward at a ten-pin bowling alley with the Shadow Chancellor of the Exchequer, and, silliest of all, Glenda and Glenys Kinnock pretending to build a wall together at the Blackburn Road Builders Training Centre. Photos show the two women crouched behind a palisade of brick and wet mortar, Glenda wielding trowel and spirit level, Glenys brandishing a supportive trowel of her own. "My father was a bricklayer," Glenda reminds the assembled media folk. "We have to build for the future," she adds, helping the tabloids toward symbolic interpretation of the event. Subsequent cross-examination of those at the training center revealed that the two Gs had laid only one brick between them, and that the wall itself, after the witnesses had gone, was to be demolished and reconstructed in a different shape.

Oliver Letwin's photo opportunities are more meager. When the real-life Chancellor of the Exchequer comes to support him, the resulting image hits only page 21 of the *Hampstead & Highgate Express*. Mrs. Thatcher's visit at least got him onto the front page–in color, moreover–and the newspaper dutifully reported the former Prime Minister's remark that Letwin had the credentials to be PM himself one day; but it still chose to headline the story GLENDA FLAYS MAGGIE. Asked about the Glenda factor over tea in a Conservative Party worker's home just south of Swiss Cottage, Letwin pronounces himself comparatively unconcerned: "I suspect Glenda is very popular with Labour voters. With Conservatives she's very unpopular. There are quite a lot of Liberals who are going to vote for us." Overall, he reckons that her presence will have "a slight negative effect" for Labour. "If she were a little more cuddly, she would convert more Tories." (I ask him about the public platforms they have so far shared: "Well, she makes up facts occasionally, but that's only in the flow of rhetoric.") More to the point is his view–and it is a refreshingly candid one to hear from a Parliamentary candidate–that "most people neither know nor care who their MP is." Letwin notes that his predecessor, Sir Geoffrey Finsberg, held the constituency for twenty-two years, and by the end of this time only 12 percent of voters proved able to name him. There are, of course, alternative explanations for such ignorance.

Letwin himself is a good choice for Hampstead and Highgate, being one of the Tory Party's prospective highfliers, able to play the Hampstead Jewish-intellectual card and also to exploit the Thatcher connection (by no means a negative factor in getting out the Tory vote); he describes himself as laissez-faire in economic matters, liberal in social policy. He is the author of *Privatising the World* (1988) and *Ethics, Emotion and the Unity of the Self* (1987). Asked for his realistic assessment of the result, he says that he expects a local swing of half the national average. Glenda needs 2.5 percent to gain the seat; the opinion polls suggest a national movement of 5.0 percent toward Labour. It is not going to take much to deflate those blue balloons at the local Conservative headquarters which ho-hoingly proclaim "Let's Win with Letwin." I ask him what fears assail him during those nocturnal moments of self-doubt. "I sleep soundly," he replies professionally.

Apart from the Labour, Conservative, Liberal Democrat, and Green Party candidates, voters in Hampstead and Highgate are offered a choice of four fringe candidates. There is nobody, alas, from the Monster Raving Loony Party, whose catchphrase is "Vote Loony"– You Know It Makes Sense," and whose leader, Screaming Lord Sutch, when asked about royal protocol if invited to form a government, replied, "Kissing hands sounds a bit too formal for the Loonies. I wonder whether Her Majesty would object to a discreet snog?" But there are other off-beam contenders. There is Anna Hall of the Rainbow Ark Voters Association, who proposes self-government for Hampstead, the striking of local currency, holistic medicine on the National Health Service, phasing out petrol-driven cars by the year 2000, the teaching of reincarnation in schools, the composting of human waste, and the increased planting of fruit and nut trees. There is Captain Rizz of the Captain Rizz Rainbow Connection, whose basic policies are "freeing the airwaves and relaxing licensing laws" as routes to "uncontrolled personal freedom." He should not be confused with Charles "Scallywag" Wilson, of the Scallywag Rainbow Party, whose more radical program includes the disestablishment of the Church of England, privatization of the Royal Family, abolition of "all laws against genuine eroticism," plus "original spiritual awakening" for Hampstead and Highgate. This last proposal might bleed a few votes from the Natural Law Party, whose candidate, Richard Prosser, makes the following statement of campaign aims: "Only the infinite organizing power of natural law that upholds the evolution of the universe can bring fulfillment to everyone." The Natural Law Party came into existence only the day after the election was called, and its 312 candidates are funded by the peripatetic Maharishi Mahesh Yogi (currently domiciled in the Netherlands). His main achievement in the campaign has been to persuade his old pupil George Harrison to make his first full-length British concert appearance since the Beatles split up in 1970. Harrison–who incidentally is the same age as John Major–declined to be a candidate, because he "wouldn't really want the karma of being in Parliament for four years." However, the ex-Beatle, perhaps remembering the days of his own famous fiscal protest song, "Taxman" ("Should 5 percent appear too small/Be thankful I don't take it all"), urged concertgoers "to get rid of those stiffs."

ON SUNDAY, APRIL 5, four days before the election, the main quartet of contenders for the constituency of Hampstead and Highgate met for the last of their public debates. The site was the church hall of St. Andrew's, Frognal, just off the Finchley Road–one of those grim barns with cut-your-throat lighting, canvas stacking chairs, and paintwork of a green long defunct on color charts. Though the contestants had already met a dozen or so times before, the place was packed with more than two hundred voters. To the outsider (and there was a professor from Stanford videotaping proceedings from the front row for his politics class), it might have seemed that British democracy was in a healthy condition, full of a zeal for debate, characterized by sage yet skeptical listening and a mutual respect among the postulants for power. In fact, the evening (and its predecessors) proved only that Hampstead and Highgate is sui generis as a constituency, one of the last remnants of how things used to be. Twenty or thirty years ago a Parliamentary candidate would expect to have a public meeting every night of the campaign, and would thicken his or her skin in the sacred rough-and-tumble of a heckling hall. Nowadays, candidates may get away with only a couple of such meetings, where they preach their wisdom to three dogs and a monomaniac. In the constituency immediately to the south of Hampstead, the safe

Labour seat of Holborn and St. Pancras, not a single public meeting was held throughout the campaign. Television is where debates take place, and local issues are accordingly diminished.

The Green Party candidate, Steven Games, was tweedy, passionate, and global. "We are losing species at the rate of one a minute," he proclaimed, and was himself treated with the sort of amused interest reserved for an unlikely, endangered animal. When he seriously suggested, "Your vote for the Greens will *frighten* the others into taking action," there were indulgent chuckles. When he invited those present to "go around your home this evening and you'll find nothing, or almost nothing, that was made in this country—perhaps clothespegs," a man in the front row heckled with infinite politeness, "This jacket was made in England." Finally, the Green was the only candidate to use the word *please*. This was a striking novelty. Politicians frequently "urge" us to do things (e.g., vote for them), and sometimes, when in a tight corner, "ask" us to do things (e.g., vote for them). But until this night I'd never heard a politician say "please." Mr. Games ended his speech, "*Please*, for the first time in your lives you have the chance to vote Green," and was rewarded with sympathetic applause.

The Liberal Democrat, Dr. Wrede, is a tall, good-looking gynecologist, able to project to the back of the hall without a microphone. You might well trust him with your uterus, but trusting him with your vote was more complicated. His set ten-minute speech was clear, ardent, and transparently well-intentioned. But he made you realize that voting for the Liberal Democrats would be rather like deliberately choosing a night of amateur theatricals when you already had tickets for the West End. What he had going for him was the glow of political innocence, to which voters genuinely respond; though it would be a mistake to think of the Liberals more generally as innocent. Just as a two-party domination of power over many decades can make both parties cynical and manipulative, so a decades-long exclusion from power can equally mildew the soul. A party with a small number of seats (no matter how many supporters) cannot go on indefinitely offering itself up as the last best hope for the country. And so Dr. Wrede zealously put the case for proportional representation, and spoke warmly of STV, which some thought a television company and others an unwelcome affliction of the nether parts until he explained it as the Single Transferable Vote. Proportional representation is, it seems, the salvation of the country; and the fact that it would also be the salvation of the Liberal Democrats as a party is merely a happy coincidence. The recession is so deep, Dr. Wrede argued, the crisis in government so acute, that it can be solved only by "a stable relationship between two parties," which in turn depends upon the stronger party's agreeing to electoral reform. It is, admittedly, a ballsy approach: things are so bad in our country that you should give the balance of power for the foreseeable future to a party that hasn't held office for more than seventy years, and whose last experience of coalition, the Lib-Lab pact of 1977, resulted in its being outmaneuvered by the larger party and ending up with nothing for something.

At one point, Dr. Wrede, seeking to explain rather ponderously the advantages of PR, pointed out, "There are ten people in the front row of this hall. It's as if these four could outvote these six, whereas under PR these six or seven could outvote these three or four." Oliver Letwin could not help observing, "It's strange how in every one of the meetings we've had there are always ten people in the front row." Letwin was the most professional politician on show in the hall, the one who spoke fluently of macroeconomics and used ugly words like *incentify*–factors that probably worked both for and against him. A dapper, quick-witted, and far from predictable Tory, he was also the only contender on the platform to suffer heckling, much of it vigorous and some of it sequential. Letwin: "Conservatives believe in the transfer of power to the people." Heckler One: "Which people?" Heckler Two: "The Rothschilds." His views on housing were interrupted by loud cries of "Cardboard boxes!" But his technique under fire was impressive. There was the direct approach: "In housing, and this is where you'd better not barrack me, because what I'm going to say will probably become Labour Party policy as well . . ." But there was also the more effective feint-and-hit-back method: "We do bear some of the responsibility for the recession." Hecklers One to Ten: "All of it, all of it." Letwin then admits what he reckons the extent of the responsibility to have been: that of reflating too much in 1987. Labour, he points out, at that time wanted to reflate much more.

While the others speak, Glenda Jackson sits with almost alarming stillness, perhaps a relaxation technique learned in the theater. No anxious shuffling around, no couldn't-disagree-more scribbling on a pad in front of her. Asked earlier in the campaign by *The Wall Street Journal* why she didn't wear makeup, she replied, "It would be a great disappointment for people if they could no longer say I looked as if I was dressed by Oxfam. I would hate to disappoint people." But tonight she is not dressed by Oxfam, and looks neat and crisp in black jacket, white collar, gray skirt, and black stockings. Her speaking style is equally crisp, and, needless to say, the microphone is unnecessary: "I'm not showing off, but if I can't be heard, who can?" She is, of course, not heckled: in British politics you rarely heckle women, and stars not at all. She also chooses her own broad-brush terms for debate: "I don't want to get bogged down in the endless exchange of details and statistics." She prefers statements like "This election is about the struggle for the nation's soul" (again, we are at a crucial moment in Britain's history), and "We are eight years from the twenty-first century and sometimes one sees things in this country which make one think we're living in the eighteenth century." She is straightforwardly moral in her approach: "What I grew up to regard as vices are now regarded as virtues. Greed is no longer greed, it is self-reliance. Selfishness is no longer selfishness, it is an entrepreneurial spirit." She is in favor of "decency, a sense of justice, fairness." Who would not be? Well, the Tories: "What we have seen is indecency, a sense of injustice and unfairness." Her stance is clear, ethical, patriotic–the political equivalent of good plain home cooking.

But Glenda Jackson is not, as Letwin pointed out, "cuddly"; and if her firmness and moral passion are often applauded, there are also times when she strikes a slight chill. She begins, for instance, by describing how she first put forward her candidacy to the local party and was asked, inevitably, "why anyone should vote for an actress." Her reply was and remains "Because before I am an actress, I am a woman, and in any twelve months of the year a woman touches more bases than any male MP. We are doctor, nurse, cook, house-keeper, decorator.... I am extremely proud of being a woman." Apart from putting off the male-decorator vote, there is something about such unadorned thinking—vote for me if you, too, are proud of being a woman—that verges on the patronizing. When the debate shifts to a matter of serious local interest—how best to govern London, and especially what to do about the traffic jams and exhausted public-transport system—this ought to give her the advantage in debate. The Tories abolished the Greater London Council in 1986, considering it an adventure playground for junior Trotskyites, but most Londoners are in favor of having some electable authority responsible for overall control of the city. Labour's plan, Glenda explains, is for a new Greater London Authority. They haven't exactly worked out how to elect it yet; all they know is that it won't be on a winner-take-all system, and the resulting statutory body will by law consist half of women and half of men. As for solving the traffic chaos, there will be extra funding for public transport, priority "green bus routes," and a determination to "get us out of our cars and onto the buses." This does not get a warm response. Labour's moral passion here shades too quickly into We Know Best. After a decade of Mrs. Thatcher's bossiness, voters are less keen to welcome any bossiness from the other side. A laid-down 50 percent of female delegates rather than, say, a guaranteed minimum? Getting us out of our cars and onto the buses? For most people, one indicator that they have got ahead in life is the ability to use their own car rather than public transport, and getting stuck in a traffic jam may even, however obscurely, be considered a modern democratic right. Though the rival Tory plan for a Ministry of Transport for London was perceived as an election dodge, Letwin's personal, nonmanifesto idea for a toll on cars going into London, the proceeds from which would fund the public-transport network, was given interested consideration. What was sniffed out in Glenda's approach was a certain strand of Labour authoritarianism. It reminded me that my own deeply unrepresentative poll of my cleaning woman had elicited the answer that though she would probably end up voting for Glenda Jackson, she found her "madamy."

* * *

IN THE WIDER CAMPAIGN, nothing very dramatic happened in the first ten days, except for the normal rituals of preening, display, and aggression, of interest only to the political anthropologist. Then–as if to confirm that the politicians were incapable of igniting things by themselves–a sudden and spectacular row broke out over a four-minute TV election commercial. It was made for the Labour Party by Mike Newell, director of *Dance with a Stranger,* and was, in his words, "a nice little sentimental weepy." Its subject was the state of the National Health Service; its message, that under the Tories the system was so underfunded that patients were sometimes forced against their natural inclinations into paying for private treatment. Like the best commercials–and unlike most political broadcasts–it told its story in images, without voice-over. Two small girls, each with the same complaint of "glue ear," go to the same crowded hospital; both need surgery, and their mothers are told of a nine-month wait for the necessary operation to insert plastic grommets. (You can't, of course, convey such concepts as "glue ear" and "grommets" in a wordless film; but within twenty-four hours of its showing, most people in the land were speaking familiarly of such matters.) One mother pays to have her daughter treated privately, the other waits for the nine months to elapse; one child quickly recovers, the other continues to endure pain, becoming both withdrawn and aggressive at school. While the second child suffers, the mother of the first is seen contentedly signing a check for two hundred pounds. The story ends with a freeze-frame of the two girls in upper and lower bunk beds; superimposed is the slogan "It's their future–Don't let it end in tiers."

The film was an excellent piece of agitprop, making its point economically while shamelessly playing on our emotions. Conservatives had known before the election that they were vulnerable on health; William Waldegrave, the Health Secretary, had written to national newspaper editors pointing out that "the exploitation of individual cases where the NHS is alleged to have failed a patient is the preferred method of campaigning by Labour." He further expressed the hope that the press would not "allow this new and ruthless form of health campaigning to pass unchallenged," adding, "It would be an-other ratchet down in electoral standards if it did." Such heavy-handed advice betokened high anxiety. Newspapers like to be ethically outraged on their own behalf, without ministerial prompt-ing; and in the event, their interpretations of the need to "challenge" the Labour broadcast varied. How, indeed, might you "challenge" it if you wished to do so? You might, for instance, condemn the exploita-tive use of children, even if only child actors, in political commer-cials—the Conservative Party chairman, Chris Patten, for instance, called the film "tacky" (he hadn't seen it at the time, but that was nei-ther here nor there). Or you might assess the narrative plausibility of the commercial—investigate the frequency of glue ear, the average waiting time for an operation, the effects of such a wait on the child's psychological condition, the cost of private treatment—and then de-cide whether or not to challenge the broadcast. This is, of course, fairly pedantic, though some newspapers followed such a line, and seemed to establish the general truth of the film, except that the cost of the operation was more likely to be between £500 and £750 (the £200 check probably being just for the surgeon's fee), thus making Labour's point even better. But newspapers do not, on the whole, op-erate in this fashion. The question they asked in response to a politi-cal row about a fictionalized infant was depressingly basic: Who is she? And "she" turned out (very quickly, with the help of a leak) to be five-year-old Jennifer Bennett of Faversham in Kent, whose father had written to the Shadow Minister for Health, Robin Cook, to com-plain about his daughter's laggardly treatment. But the newspapers also discovered that reality is messier than a TV commercial. For if Jennifer's father was a disgruntled floating voter, his wife was a Con-servative, and *her* father turned out to be a former Tory mayor of Faversham and friend of the sitting MP. Worse, he had faxed the Conservative Central Office more than a week before the broadcast warning them of Labour's plans and disagreeing with his son-in-law's interpretation of events.

The War of Jennifer's Ear, as it swiftly became known, dominated the election coverage for several days. Jennifer Bennett was on the front page of every paper, even *The Times;* the family was endlessly doorstepped; the grandfather, in a moment of pure soap, even burst in on a TV interview with his son-in-law. "Is it true?" had quickly lost out to "Who is she?" which in turn gave way to "Who leaked what?" Did Kinnock's press secretary divulge the girl's name? Did Waldegrave's office put the surgeon who conducted the operation in touch with the *Daily Express?* And was Jennifer's case just a simple administrative error, as was now claimed, rather than a direct result of underfunding? And so on. Waldegrave stupidly compared Newell's film to a piece of prewar Nazi propaganda. Patten claimed the film showed a "colossal error of judgment" on Kinnock's part and questioned Kinnock's "fitness to hold any public office." Cook naturally called for Waldegrave's resignation on the ground that the Tories had led the press to "the door of the Bennett family and caused them that distress."

The Liberal Democrats watched the scuffle from a high moral stool. Labour cursed itself for not having researched the Bennett family more carefully in the first place. The Tories screamed and shouted and threw bagfuls of dust in an attempt to obscure the film's original campaigning point. But their pained yelps indicated how vulnerable they felt. The British are proud of their National Health Service and react proprietorially if they think it is being messed around with. No one would claim that under Labour waiting lists would be abolished or politically embarrassing cases would never arise. But Newell's film and the subsequent War of Jennifer's Ear did successfully illuminate one fundamental question. Given that two patients suffering from the same condition may within the existing health system be treated at different speeds, and that the determining factor in that speed is the patient's bank account, does this differentiation indicate, as the Tories would maintain, that the citizen has a philosophically desirable freedom of choice in medical treatment as in so many other spheres of life under the liberty-loving Conservatives, or is it, as the Labour Party claims, straightforward proof of a two-tier system in which priority of treatment is based not on medical but on financial factors? And which party is more content that this should be so? The British do not, on the whole, like the intrusion of morality into politics, but when Labour's deputy leader, Roy Hattersley, declared the whole case a "moral" one, and when Neil Kinnock cried, "A sin, a sin," they were on the safest political ground.

A WEEK BEFORE ELECTION DAY, I went canvassing with my friend and neighbor Lisanne, a political scientist and resolute Labour supporter. Badged with our red-and-yellow Glenda Jackson lapel stickers, we addressed ourselves to nearby Chetwynd Road, NW5, a narrow, hilly street from whose highest point you look across to Hampstead Heath (or at least to the big NHS hospital beside it). Originally, Chetwynd Road must have had a certain terraced elegance, but since its discovery by motorists as one of the few east-west cross routes in this part of town, it has become a clogged rat run. Traffic used to barrel along here as fast as it could go, until a couple of years ago Camden Council decided to put speed bumps in the road. This measure is known in planning jargon as "traffic-calming," but it is, of course, also tremendously traffic-irritating, as drivers roar between the bumps, then stamp on the brakes so as not to lose the underside of their chassis.

As Lisanne and I plunged hip-deep into the carbon monoxide, I remembered Oliver Letwin's observation about canvassing. From the moment he approaches a house, he says, he can usually judge whether its inhabitants vote Tory or Labour. "You can tell the Tories from the neatly clipped hedge, the little pots of geraniums, from the fact that the front porch is tidily swept." It has nothing to do with grandeur—indeed, if a large house isn't neat on the outside, its inhabitants will never be Tories—or with the beauty or value of the property. It has purely to do with tidiness. (The Letwin front-garden principle, by the way, applies only in the South of England, he says. In the North, they're all tidier, regardless of politics.)

There are about 120 houses in Chetwynd Road, some owner-occupied, many divided into flats. The object of canvassing is not (as I had imagined when I stood on my front step with Glenda) to convert people, or to indulge in far-ranging discussions of foreign policy, but simply to identify your own supporters. A printout of the electoral roll gives you a list of all registered voters. This, you quickly realize, does not tally with the people who actually live in the street.

"I'm just over from Hong Kong," replies the first man whose electoral intentions we inquire about, "and I *can't wait* to get back there." An elderly woman opens the door, peers at our red-and-yellow lapel stickers, and wordlessly closes the door again. "Not one of us," hazards Lisanne, annotating her printout accordingly: *T* for Tory, *S* for Liberal Democrat, *L* for Labour, *P* for Possible Labour, *M* for Moved Away or Dead. We are in a demographically Macedonic area: there are Greek and Irish names, Italians and Indians, a girl whose unfamiliar Christian name turns out to be Maori. The Letwin front-garden test seems generally to hold up well: extreme tidiness in the face of this traffic-wrecked, fume-ridden street where cars are parked all over the pavement is often topped off by a neat Letwin advertisement. But mainly the posters are red-and-yellow ones; we mark *L* on the printout and move on to the next house without knocking. A fair number of voters are wary of opening their doors as the light fades on an April evening; some lie doggo, others throw up top-floor windows. Nowadays, holding a conversation through the entry phone is a key political street skill. "I'm a Liberal Democrat," squawks one metal box in reply to our ring.

"Well, let me tell you," Lisanne bellows back, "that we have very good friends in Richmond who are Labour and who will be gritting their tiny teeth and voting Liberal Democrat to get the Tory out, so why don't you return the favor?"

"I'll think about it," squawks the box.

"We don't want Mr. Letwin, do we? Not the man who invented the poll tax?" Lizzie eyes the box fiercely.

"You may have a point," it answers, rather cravenly. Is this a *P* or just an *S* being polite? It's hard to tell. One house worryingly displays both Labour and Tory posters side by side; only when we get close do we see that Oliver Letwin's youthful features have been disimproved with a burlesque Biro mustache, while a large arrow penetrates his skull; we mark *L* and move on. An Indian paterfamilias with sticker-free windows mutters, "Yes, Labour, all four of us," and Lizzie triumphantly marks four *L*s. I am less sure; he replied with dubious speed, and his front garden is suspiciously tidy.

We start down the other side of the street. "I'm still making up my mind," answers a gentleman in slippers, dressing gown, and pince-nez. "But not for us, I think," Lisanne adds quietly after the door is closed. Then we meet "I'm deciding on polling day," and "I'm a Liberal Democrat, but I'll be voting for Glenda Jackson unless it looks as if she's going to win easily, in which case I'll vote Liberal Democrat," and again, "I'm making up my mind on polling day." (What is it with these people? Thirteen years of Tory rule and they still haven't decided whether more of it is a good or a bad idea?) According to the electoral register, several voters live over the launderette, but, if so, they must come and go by rope ladder. A large West Indian at a top-floor window gives us a thumbs-up sign, then yells, "But I haven't paid my poll tax." "Doesn't matter!" we yell back. "It's not connected!" Most of the exchanges are perfectly friendly. "I'm not going to vote for you," says a young man, "but anyway I vote in Islington." "Good," mutters Lizzie as we walk off. "*That* won't make any difference either way." We get a friendly hello from a pair of blue-rosetted Tory canvassers, and are briefly abused with shouts of "Tory, Tory, Tory, we're gonna win" from three teenage girls, fortunately below the age of electoral consent.

At almost the last house in the street, we come across the first positive evidence of a changed electoral intention. "I always vote Tory, but I'm probably going to vote Labour this time," a young woman says. "What's your party's position on blood sports?"

Lisanne rises splendidly to this request. "As part of our program to outlaw cruelty to wild mammals," she recites, straight from the manifesto, "there will be a free vote in the House of Commons on a proposal to ban the hunting of live quarry with hounds."

"But what does your candidate think? How is she going to vote?"

"I think you'll find Glenda *very sound* on blood sports," answers Lisanne, crisply guessing.

Overall, she is cheered by the canvass: one almost certain switch to Labour, one probable, plus the guy at the end of the entry phone who might do a tit-for-tat tactical vote with someone in Richmond he hasn't met. Not a bad evening's work. Yet what made the strongest impression on me was the number of people living in Chetwynd Road who weren't on the electoral roll. One house was almost certainly empty, but several more, all in multiple occupation, contained not a single resident authorized to vote. Here were members of that missing five thousand. Some were no doubt just passing through the borough, or were, in any case, apolitical, but what if, say, a quarter of them were natural low-income Labour supporters who failed to register because of a desire to avoid the poll tax? Would their significant silence thwart Glenda and ease Letwin home?

IN THE LAST WEEK of the national campaign, to everyone's surprise, a genuine issue emerged, one on which all three main parties had differing opinions: electoral reform, and, specifically, the issue of proportional representation. When Paddy Ashdown first tried to get the question of PR rolling in the campaign, John Major had mockingly dismissed the initials as standing for "Paddy's Roundabout." But with some help from the pressure group Charter 88, and more from opinion polls that still pointed firmly to a hung Parliament, Ashdown managed to get PR discussed. What, he demanded twice daily, did the other main parties intend to do when Parliament was deadlocked after April 9? And on every occasion he repeated the Lib Dem message: stability for a full term, a five-year partnership, with PR the price of the deal.

Despite the questionable logic (is there anything inherently stable about coalition government?), Mr. Ashdown's cheek and verve in making strong demands from a weak position drew other parties into the argument. The Conservative position was explained by the Prime Minister without ambiguity: we do not believe in PR, there will be no PR under the Tories, the present system works perfectly well, thank you very much and good night. Ergo, the voter deduced, there could be no Tory pact with the Liberals unless Ashdown retreated utterly. So what about the Labour Party, still tipped to be the largest grouping in the new Parliament, if without an overall majority? Labour was, in any case, a more natural ally for the Lib Dems. The official Labour answer, as given in St. Andrew's, Frognal, by Glenda Jackson, was "Well, there won't be a hung Parliament." Labour's fallback position was that no one could say what the Party's position on PR was because it hadn't yet been decided. The leadership had commissioned a report on the matter two and a half years previously, and was still waiting for the outcome. Some Labour candidates, like Glenda Jackson, were in favor of PR; some were against it; Neil Kinnock, when quizzed, said it wasn't very easy to say where in particular he stood, while emphasizing that his was of course the party that was always open to discussing new ideas. The cynical or politically realistic interpretation of all this was that the Tories were against PR because it would mean an end to their ability to form a majority government on a minority of the votes, and that Labour, while also hoping to pull the same trick this time round, was keeping open the option of being principled in case of failure. The issue of Paddy's Roundabout made the Tories seem hostile to new constitutional thinking, Labour fuzzy-minded if not actively shifty on it, and the Liberal Democrats clear-sighted, pragmatic, and committed to electoral justice. They were also, no less than the other parties, committed to their own self-interest—a permanently hung Parliament, permanent third-party influence, and a permanent job for the increasingly statesmanlike Paddy Ashdown.

The last-minute omens looked good for Labour. The *Financial Times* came out in their favor; the afternoon before Election Day a horse called Mister Major was withdrawn from the three-forty at Ascot because it was discovered to be "unsound"; and the morning of Thursday, April 9, dawned bright and sunny over most of the kingdom. The blue of the sky seemed bad news for the Tories, who are normally held to gain an advantage of up to 1 percent at the ballot box if it rains: Tories drive to the polls, Labour supporters walk, according to the received wisdom. On the other hand, there were keep-your-spirits-up murmurings about a "late Tory surge." Conservatives reminded one another, as they had done at disheartening moments during the previous four weeks, that John Major (unlike his equine namesake) was "a late finisher." Look how late he had finished in the leadership election, and look how late he had snatched victory at the Maastricht summit. Whether these signs were truly comforting was another matter: in the leadership contest he failed to get an overall majority, and at Maastricht he merely established the right of his country to be, on some matters, in a minority of one.

The Guardian, reckoning that if voters hadn't made up their minds by now on the weightier isues, they might as well be given some frivolous reasons for doing so, canvassed candidates in marginal constituencies as to their favorite books, films, and music. Glenda Jackson proposed *Persuasion, Les Enfants du Paradis,* and Stravinsky's *Symphony of Psalms;* her Conservative opponent chose *War and Peace, Dr. Zhivago,* and Mahler's Fourth Symphony; the Liberal Democrat listed Bellow's *More Die of Heartbreak,* the film *Stalker,* and Sibelius's Violin Concerto. Light relief from *The Times* came in a different form— that of a special Election Day poem by the Poet Laureate, Ted Hughes. It is, of course, by now traditional for any Laureate's official offerings to be bewilderingly bad, and Hughes certainly obliged with a jocose number about the effect of toxic chemicals on the sperm count of Western males. Specimens going off to vote might have been downcast to learn from the Laureate that their "virility packet" was only half as spunky as it had once been, yet more than a touch skeptical about the likely efficacy of Hughes's gonadic appeal to the incoming Prime Minister.

You wouldn't have thought there was much wrong with the sperm count of British males to judge by the end of the campaign. The three party leaders raced about in a fizz of testosterone, leaping into helicopters, bouncing out of cars, promising firmness, forcefulness, resolution, courage. But all the opinion polls pointed to neutered deadlock; so did the Poll of Polls, that source of wisdom as sure as the King of Kings; so, too, did the exit polls. But when the first actual results came in, around 11:00 P.M. on Thursday, April 9, computer predictions began to suggest—contrary to all previous commentatorial wisdom and psephological savvy—that the Tories might actually form the largest party in the new Parliament. The media pack ensconced on the press balcony at the Camden Centre to await Glenda's declaration shuttled incessantly to the wonky TV set in the Council Chamber for an update on the baffling results. As we watched, strange things continued to happen. For a start, swings varied enormously– one moment 7 or 8 percent to Labour, then suddenly 1 or 2 percent to the Conservatives. What was this about? Was it the result of tactical voting? The computer which claimed to make sense of everything was now suggesting that the Tories might even end up with an overall majority of one seat. The Liberals picked off a couple of Tory bastions in the West Country, then started shedding constituencies of their own that they'd gained in recent by-elections. The Tories seemed to be doing much better than expected in Scotland; female Labour candidates were showing well, black Tory males were going down. The Tory Party chairman, Chris Patten, lost his marginal seat in Bath; senior Conservatives mourned him in the language of classical tragedy.

Throughout it all, Glenda's result (as we had come to think of it) kept being delayed, from 1:30 A.M. to 1:50, to 2:20, to 2:50, and the caffeine-fueled remnants of the press began to fret about deadlines. Meanwhile, the calculated size of the Tory majority continued to rise: one, two, nine–until, by three o'clock, it had reached double figures. Hampstead and Highgate, twenty-fourth on the list of Labour's key marginals, was by now only of local interest; it couldn't arrest the remorseless Tory advance. So it was in an atmosphere of slightly reduced excitement that the Returning Officer at 3:15 A.M. finally led the eight candidates up onto the stage for the announcement of the result. They stood in a line with a large black curtain behind them, the only decoration a vast funeral-parlor vase of white flowers: lilies, carnations, and daisy chrysanthemums. Glenda Jackson wore the same outfit as she had at St. Andrew's, Frognal, with the addition of a spray of red roses on her left lapel. Captain Rizz looked dashing in red-and-yellow top hat, red frogged jacket with tails, and dark glasses. In alphabetical order of the candidates' names, the Returning Officer read out the number of votes cast. The Green Party got 594 and the Rainbow Ark Voters Association 44, putting a damper on the plan for

Hampstead to have its own currency. Glenda May Jackson received "nineteen thousand, one hundred and ninety-three votes," Oliver Letwin "seventeen thousand . . ." The extra numbers (753, to be exact) were lost in a great roar, while Glenda stepped forward and gave a curious gesture: she raised her arm, though not with masculine aggression, and closed her fingers on her palm, but without making a tough fist. A sort of soft-left victory salute, presumably.

The other figures were then announced. The Liberal Democrat got 4,765, a fall of nearly 50 percent, and an indication that tactical voting had reduced his pile. Captain Rizz got a mere 33 votes, and Charles "Scallywag" Wilson, whose name was greeted with an enthusiastic cry of "Yeah, Scallywag" from the hall, received only 44. This serious three-way split in the Rainbow vote (which in 1987 had tallied 137) eased the Natural Law Party representative, a man in a deeply nonpolitical white suit, into fifth position, with 86 votes. The candidates made brief speeches. Glenda Jackson said, "Never before has the Labour Party been needed as it is now." Oliver Letwin consoled his supporters with the traditional remark that "this seat is on loan to the Labour Party for perhaps a few years"; but the figures were not prima facie encouraging. If Hampstead and Highgate traditionally swings at half the national average, Glenda Jackson had done four times as well as had been expected. The Green candidate, after making his speech, gave the new MP a bottle of champagne, on the ground that she must be a champagne socialist; though he missed a trick by not asking her to recycle the bottle. Then the candidates were led off, and in a moment of tiny metaphor Glenda Jackson was seen beginning her political life by leaving a theatrical stage.

BY LUNCHTIME ON FRIDAY, with only a few Ulster results left to be declared, John Major's majority had grown to the comparatively decent—and, in terms of all predictions, incredibly enormous—size of twenty-one. It is effectively larger, given the inert status of Ulster Unionists in mainland politics, so Mr. Major will not have to worry overmuch when a backbench MP gets stuck in a traffic jam on the way to vote or starts complaining of chest pains. The Prime Minister will be able to ride out a few by-election losses and govern without much Parliamentary threat for up to five years. Not even Andrew Lloyd Webber's threat to leave the country in the event of a Labour victory had persuaded enough people to vote for Neil Kinnock.

Labour optimists pointed out that they had needed a swing of 1945 proportions to oust the Tories, and that the reduction of the Conservative majority from 101 to 21 was a fine achievement. Labour had nearly climbed the mountain; one more push next time and they would surely make it. But this line of consolation fails to convince. Apart from anything else, next time the mountain will have grown even higher. The recommendations of the Boundary Commission will have been implemented by the next general election, adjusting the size and shape of many constituencies. The effect of these changes, it is generally assumed, will be to hand the Tories from fifteen to twenty extra seats without any more work.

The situation facing Labour is therefore brutal. If the Party spends eight years reorganizing itself under Neil Kinnock, outlawing the word *socialism,* expelling left-wing extremists, accepting the free market and the principles of nuclear deterrence, weakening the obvious links with trade unions; if the party leadership does everything to cuddle up to prospective voters made apprehensive by previous Labour attitudes; if, banker-suited and pro-Europe, they pitch themselves as a nicer, more compassionate version of the Tories; if they fight an excellent campaign, well-organized and well-publicized; if the election comes at the right time for them, in the depths of a recession, with a lot of old-lag Tories seemingly attached to power only by their fingertips; if all the polls and all the analysts agree that Labour will at least end up with a share of power; and if, when the results come in, despite an increase in seats, Labour has captured only 35 percent of the vote, and the Conservatives are just as solid on 43 percent as they were five years earlier—then the question arises as to whether Labour has become unelectable. Or at least unelectable under the present system. Perhaps jumping on Paddy's Roundabout is the necessary solution? Whereupon a second brutal truth asserts itself: in order to change the electoral system to a new one which favors you better, you first have to win power under the old system. Which is what Labour seems incapable of doing.

What has changed? The Labour Party is like a lover who, rejected for being scruffy and high-minded by the girl he seeks, goes out, gets a haircut, a new suit, a proper job, a mortgage, and a portable phone, and then comes back only to be rejected again, in favor of some other man with a haircut, suit, job, mortgage, and portable phone. Better the devil—or the man in the suit—that you know. Casting around for explanations, Mr. Kinnock complained about the tabloid-press denunciations of Labour. But the tabloid press always denounces Labour. Others pointed to "the Kinnock factor"—a suspicion of his malleable principles, combined with a prejudice against him as a Welshman. But the British do not hold an ability to change one's mind, one's principles, even one's political party, against somebody who really wants power. And, while there is a certain low-level anti-Welsh prejudice among the English, and there could not have been a greater contrast than that between the hey-boyo Kinnock and the permafrost upper lip of the Prime Minister, this explanation is strictly one of last resort.

A more likely solution is that the British themselves—or an electorally significant percentage of them—have changed. Surveys of social attitudes tend to show that the Thatcher years have not much altered what people claim they want and expect from society. But people's behavior has changed. For a start, they have clearly started lying to opinion pollsters, which is probably a sign of a new political maturity on their part, and might even lead to the healthy disgrace and eventual abandonment of polling. (Of course, if they lie to political pollsters they might equally lie to social-attitude pollsters.) And in other respects a significant portion of the voting public has been altered by Thatcherism. As I waited for Glenda's result in the defiantly unstimulating atmosphere of the Camden Council Chamber—no alcohol allowed, smoking forbidden, the coffee machine run dry—and as John Major's prospects rose by the minute, a TV technician said to me, a little apprehensively, "I instructed my bank manager to buy me nine hundred pounds' worth of BT shares if the Tories won." He was worrying about the fact that on the eve of Election Day the City had scented a possible last-minute Tory rally and share prices had taken off; even so, he reckoned that his shares in British Telecom, the privatized successor to a section of the state-run Post Office, were a good buy. Fifteen or twenty years ago, the idea of a BBC technician instructing his bank manager to up his holding in BT would have seemed a strange dystopian fantasy. Now it is unavoidable here. Oliver Letwin wrote a book called *Privatising the World;* Mrs. Thatcher famously remarked, "There is no such thing as society" (there being only individuals and families in her view). The change in British political reality is not as complete as these two phrases imply, but a shift has certainly taken place—one that will have led, by the end of Mr. Major's immediate term of office, to seventeen or eighteen years of nonstop Conservative rule. This long period of single-party power makes Britain, depending on your view, either a stable and economically realistic nation of enterprise and individualism, or else "Japan without the prosperity."

On the Monday following his defeat, Neil Kinnock resigned as Labour leader. Eight days earlier, his last major London rally before the election was a gathering of the fairly high-profile faithful—self-satirizingly dubbed "Luvvies for Labour" by the comedian Ben Elton. Kinnock preceded his speech by pulling from his pocket Shakespeare's Sonnet No. 29, which, he said, he habitually carried around with him. It was an odd and proleptic choice:

> When in disgrace with Fortune and men's eyes
> I all alone beweep my outcast state,
> And trouble deaf heaven with my bootless cries
> And look upon myself and curse my fate . . .

The poet, in despair, reflects upon the one he loves, just as Mr. Kinnock, in a dignified farewell, was to pay warm tribute to his wife, Glenys: he was not to be pitied, for he had much richness in his personal life; it was the country that was to be pitied. The sonnet ends:

> For thy sweet love rememb'red such wealth brings,
> That then I scorn to change my state with kings.

–which was, more or less, exactly what he'd been trying to do for the last eight years as Labour leader.

Asked what went wrong for him in Hampstead and Highgate, Oliver Letwin replied, "Very simple. The Liberals collapsed and the bulk of them went to Labour." Why? "I don't know." The Glenda Jackson personal vote he still rated an insignificant item; he thinks there might have been "a marginal anti-me factor," because of his association with the poll tax, but the result was all "more to do with the big national questions." Liberal Democrats voted tactically "to get out the Government," and while his own vote held up well, the Lib Dem switch finished his chances. Unlike those of us who waited until 3:15 A.M., Letwin knew "as soon as the ballot boxes were opened" that he had lost: not from counting his own votes or Glenda Jackson's but from the rarity of crosses beside Dr. Wrede's name. If it's any comfort to Labour, Letwin judged it "absurd" to talk about the Party's long-term unelectability–politics being simply too fluid and hazardous a business. Asked finally about the victor, he agreed that she will probably make a good constituency MP. "The danger is she might get bored. She's been on a big stage, and she might find Parliament boring and trivial."

Her stage has indeed been big. Apart from anything else, there can be no other member of either House of Parliament who has inspired a piece of South American fiction. Julio Cortázar, in his story "We Love Glenda So Much," describes a group of film fans who so adore the actress that they are unable to bear the fact that some of her films are less than perfect. These club members therefore buy up copies of her unworthy movies and, with a cut here and a sly addition there, give them a perfection that their incompetent directors had initially been unable to provide. When Glenda announces her retirement, their happiness is complete: her oeuvre is perfect and their love impeccable. Except that one day, a year later, the actress announces her return to the screen. The fans are shattered. They cannot start their work all over again, and so they decide on the ultimate solution: in order to defend both Glenda's oeuvre and their love for her they must ensure that she doesn't live to make another film. . . .

If such a group of fans exists, they will surely be pleased with the result on April 9 in Hampstead and Highgate. The work of the death squad in closing off the film career of Glenda Jackson has been done instead by 19,193 North London voters.

May 1992

The Boundary Commission changes proved less damaging to Labour's prospects than had been predicted. Mike Newell went on to direct Four Weddings and a Funeral.

▪ 7 ▪

Traffic Jam at Buckingham Palace

A couple of years ago, I was driving west out of London, saunter-ing down the middle lane of the M4 at no more than ten miles an hour over the speed limit, when two search lights lit up my offside wing mirror. They turned, all too rapidly, into police motorcyclists. I was beginning to console myself on the unfairness of my random ar-rest when they growled past unheeding. They were far too busy sweeping the fast lane for the car they were escorting. It duly ap-peared in its swift bulk, pounding along at between ninety and a hun-dred miles an hour: a large black saloon flying a royal pennant on its bonnet. When the rearguard had passed, my companion and I specu-lated on the limo's occupant and the reason for such ostentatious speeding. The Queen late for a state lunch? Princess Anne late to feed her horses? The Queen Mum late for a gin and tonic? And so on. But the encounter also made me recall one of Prince Philip's obiter dicta: he once remarked to an interviewer that the Royal Family would "lose its dignity" if its members were caught in traffic jams like ordi-nary citizens.

Over the last few years, the Royal Family has shed quite a bit of its dignity, and the fault has not been that of its motorcycle outriders. The latest revelations, or allegations, or filthy gossip, about the marriage of the Prince and Princess of Wales may have induced disbelief, rage, pity, and schadenfreude, but they did not come out of a clear blue sky. Most of the recent domestic bulletins about the House of Windsor have been of matrimonial misfortune. There is a probably apocryphal story of a British matron watching Sarah Bernhardt play Cleopatra and commenting, "How very different from the home life of our own dear Queen." Until not long ago, the remark could be, and was, still applied waggishly to the stodgy, dull, decent, seemingly chaste House of Windsor. Not anymore. For a mother of four children to see one of their marriages break up is probably a statistical normality in present-day Britain; two looks like positive misfortune; three begins to argue that there is something seriously wrong with the family itself. When that woman is the Queen of England, the follow-up questions have a wider resonance.

The fact that Prince Charles himself has been afflicted with marital blight is particularly ironic. The British monarchy, which over the centuries has put its fair share of blackguards, adulterers, and madmen on the throne, and has endured mockery and criticism up to the severest censure of regicide in 1649, has been enjoying for the last half century a remarkably placid and uncontested phase of its existence. One factor in this, even committed monarchists agree, has been genetic good fortune. The line of thinking goes as follows. Jolly lucky we got rid of that unstable and potentially ruinous Edward VIII, plus his foreign, fortune-seeking Mrs. Simpson, and traded him in for the solid stamp-collecting George VI. Jolly lucky that his eldest daughter was the dutiful Elizabeth, and that we got her as Queen rather than the flighty Margaret, who fell in love with a divorced man, liked smoking cigarettes, and hung around with arty types. Jolly lucky, finally, that Charles, an earnest worrier with a proper sense of his ancestry, is going to inherit, rather than the headstrong Anne, the larky Andrew, or the seemingly unmarriageable Edward. And, besides, we don't just get Charles, we also get Princess Di, the most popular woman in the country. How can the show not run and run?

The main allegations in *Diana: Her True Story*, by Andrew Morton, formerly a *Daily Star* journalist and now a rich man, are: that the marriage of Charles and Di collapsed early and is currently a sham; that Di became acutely depressed and made five "suicide bids" (or, at least, pathetically frenzied cries for help, such as throwing herself against a glass display cabinet and cutting herself with the serrated edge of a lemon slicer), which Charles declined to take seriously; that she suffered from bulimia nervosa for many years of her marriage and was treated by a consultant psychiatrist; that she does not believe she will ever become Queen, an apprehension confirmed by the astrologers she has consulted; that Charles is a cold and unsupportive husband, who throughout his marriage has continued his long-standing "friendship" with Mrs. Camilla Parker-Bowles despite his wife's protests and jealousy; and that when, after years of painful matrimony, the Princess asked her husband, "But did you ever love me?" he is said to have replied, "No."

If these disclosures were merely the backstairs chatter of a disgruntled parlor maid, as used to be the case with "royal revelations," they might have made no more than a deniable early-summer scandal. But Morton was allowed to tape interviews with one of Diana's sisters and her younger brother; he talked to her former flatmates and Chelsea friends; the publisher of the book was sold eighty previously unseen photos by her father, Earl Spencer; and a slice of profits from the venture will go to a drug-abuse charity of which Diana is patron. In other words, this is as close to *Diana: My Story* as we are likely to get; and if the Princess now finds her life sensationalized and its emphases skewed, then that is the price celebrities often pay for not writing their own stuff.

Morton's book, as serialized in the *Sunday Times* before publication, was received with fascination, wrath, and a large amount of cant, not least from fellow journalists. The day after the first episode appeared, Donald Trelford, editor of the rival Sunday *Observer*, was quoted as saying of Morton's book, "It looks like trash to me. I can't stand stories about Royals who can't answer back. I don't know if it's true or false." But such sentiments, however worthy, had bowed to the exigencies of journalism the previous day. The *Sunday Times*'s front page had been dominated by a color photo of a rather melancholy Diana in her finery, beneath the headline DIANA DRIVEN TO FIVE SUICIDE BIDS BY "UNCARING" CHARLES. The *Observer*'s was dominated by an even larger color photo, of a grim-looking Princess at the wheel of her car, beneath the headline DEPRESSION "DROVE DIANA TO FIVE SUICIDE BIDS." Devotees of the codes and conventions of British headline writing might have noticed the position of the quotation marks, which separate those parts of the story which are only alleged to be true from those which the newspaper itself endorses: so the *Observer* was confirming the depression but hedging its bets on the suicide bids; whereas the *Sunday Times* was confirming the suicide bids but hedging its bets on whether or not Charles was a heartless husband. The average reader, of course, would come away from each front page with exactly the same impression of what had happened, and probably the same percentage of conviction as to the truth of the story.

But whether the other papers were sniffy-nosed, emulative, or spoiling, none managed, or perhaps tried very hard, to discredit the story in the first few weeks; they were too busy selling newspapers. Nor were there any denials from the Palace. So with the question "Is It True?" on hold, attention turned to "What Does It Portend if True?" and "Should the Bastards Have Been Allowed to Do It?" In constitutional terms, the story portends very little. The couple could separate, they could divorce, Prince Charles could even marry again, and there would be no constitutional crisis. If Henry VIII is anything to go by, he could marry again to his heart's content; the only disadvantage would be that he couldn't remarry in church, and therefore couldn't act as Supreme Governor of the Church of England. So the portents were all more local: to do with the future stability and popularity of the monarchy if its current juve lead withdrew from the production.

This left the question "Should the Bastards Have Been Allowed to Do It?" Though a regulation amount of smarmy humbug oozed from the *Sunday Times*, it was exceeded by the hypocrisy in some of the responses. If the message is bad, shoot the messenger. There were widespread denunciations of gutter-press intrusiveness, although the story first appeared as a book, from which a broadsheet serialization was made. There were renewed calls for a law of privacy, a subject which thereby climbed higher up the reformists' agenda than more fundamental matters of government secrecy and freedom of information. There was the reminder that the Royals could sue for libel. (Minor ones, like Lord Linley, Princess Margaret's son, have already done so.) The Archbishop of Canterbury burbled away in disapproval. So did the Press Complaints Commission, a rather ludicrous body set up by the industry out of the fear that if it didn't regulate itself the government would come in and do the job less indulgently. The commission condemned what it called "an odious exhibition of journalists dabbling their fingers in the stuff of other people's souls in a manner which adds nothing to legitimate public interest in the situation of the heir to the throne." This stricture was not treated everywhere with proper gravitas, given that two of the commission's members are the editor of the *News of the World*, historically the market leader in Sunday salacity, and the editor of the *Daily Star*, whose front page that very day had finger-dabbled, with the headline CAMILLA'S ROYAL OK, claiming that "Di's love rival," Mrs. Parker-Bowles, had won a "big smile" from the Queen at a polo match.

There was even a droll side tiff between Mr. Andrew Neil, editor of the *Sunday Times*, who had fronted the story much more than Mr. Morton himself, and Sir Peregrine Worsthorne, former editor of the *Sunday Telegraph*. The two had previously confronted each other in the libel court, when the self-consciously old-style Worsthorne had been obliged to pay the self-consciously new-style Neil a thousand pounds for implying that when Mr. Neil had squired a certain Pamella Bordes around town he knew that she was not just a glamorous model and an ex–House of Commons researcher but also a high-class tart. Sir Peregrine, who despite his parodically English name is of Belgian extraction, and who despite his chivalrous defense of the decencies of life was one of the first people to use the *F* word on television, returned to the subject of Andrew Neil with gleeful disgust. "Twice last week," he wrote in his *Sunday Telegraph* column, "have I had to see Mr. Neil on television. It is not quite a case of 'see Mr. Neil and die' but see Mr. Neil and throw up. Has there ever been a more confusing face? With an expression half-bovine and half sheeplike he stares out of the screen in such a way as to leave us all uncertain whether he wants to cut our throats or lick our boots." It is true that Mr. Neil is not exactly a looker, but connoisseurs of comic physiognomy would do well not to bypass the flamboyant Sir Peregrine: in any Daumier series, he could safely model for the Languid Epicure. As for Miss Pamella Bordes, she is a good example of how the lives of celebrities intertwine. I was in Delhi this February, and seeking conversation with a taxi driver, I remarked that Princess Di happened to be in town, too. (She had visited the Taj Mahal and pronounced it "a very healing experience"–a remark that made no sense at the time but a little more in retrospect.) The driver was indifferent to the Princess's visit and proclaimed himself much keener on Pamella Bordes, the famous model, who was also visiting Delhi. Our conversation took off when I shyly confessed that I had myself met Miss Bordes, and even shaken her hand. I did not mention that at the time she was in the company–how the names come around again–of Mr. Donald Trelford.

A further question that the moralistic harrumphers chose not to answer was this: what if the "dabbling in other people's souls" is actually connived in by the so-called victims? It may be a well-known fact that the Royal Family, as Mr. Trelford reminded us, "can't answer back"; but like most well-known facts, this one is partly untrue. For a start, Buckingham Palace and its coroneted outposts have a very large slice of Fleet Street–including Sir Peregrine Worsthorne–already in the position of thrilled obeisance. The Royal Family may not come to the front door and give interviews, but it carefully chooses what to throw in its dustbins, confident that they will be rootled through before dawn. Princess Di seems to have given the Morton story tacit approval before publication; subsequently, she gave it active encouragement. For instance, on the Wednesday after the news broke she telephoned her old friend Carolyn Bartholomew (one of Morton's sources) and invited herself round that evening. Shortly afterward five newspaper picture desks and one royal photographer were alerted and told to be outside the Bartholomews' house at eight-fifteen. The Princess arrived, spent forty-five minutes with her friend, and then lingered on the doorstep long enough for every snapper to get his picture. The next morning the Bartholomews spoke openly to journalists about the visit. Now, this may not technically be a press conference, but it goes as near as royal protocol allows, and probably nearer. To take another example: last summer the tabloids discovered that the Princess was spending her thirtieth birthday in a surprisingly subdued and Charles-less manner. "Friends of Prince Charles" had told gossip columnists that the Prince had offered her a birthday party but she had refused; at about the same time, news began to leak of the Princess's friendship with a certain major. One theory is that Diana used the Morton conduit as a way of replying to "Friends of Prince Charles." More generally, she might be seen as appealing over the heads of Palace apparatchiks to her loyal British public, making a cry for help on a national scale.

The tabloids do, it is true, frequently behave in a disgusting manner; they define the phrase "the public interest" as meaning "whatever the public happens to be interested in, particularly sex." The feeding frenzy of paparazzi, the heaving shoal of photographers eager for a snap of misery or a surprise bikini shot do not constitute a group overtly concerned with the sensitivities of their subjects; nor should we imagine that Mr. Morton is unconcerned with financial reward or Mr. Neil indifferent to a thumping rise in circulation (210,000 extra copies for the first installment of his serialization). But the image of the Royal Family as mute manipulatees is far from the truth. For most of the time, the Palace successfully works a pliant and monarchistic press. Few complained when the popular newspapers a decade ago built up Charles and Diana's courtship and marriage in the most treacly, sycophantic, and, it now seems, mendacious fashion: the Cinderella Princess, the Romance of the Century, and all that guff. Morton offers a few corrective details about that supposedly enchanted time. Before the wedding, Diana discovered that Charles was offering Camilla Parker-Bowles a bracelet with their self-given nicknames Fred and Gladys on it, which made her discuss with her sisters the possibility of breaking off the engagement. On her honeymoon, she saw photos of her "love rival" fall out of her husband's diary, and noticed a pair of cuff links, with two *C*s intertwined, given to Charles by Mrs. Parker-Bowles. Even during her engagement, she had begun to display symptoms of bulimia, which were put down to prenuptial nerves. This may all be intrusive tittle-tattle, which the nation's newspaper readers shouldn't have the right to know. But if there is a choice between happy lies and sad truths, which do the more harm? And the sad truths, when they inevitably arrive, appear sadder because nobody sought to curb the pornographic panegyrics in 1981, to moderate the press's mawkish epithalamia.

A thumbnail guide to the current fortunes and popularity of the Royal Family—or, at least, of its most visible members—would go something like this:

Queen Mother. Top Royal. The nation's favorite granny. Gracious, smiling, professional, still carries off pastel colors even at an advanced age.

The Queen. Popular, respected, thought to be "good at her job." Suspected of having a secret sense of humor. As she has got older, she has been less mocked for her tweediness, for her high voice and low dogs. General attitude among skeptics: if we've got to have a monarch, she seems to fit the bill better than anyone else.

The Duke of Edinburgh. Not much loved, though not much disliked. Given to making ducal gaffes, like being overheard on an Eastern tour referring to "slitty-eyed" Orientals. This tends to confirm prejudice among fans and critics equally.

Princess Margaret. Less in the public eye nowadays. Regular supplier in her day of emotional drama—Peter Townsend, Lord Snowdon, divorce, Mustique, Roddy Llewellyn, etc. Now a neutral figure. Popular with the tobacco industry, no doubt.

Prince Charles. Provokes ambivalent reactions. No longer the gauche youth with sticky-out ears who played the cello. But what is his role as he waits in limbo, knowing that he can become what he was born for only by the death of his mother? He supports organic

farming, talks to plants, dislikes modern architecture, is a disciple of
the Jungian trekker Laurens van der Post. Bit of an odd fish, who was
humanized for the nation by his marriage to Diana. Now whither?
Will he be seen as just another off-beam aristo who didn't know how
to make his wife happy?

Princess Di. Fairy-tale princess, virginal, sweet. Frequently called
herself "as thick as a plank" in early appearances. Suspected initially of
not taking her royal status seriously enough, not paying her dues in
return for the treats, but then buckled down, and after she shook
hands with AIDS sufferers her standing was fully restored. Now
largely pitied for her plight, but who is to blame? The royal system?
The journalistic rat pack? Her own lack of psychological hardiness?

Princess Anne. For years, disliked as haughty. Once told press
photographers to "naff off," thus popularizing the euphemistic phrase,
which she may have used in the full original. Was married to Capt.
Mark Phillips, known as Fog, because he was thick and wet. Marriage
dissolved. Perhaps the only Royal with actively rising popularity, after
work for the Save the Children Fund. Now perceived as mature, in-
dustrious, her own woman. Expected to remarry.

The Duke of York and *Fergie.* Known variously as the Duke and
Duchess of Yob (this from a regular *Times* columnist) and, for their
contented-looking chubbiness, the Duke and Duchess of Pork. Builders
of a large and vulgar ranch-style house. He a naval officer and couch
potato, she an enthusiastic consumer of royalty's perks: she likes the
skiing, the travel, and the writing of fatuous children's books about an
anthropomorphized helicopter called Budgie. She untraditionally
accepts royalties—well, why else would they be called that?—on her
literary output, and in late June signed a TV-and-merchandising deal,
which, according to industry sources, could net her as much as £3
million. Briefly popular after their marriage, the couple are now officially separated and held in low esteem.

Prince Edward. The youngest child, but already balding. Joined
the Marines but didn't stay the course; was found a job instead by
Andrew Lloyd Webber (recently knighted). Suspected of artistic leanings and possible unmanliness. Has denied that he is gay. Not much
public rating.

Duke of Kent (the Queen's cousin). Mason. Recently photographed in his apron. Not much else is known.

Duchess of Kent. Wife of above. Has rather ethereal graciousness; thought to suffer mood-related problems. Only appears at Wimbledon fortnight.

Princess Pushy. Nickname (supposedly affixed by Queen) for Princess Michael of Kent. Married to an obscure man with beard (also a Mason). Foreign divorcée who makes Fergie seem austere and self-denying in her attitude toward the perks of royalty. Wrote a book that bore dubious similarities to other people's books on the same subject. Positively unpopular.

Given this colorful dramatis personae, it's tempting to think of the Royal Family as a supersoap, Britain's longest-running TV export, the PBS hit that outgrossed *Brideshead Revisited*. But the Royals are not played by actors; they merely (however hammily at times) play themselves. Equally, comparisons with international stars like Dietrich or Sinatra or Liz Taylor, which are closer in terms of money, perceived glamor, and distance from reality, are misconceived. With figures like these, it is always possible to go back to the original performances from which the legend derived, to say that So-and-So acted or sang badly or well. With the Royals, there is no original talent that gave rise to their myth, simply the myth itself, which arises from the awful luck of being born or marrying into this extremely rich, well-connected, landowning family. They cannot do, they can only be; so mythic reality is all they can have for us.

And also, presumably, much of what they have for themselves. If we try to imagine what it must be like to be a Royal, we usually stop at the rewards and the inconveniences: on the one hand, the tax-free status and the ability to swish past in the fast lane; on the other, the nuisance of having the plebs stare at you, take photographs, and feel that they have a stake, however small, in your life. But imagine what such an existence must do to your sense of identity. You don't have anything like a job, though you may make the odd speech (usually written by someone else) and open the occasional factory. You have a semblance of power but no reality of power, and a shivering memory of what happened to your ancestors who governed too greedily. You are expected to be noncontroversial, while knowing that your slightest preference, for primrose yellow in a summer frock, or for domestic-revival over postbrutalist architecture, will be heeded as if it were an addendum to the Ten Commandments. You travel the world like an animated shop-window dummy advertising the unique, the mysterious product of Britishness. You are feted and groveled to and kept out of traffic jams. But in a sense you do not exist: you are what others decide that you are, you are only what you seem to be. And therefore you depend for your existential reality on the whole myth making, knee-bending, lie-telling business of promotion and packaging, on the Buckingham Palace spin doctors and the megaphonic exaggerations of the media.

You are, for instance, a rather gawky, shy, big-nosed girl from a posh family, not very bright, with no obvious fashion sense and with a taste for Barbara Cartland novels; you are, perhaps, one of the last virgins of your age in the country. (If you are not, someone will later find out and publish the fact.) You meet an equally gawky, big-eared boy, also from a posh family; he is older than you, rather serious-minded, not a spectacular wow with girls, and he just happens to be the heir to the throne. Therefore, and immediately, you become a fairy princess and fashion icon; you are 50 percent of the Romance of the Century. True, there are disadvantages, since you are inspected every moment of the day, inspected even by the royal gynecologist for your fitness to produce new young Windsors. But you have been transmuted from an unformed Chelsea girl who likes teaching small children into the bearer of a vast weight of the nation's emotional overload. Some people see in you a perfect example of the tremendous thing they hope will happen to them; others, for whom the business of love and marriage went wrong or is old history, are fiercely consoled by the fact that it went right for you. You have stepped not out of but into the world of a novel by Barbara Cartland—who, just for symmetry, happens to be your stepgrandmother.

So what then if things start to go wrong for you? There is nothing in the myth book to fit your case. It seems to contain only items such as Royal Romance of the Century, Prince Weds Commoner,

Princess Gives Up Unsuitable Suitor out of Duty, King Abdicates for Love of Foreign Divorcée, and so on. You can have Triumph or Tragedy, or (better still) Tragedy that becomes Triumph. What you can't have is the banality of My husband doesn't understand me, he's still seeing his old girlfriend, he's stuffy and doesn't want to have fun, my marriage is emotionally like lots of other people's marriages. The myth book has something about a Princess in a Gilded Cage, but such princesses tend to be liberated by handsome troubadours who help them fly the coop. The trouble with Prince and Princess Together in a Gilded Cage is that it's far too close to Marital Tiffs at No. 24 Laburnum Drive. Less than the stuff of myths.

The problem for the modern monarchy is how to hold in balance the demands of myth and ordinariness. The Queen is no longer seen as God's appointee; her role as Defender of the Faith is marginal, her position as Head of the Commonwealth probably less influential than that of nonplaying captain of a Davis Cup team. Yet she and her family are wanted by a majority of the population; their presence, and their continuity, are considered a defining mark of the nation. Republicanism remains a spindly growth, and the low regard in which politicians are held confirms many people in their view that the Head of State should not be just another elected official. So the main danger to the monarchy is that of auto-destruction—if it flaunts its cash, enjoys its perks too openly, fails to look useful, or seems too fallibly ordinary for the survival of its own myth.

When I was growing up, the Royal Family still operated as a moral and domestic exemplar for most of Her Britannic Majesty's subjects. This function is currently in abeyance. You could try to argue that Elizabeth's children are showing how democratically close to ordinary people they are by their ability to screw up their own lives; but that would be sophistry. Part of the unspoken deal between the Royals and the populace is that the Royals, in return for privilege, wealth, and adoration, must occasionally be seen to suffer, or give the appearance of suffering; they must also indicate from time to time that they are subject to burdensome duty, to long-term conditions and restrictions that the rest of us do not envy. They can't be seen to wallow in the benefits and then walk away when things get sticky. Therefore, the best scenario for the Royal Family–at least, the one that will best enhance its durability–is for Diana to stay with her husband and be seen to be making a painful go of it; for the Duke and Duchess of Pork to call off their separation and develop a sudden interest in charity work; for Prince Edward to make a tactical marriage; and for Princess Pushy to take the veil. Otherwise, the Royal Family will quickly decline into mere illustrators of what is known in advertising jargon as an aspirational lifestyle: this is how we plebs could and would live, had we the luck, the history, the tax breaks. Whether this would be a strong enough philosophical justification for the House of Windsor's continuance is doubtful.

July 1992

The Royal Family puzzlingly declined my advice, and its capacity for public fission continues.

■ 8 ■

The Chancellor of the Exchequer
Buys Some Claret

History, even when in trivial, jesting mood, often comes in incompatible versions. So during the last week of November the British public hunched frowningly over the following conundrum. Did a short, plump, middle-aged man, his hair mashed into a rather ridiculous graying quiff, enter Thresher's "off-license" in Praed Street, Paddington, on the evening of Monday, November 16, and there purchase one bottle of Bricout champagne, plus a packet of Raffles cigarettes (total cost £17.47), or did the same man go into a different branch of the same liquor chain on the previous day and there buy three bottles of wine (total cost also £17.47)? It would matter very little to most of us, but it mattered very much indeed to the man in question, Mr. Norman Lamont, the Chancellor of the Exchequer.

The story began on November 26, when *The Sun* published an irresistible tip-off from a mole inside the National Westminster Bank. The Chancellor, the informant disclosed, was currently £470 over the limit on his Access credit card; not only that but Mr. Lamont had breached his limit twenty-two times in the previous eight years, and had received no fewer than five written warnings after failing to make the required monthly payments. Downing Street huffed and puffed at the news, denouncing the breach of confidentiality, and claiming that the latest unpaid bill had only gone astray because of building work at No. 11, the Chancellor's official London residence. Few were impressed by this flimsy defense, and opinion varied from those who saw a shocking failure of security on the bank's part, plus a shocking intrusiveness by the press, to those who professed deep un-surprise at the financial revelations, given the wider state of the British economy under Mr. Lamont's stewardship.

Tucked away in *The Sun*'s report, however, was a small para-graph about Mr. Lamont using his Access card in the Paddington area the previous Monday. The *Evening Standard* sent out a reporter and turned up John Onanuga, an assistant at the Praed Street branch of Thresher's, who vividly recalled serving the Chancellor. Accord-ing to Mr. Onanuga, Mr. Lamont had first examined a bottle of £11.99 Tescombes Brut champagne, the cheapest in the shop, and then moved up to the midrange £15.49 Bricout, which was being promoted, appropriately enough, as a "recession-busting" item. The Chancellor also bought a packet of Raffles 100s, a low-tar cigarette retailing cheaply at £1.98. Mr. Onanuga said that he had recognized Mr. Lamont, as had a woman in the shop, and had also noticed the House of Commons pass in his wallet; he added that the Chancellor had particularly wanted a bottle of champagne that was already chilled.

All this seemingly trite substantiating detail was in fact poten-tially lethal. Mr. Lamont is known to smoke only small cigars; his wife does not smoke at all. Raffles, in any case, is hardly a brand ei-ther of them would be likely to smoke; the cigarette's image is one of down-market attempted glamor—you might expect a man who smoked Raffles to have a rusting car with a Playboy badge on the back, and a woman who smoked Raffles to dream of ensnaring her boss behind the filing cabinets at the Christmas office party. And what, moreover, about the chilled champagne? This hinted at—no, screamed—immediate consumption. On the Monday evening in ques-tion, Mr. Lamont had apparently left a civil-service select committee at six-fifteen, and was next seen at an official reception at No. 11 a while later. Journalists muttered about "the missing hour and a half," which translated into newspaper headlines like WHAT WERE YOU UP TO NORM? (*Daily Star*).

Fleet Street can scent the possibilities of sex like a tile-tripping tomcat; and while sex—by which we mean, of course, extramarital or otherwise nonconformist sex—is not in itself enough to burn a minister at the stake, it makes excellent kindling. The best way to bring down a member of the government in Britain is to link private indiscretion to public incompetence. Here the argument does not go: Ah, I see the Minister was engaging in sexual activity—well, that's probably relaxed him after a tough week of decision making and sent him back to his desk with a fresh mind. No, the argument tends to run: Look what the Minister was up to when he should have been contemplating great affairs of state. At times, of course, the Minister in question aids and abets this latter interpretation. The last of John Major's close associates to fall, David Mellor, then Secretary of State for National Heritage, made a phone call to his actress girlfriend in which he maintained that their previous sexual encounter had been so exquisite and so prolonged that he did not have the energy to write his next ministerial speech. Now, this could have been mere intimate praise, a lover's courtesy, but the phone happened to be tapped, and British puritanism supplied the textual exegesis: Minister too shagged out to think straight. The illegality of the phone tap was a mere side issue in Mr. Mellor's subsequent fall. So was the fact that most ministerial speeches are of such low quality anyway that an outside observer would be hard-pressed to judge where in the politician's private sexual cycle any particular speech resided. Germaine Greer, when put up in debate against the sort of crusty old male who argues that women can't do really complicated and demanding jobs, like fly an airplane or run the country, because, well, er, you see, the fact of the matter is that every so often, about once a month, actually, they, how shall we put it, become a little unreliable—Ms. Greer would on such occasions look the geezer magnificently in the eye and say, "Am I menstruating now?" Ministers might in turn try a similar ploy when congratulated on an effective speech: "Fact of the matter is, old boy, had a spot of how's-your-father last night, properly sets you up for speechifying, y'know."

The most politically wounding part of the story ought to have been the details of Mr. Lamont's Access account. If you want to connect private and public spheres of activity, and allege that behavior in one affects behavior in the other, then here was a vast opportunity. A private individual who heedlessly runs up debt, and by not paying off that debt incurs a punitively hefty rate of interest, who has to be booted into line by the credit authorities, and blames the builders for his failure to respond to his latest bill? Could there be any connection with a chancellor who presided over a whacking hike in public-sector borrowing, who kept the pound at an indefensibly high level, who maintained that Britain would never leave the exchange-rate mechanism until the day Britain left the exchange-rate mechanism, and who likes to blame everything on the Germans and the Bundesbank? Does this or does this not sound like the same man?

Mr. Lamont has not been one of the more impressive Chancellors of recent decades. He is said to be "overpromoted." Apart from anything else, he never seems to exude much confidence that he *is* the Chancellor. I once saw a game show on television in which the same piece of music was played three times by a studio band, with a different conductor each time. The contestants had to guess which of the baton waggers was a real musical conductor, the other two being by occupation bus conductors. Mr. Lamont has always seemed the bus-conductor type of Chancellor: one who scoops his hands up and down while music is played but has no special idea what tune is coming out, or how the musicians manage their instruments. Most people admit to little understanding of economics, while worrying a fair deal about it; so public confidence in the Chancellor depends on more than just his choice of policy. An important part of his function is to look as if he knows what he is doing while blaming others—France, Germany, the world—for the economic ills of the nation; to maintain grandly that "we shall not be blown off course," whatever the barometer indicates; and to reassure the public with an air of weighty savvy.

But what if the nation knows that it is suffering the worst recession in sixty years, that bankruptcies and mass redundancies continue unabated, and that the man in supposed charge of it all, who claimed to spot "green shoots" in the economy when others saw only a trampled mud field, doesn't appear able to keep a grip on his own small private finances? In such a case, statesmanlike posing from the Chancellor is likely to carry less conviction.

But this is, of course, a position, an editorial statement, rather than a running story. Downing Street did not attempt to rebut the disclosures about Mr. Lamont's lamentable credit record, because they were irrebuttable; the battle was fought over Mr. Lamont's moral rather than financial creditworthiness, and took place amid the stacked pre-Christmas shelves of West London "off-licenses." The full power of the British Treasury was now ranged against Mr. Onanuga. Officials telephoned newspapers with the Downing Street version of events: Mr. Lamont had never set foot in the Praed Street Thresher's but had called in at another branch the previous day on his way back from his official Buckinghamshire residence; nor, of course, had he bought chilled champagne and a pack of Raffles—just three bottles of wine. Needless to say, this primary denial was little believed: would you take the word of an unnamed Treasury spokesman against that of an assistant in your local "offie"? Almost certainly not. Besides, Mr. Onanuga had apparently told his store manager and his girlfriend that he had served Mr. Lamont days before *The Sun* broke its story.

Thresher's is a subsidiary of Whitbread, a large brewing company that is also—as conspiracy theorists were quick to point out—a major donor to the Conservative Party. (This last detail is probably not as significant as it seems: you would be hard put to find a company as large as Whitbread giving money to any party other than the Conservatives.) Thresher's held an emergency board meeting at its Welwyn Garden City headquarters; thousands of credit-card vouchers were examined by staff; and at the end of it the company confirmed the Treasury's version of events, while continuing not to specify the branch where Mr. Lamont had shopped, and denouncing its own employee's story as "wholly inaccurate and without foundation."

On the night of Sunday, November 29, in a final attempt to put the cork in the bottle, the Treasury released a copy of a Thresher's register receipt bearing the Chancellor's signature. This showed the date as November 15 (the Sunday), the time as 7:19 P.M., and the amount paid as £17.47; it itemized two bottles of J. P. Bartier claret at £3.99, plus one bottle of 1990 Margaux from Sichel at £9.49. Mr. Lamont then released his own copy of the receipt, which added a final detail: the identity of the Thresher's branch in question, one in Connaught Street, a few blocks away from Praed Street. Finally, a Thresher's spokeswoman announced that Mr. Onanuga and his store manager had admitted that their story was "totally fabricated" but said that they "did not mean to cause Mr. Lamont any trouble." So why might they have done it? Were they part, wittingly or unwittingly, of some wider conspiracy to undermine the Chancellor? Did they simply wish to wind up the press and set it running in best headless-chicken mode? Either way, the men were not produced for journalistic cross-examination and were suspended "in line with normal disciplinary procedures"—as if there had been anything normal about the preceding tale. Only a couple of minor points remained. When journalists tried to obtain from Thresher's the two wines Mr. Lamont had bought only a fortnight earlier, they discovered that both had been taken off the shelves for what was described as "precautionary quality control." And, lastly, it seemed strange that, given all the publicity, given knowledge of the exact date, time, and location of Mr. Lamont's purchase, no one had come forward from the Connaught Street shop with any memory of having served the rather recognizable Chancellor.

So, after a week of vintage quibbling, the story petered out, with an appropriate tasting note from the wine writer Jancis Robinson. Asked if she had come across Mr. Lamont's cellar selections, she consulted her records and found that she had dismissed the J. P. Bartier claret in a single word: "dirty." The story was now also dismissed, though only in the sense that a small cloud can be swallowed up by a larger one. For it was at precisely the moment of the Praed Street affair that an earlier embarrassment in Mr. Lamont's tenure as Chancellor bobbed up again, like a dead dog in a dirty river. This one involved, well, yes, sex, though even the most prurient mind did not finger Mr. Lamont himself in this context. It began when he was appointed Chancellor in November of 1990; the job brought with it a salary of £63,047, a government car, and the use of two houses: 11 Downing Street for work, and a forty-five-room Buckinghamshire mansion for weekends and holidays. This superabundance of housing meant that Mr. Lamont was able to rent out his own dwelling in Notting Hill. The following April it turned out that the tenant in his basement, one Sara Dale, who had described herself in her rental agreement as a "therapist dealing with stress and nutritional management," was, in the language of the *News of the World*, a "busty hooker," and that her therapy involved punishment and payment (ninety pounds per hour) of an all too predictable nature. Neither Mr. nor Mrs. Lamont had met this professional lady; she had been found, it seems, by reputable agents who had taken personal references from "solicitors, a bank, and a building society." When he heard that the story was about to break, Mr. Lamont not unnaturally went to see a solicitor. What was surprising was his choice of Peter Carter-Ruck & Partners, one of Britain's best-known and supposedly most expensive libel firms. Their job was (1) to evict the embarrassing woman (not their normal line of business); (2) to handle press inquiries (though there was also the Treasury press office, which would not have charged for this service); and (3) perhaps most important, to warn newspapers to be careful what they wrote. As a further incentive to speed Miss Dale, Carter-Ruck took out a quite extraordinary writ for defamation against the therapist, alleging damage to the reputation of Mr. Lamont's property caused by her presence in it. It seems that in British law you can libel a building. Whether prospective buyers or tenants might have thought that the property's reputation had already been sufficiently diminished by having a politician living in it was not, alas, tested in court.

The solicitors' bill for this work—an unopposed eviction case, some phone answering, plus a bit of watch-your-step to Fleet Street—came to a staggering £23,114.64, the equivalent of 257 hours of "stress therapy" from Miss Dale, or approximately 5,800 bottles of J. P. Bartier claret. Not a penny of this was coughed up by Mr. Lamont himself. Most of the bill was paid by a generous but unnamed Conservative Party supporter, while £4,700 came from Treasury funds. The justification for this latter contribution, which for a year and a half was successfully concealed from the public, ran as follows: if ministers are involved in legal actions relating to official duties, they may, under a Cabinet Office code of guidance, be indemnified with taxpayers' money. Apparently, the then Permanent Secretary to the Treasury, Sir Peter Middleton, told Mr. Lamont that it was "reasonable and proper" for the Treasury to meet a portion of the bill: the £4,700 thus paid was for Mr. Carter-Ruck's firm to issue a statement about potential libel and handle subsequent press inquiries (at £200 per hour, in case you are planning to use them). There seem to be three problem areas in all this. First, whether "legal action" can be stretched to include "preemptive legal strikes against possible libels"; second, whether Mr. Lamont should have chosen a famously expensive firm when some of his bill was being footed by the public; and, third, whether his case fell remotely within the Cabinet Office guidelines. It's true that if he had not been appointed Chancellor he wouldn't have been able to rent out his own house and therefore wouldn't have been obliged to evict the stress therapist, but it's hard to see how this domestic irritation could be said to have anything in the world to do with his official duties.

Mr. Lamont is currently being described as "accident-prone"–political shorthand for "incompetent beyond the dreams of the Opposition"–and is sternly announcing that he will not resign (often a prelude to resignation). But his predicament is far from unique. Consider its elements: unfortunate image, doubtful competence, public unpopularity, plus a willingness to let others pay your bills. Who else fits this profile perfectly? The British Royal Family, of course. And in the very week that Mr. Lamont was desperately defending his reputation and his job, the Queen was defending hers, too. In a speech at the Guildhall to commemorate the fortieth anniversary of her accession to the throne, she made a rare public appeal for sympathy, and even acknowledged that there was room for debate over the nature of the organization she heads. "There can be no doubt, of course, that criticism is good for people and institutions that are part of public life," she said. "No institution–City, monarchy, whatever–should expect to be free from the scrutiny of those who give it their loyalty and support, not to mention those who don't. But we are all part of the same fabric of our national society and that scrutiny, by one part of another, can be just as effective if it is made with a touch of gentleness, good humor and understanding." This may seem bland and banal to a reader living in a republic, but in a British context it was positively self-lacerating.

Her Majesty admitted that 1992 had been for her an "*annus horribilis*." The sexual and marital tomfoolery among her whelps was indeed terrible PR for Windsor Inc. And the year closed with bad news feeding off bad, so that even a potentially blithe event was thrown out of kilter by the murk surrounding it. This was the case with Princess Anne's remarriage on a raw and snow-threatening Scottish afternoon. It could have been a mildly upbeat affair, contributing a speck of much-needed image modernization to the family: here, after all, was a divorced woman in her forties marrying a chap five years her junior, and also introducing a few welcome (if dilute) Jewish molecules into the Saxe-Coburg-Gotha blood royal. Instead, the union was swamped by the backwash from Charles and Diana's separation, and the fact that the event took place in Scotland merely pointed up the current impossibility of royal remarriage within the Church of England. What was billed necessarily as a "quiet family affair" smacked instead of a dynasty hunkering and bunkering down against misfortune. The rare dispatch with which Anne married Comdr. Tim Laurence even depressed the normally buoyant memorabilia market. Previous royal hitchings produced hundreds of commercial supplicants to Buckingham Palace, asking permission to vend jaunty mugs and smile-filled T-shirts. By the time Anne and Tim had signed the register, however, only a single such request had filtered in to the Palace. One manufacturer from Stoke-on-Trent commented glumly, "We didn't think anyone would want to buy Anne and Tim tea towels."

Whether there will be Royal Worcester oil-and-vinegar cruets to mark Charles and Di's official separation remains to be seen. This public acknowledgment of a widely reported reality was no doubt designed as some kind of solution; but at best it is a holding operation, and one which opens up more possibilities than it closes down. (Separate lives, separate courts, separate lovers? A tabloid editor's dream.) Worse, it refocused the same problems as in the Lamont case: the tie-in between the private and the public life. If you don't view the Royal Family as the privileged descendants of a bunch of brigands and main chancers airbrushed into respectability by high-quality PR (with even Shakespeare & Co. engaged on the account), then you tend to invoke symbolic identity, public service, duty, and so forth. During various official junkets (the Coronation, the Investiture of the Prince of Wales), various Royals pronounce various vows whose texts are rarely scoured. But roughly they say: we promise to do our duty as symbolic top people, figureheads of the nation, defenders of the established church, and in return you give us your fealty, some of your money, and applause ad libitum. This larger pledge for the most part wafts mistily in the air, while groundlings pay closer attention to the lesser pledges: for instance, the marriage vows, promises to forsake all others and so on, made before a television audience and a priest of the said established church. So what happens when the marital log of Elizabeth II's children shows a 100 percent failure rate? Do we merely blame the press? Do we look with a darker, different eye upon the parents? Or do we say that this is the royal equivalent of Mr. Lamont's infraction, and that the family is recklessly running over the credit limit of its moral Access card?

And the fact that "we" are talking about it in this newly authoritative way indicates that another shift has taken place. As at the time of the 1936 Abdication, there is now talk of a constitutional crisis. There isn't one, inasmuch as there is very little constitution to refer to; rather, there are the adipose opinions of a group of political and spiritual power brokers who take it upon themselves to be moral arbiters. When Edward VIII–like Charles, a late marrier–was forced out, the viziers involved were the Prime Minister, the Archbishop of

Canterbury, and the editor of *The Times*. The historian A. J. P. Taylor described these three "directors of public life" as talking subsequently "as though they had triumphed over the laxity inherited from the nineteen-twenties."

Currently, the main pseudoconstitutional questions being asked are: Can Diana be crowned Queen if she and Charles are living apart; and shouldn't Charles give up the throne in favor of his elder son, William? The directors of public life have in the meantime changed. Rupert Murdoch's *Times* is much less influential, the Prime Minister is an easygoing loyalist, and the Archbishop of Canterbury is a member of the happy-clappy persuasion. With the Palace having lost the knack of setting the agenda itself, a loose crew of tabloid editors, opinion pollsters, and royal experts has taken over. So Charles is being and will continue to be tried in some informal court of morals and popularity. No matter that he is the legitimate heir to the throne, that he is still of sound mind, and that he has been trained all his life to assume the function of monarch. How will this stack up against the fact that he two-timed the most popular woman in Britain?

And then, on top of all this domestic drama, there is the question of money. This arose with a vengeful suddenness in the wake of the Windsor Castle fire. Normally, a good blaze plays in a predictable fashion, producing a sort of subdued Reichstag effect. (One could even imagine a junior Royal torching the castle to reattract public sympathy.) But this time the opposite occurred. Peter Brooke, Secretary of State for National Heritage, no doubt imagined he was being a loyal minister and an uncontroversial citizen when he announced the next day in the House of Commons that the state would pick up the estimated £60 million tab for restoring "this most precious and well-loved part of our national heritage." Buckingham Palace confirmed that the Queen herself would pay only for the repair of damaged artifacts from her private collection—which seemed to come in at a few carpets and chandeliers, plus various items dented by the firemen. Both sides agreed that the financial position was clear. Windsor Castle belonged not to the Queen as a private individual but to the

Crown; therefore, the Crown, meaning the state, meaning the tax-payer, would have to fork out.

However, the taxpayer was not very impressed by what was being done in his or her name. It's true that £60 million, spread over a number of years, is nothing in terms of the national budget–about the equivalent of a couple of bottles of dirty claret from a Paddington "off-license." But the taxpayer has had many years now of being told by a Conservative government that public services must slim down, be efficient, give value for money–political cant constantly wheeled out to justify closing down hospitals, schools, libraries, and so on. Why should this principle and these phrases not apply equally to the public services provided by the Royal Family?

Of course, it's often difficult to assess what "the public" thinks. In royal matters, "public attitudes" seem to be assembled from ad hoc opinion polls plus the shifting editorial viewpoints of normally mon-archist newspapers. In a February 1991 poll, nearly eight out of ten people interviewed thought the Queen should pay tax; more recently, *The Sun* found that 59,553 of its readers believed that the Queen should fund the repairs to Windsor Castle, while only 3,843 believed that the state should do so. No one, it must be emphasized, took to the streets on this matter; no pikes were waved with blades greased for inserting in severed Windsor heads. But the monarchy's advisers can tell what is just a straw in the wind and what looks more like a whole damn haystack. So it was not exactly a coincidence that two days after the Queen's unprecedented appeal for sympathy the Prime Minister announced that she and the Prince of Wales had agreed to pay tax on their private incomes, and that five lesser Royals–Princess Anne, Princes Andrew and Edward, Princess Margaret, and Princess Alice–would in future be paid out of the Queen's pocket, thus sparing the Civil List £900,000 per annum. Mr. Major indicated that the Queen herself had initiated discussions on this matter back in the summer, long before the smoke rose at Windsor. *The Sun* congratu-lated its readers with the voluptuously smug headline YOU SPOKE–SHE LISTENED and acclaimed the victory of "People Power."

It was a tiny triumph, a successful protest squeak after decades of barnacled deference. A nation that three and a half centuries ago didn't shrink from executing Charles I has for too long winced at the idea of examining the sovereign's check stubs: the Queen's untaxability has been seen as somehow part of her separateness, her magnificence, her magic. Royal cash is best discussed both in hugger-mugger and on bended knee. The last time the Windsor stipend was renegotiated—in 1990, when Mrs. Thatcher was Prime Minister and Mr. Major her Chancellor of the Exchequer—a ten-year index-linked, inflation-proof deal was signed, with a special promise from the government that no new accounts of how the Queen spent her money would be published before the year 2000.

Most people waking up to the Queen's nod of fiscal submission probably believed that exposing Elizabeth to the lads from the Inland Revenue was a major constitutional breakthrough. But when income tax was first introduced on a permanent basis in 1842, the then Prime Minister, Sir Robert Peel, persuaded Queen Victoria to pay this new levy on all her income, from whatever source. She did so until her death in 1901, since when the principal narrative line has been of the monarchy trying with increasing success to be let off as much tax as possible. Edward VII made the first move on his accession, but was fobbed off by a government fighting a money-intensive Boer War at the time. However, George V managed to get the Civil List exempted from tax, and George VI, in a series of agreements concealed from Parliamentary scrutiny, had his private income declared untouchable as well. This has been the position for the past fifty-six years.

Income tax was trifling throughout the nineteenth century, so Queen Victoria could well afford to pay it. Serious increases began only in 1906, when Lloyd George introduced his first budget and sought money to lay the foundations of the welfare state. What has happened since then is that the tax burden has been greatly increased—rising to 97.5 percent between 1941 and 1953, and reaching 98.0 percent between 1975 and 1979—while the Royal Family has progressively argued itself out of contributing to the state over which it has presided. Part of the current sovereign's private wealth arises directly from this exemption. If £1 were invested in averagely producing shares in 1936 (the last year the monarch paid tax), an investor who had paid tax at the top rate down the years would today find his or her stake worth £42, whereas a nontaxpaying king or queen would find the same portfolio worth £418. To put it another way: the lowest estimate of the Queen's private wealth is £50 million, a sum that could have been generated had her father, George VI, invested a mere £119,000 in a spread of British shares back in 1936.

Queen to Pay Tax! Triumph of People Power! Yes, up to a point. But how much she will pay, and on what, is an altogether different matter, not to be decided by newspaper phone-ins. Discussions will now proceed in extreme secrecy as to what exactly belongs to the Queen (Balmoral, Sandringham, her racing stables) and what belongs to the state and is merely used by the Queen (Buckingham Palace, Windsor Castle, the royal yacht). Then there is a third category of items, like the Crown Jewels, the Royal Art Collection, and even the Royal Stamp Collection, which are generally deemed inalienable, vested in the sovereign rather than the individual, and therefore not taxable. And after the division of the spoils has been made, there will presumably be meaty arguments about the Queen's professional allowances. What will the Revenue permit her? How many frocks and shoes are deemed essential for the job? She will, of course, be able to claim a personal exemption of £3,445, and if she can successfully argue that her husband does not work, she will benefit from an additional allowance of £1,720.

Estimates of the Queen's wealth vary according to how you do the sums. At one end, £50 million; at the other, £6.5 billion—a figure dismissed rather pertly by young Prince Edward as "absolute crap." That in some sense his mother lives frugally (worn stair carpet, or whatever) is not in dispute; nor is the fact that she is one of the richest women in the land. She has of late, it seems, had to dig into her reserves of capital to provide for her errant brood; and her other bloodstock business—that involving horseflesh—is said to lose £500,000 a year at the moment. So early estimates suggest that the Exchequer may be enriched by no more than about £2 million a year from Mrs. E of Windsor. The agreement to pay tax will hardly rescue the next budget of Mr. Lamont (or his successor). Nor, on the other hand, will this small symbolic step turn the Windsors from a stuffy, horse-drawn, quasi-imperial, knee-breeched organization into a modern, open, accountable, bicycling monarchy all set to greet the twenty-first century.

Her Majesty is currently being investigated by an elite squad of tax inspectors based in the northern suburbs of Cardiff. Norman Lamont is currently being investigated by Sir John Bourn, the Comptroller and Auditor General, who knew nothing of the concealed £4,700 payment and is deciding whether or not it can be justified under Cabinet Office rules. Mr. Lamont in his continuing difficulties has once more engaged Peter Carter-Ruck & Partners to act for him, and the firm is demanding apologies–plus, no doubt, impressive lawyers' fees–from half a dozen newspapers. This time, we are assured, Mr. Carter-Ruck's bill is to be met from Mr. Lamont's own pocket. And presumably he won't try using his credit card.

December 1992

Norman Lamont survived as Chancellor until May 1993, when he was reshuffled (or sacked) by John Major.

■ 9 ■

Britannia's New Bra Size

Pious moralists and historical depressives like to comfort themselves with the notion that Britain is downwardly mobile. This is abundantly true in the geopolitical sense: Dean Acheson's 1962 remark that "Great Britain has lost an empire and not yet found a role" continues to sting, because it continues to be accurate. But snufflers after signs and symbols often prefer the small instance to the large denunciation. So what better news than that Britannia herself, the very image of the nation, had become déclassé? Last month, a new ten-pound postage stamp was put on sale, and its design featured a new Britannia. In France, a replacement for the seriously sexy national figurehead of Marianne might have led to an open competition, a national canvas, a TV phone-in; the Minister of Culture, if not the President himself, would have felt a duty to interfere before the announcement of a successor to Brigitte Bardot, Catherine Deneuve, and Inès de la Fressange. In this country, too, the corporeal model for Britannia has had her moments of social glitter. When she was reintroduced onto the coinage of modern times in 1672, King Charles II used the occasion to promote his mistress Frances Stuart, Duchess of Richmond and Lennox, as the national icon. Samuel Pepys had seen her image on a commemorative medal a few years earlier and written in his diary for February 25, 1667, "At my goldsmith's did observe the King's new medal, where in little there is Mistress Stuart's face as well done as ever I saw anything in my whole life, I think: and a pretty thing it is that he should choose her face to represent Britannia by." In looking for a successor to the Duchess of Richmond, the "pretty thing" might have been to choose Prince Charles's longstanding friend Mrs. Camilla Parker-Bowles. But nowadays the royal writ does not run so far; we live in times that are more squeamish, or hypocritical, or democratic. And so in 1993 the tufted helmet of Britannia alighted on the head of Karin Craddock, photographer wife of the illustrator Barry Craddock. The unexpected icon and her husband dwell in Deptford, a less than fashionable quarter of southeast London.

Charles II chose his own Britannia, and also his own designer, Jean Roettiers, whom he invited over from Antwerp to work at the Royal Mint. Nowadays, the process has become bureaucratized. Royal Mail Stamps auditioned several design teams before choosing the Roundel Design Group. Roundel, in turn, considered the work of several possible illustrators before selecting Barry Craddock, one of whose strengths is an ability to draw in a way that resembles engraving. ("Brush on white scraperboard and then cut back with a tool," he explains.) His contribution is the first thing that strikes you about the new stamp, but in design terms he was last on the timetable. The Royal Mail's Stamp Advisory Committee and the Roundel Design Group worked together for almost two years; Mr. Craddock was only involved in the final six weeks of the process. Three weeks of discussions; then three weeks of putting brush to paper. Not surprisingly, given such a deadline, the illustrator did not scour the model agencies looking for some breakthrough Face of the Nineties; he whistled up his wife. Did he pay her? "No," she replies. "We don't work like that."

Mr. Craddock is a short, dapper man with discreetly graying hair and a neat mustache; the unpaid Britannia is delightfully unregal—a cheery, direct woman with the sort of London accent recently classified by a linguistic demographer as Estuary English. They are both out of their thirties, but pedantic impertinence about establishing Britannia's precise year of birth is laughingly met with the answer "55 B.C.," that being the date of the first Roman invasion of our islands. The Craddocks live in surroundings of appropriate Englishness: William Morris wallpaper in the hall, bronze plaque of Queen Victoria in the kitchen, and down on the lawn the lolloping figure of a large pet rabbit, white with black ears and an uncannily thin black line along the backbone. The breed, fittingly enough, is called Old English, though the Craddocks suspect it to be Chinese. Equally confused are the racial origins of the new Britannia, who would certainly be failed by some vetting committee obsessed with *pur sang*. Karin is half Danish, with a "possibly Lapp grandfather," and on her other side there are smidgens of Yugoslav, Irish, and French blood. Still, at least she has a patriotic modeling pedigree, having previously featured in a TV commercial as Queen Victoria sitting on a beer barrel.

On this occasion, she posed for Barry in a domestic parody of her mythical embodiment. She sat, draped in a sheet, on top of a board balanced on a picnic hamper and a pile of books; the trident in her right hand was a garden rake, the circular shield against her left hip an old tabletop; in her left hand a chunk of tree from the back garden served as her olive branch. In this context, of course, modeling doesn't mean twitchless pose holding but rather trying out stances for a series of photographs from which the final drawings would be made. Even so, did Karin Craddock, in the gravity of the moment, reflect that she might be defining the nation's image for the next generation? "I didn't think about it," she replies with an insouciant grin. "It was just a job of work, helping him to get it right."

Barry already had a track record with the national image, having depicted Britannia in various commercial settings. This time, "getting it right" was a more complicated process, not least in terms of constant consultation—or, if you prefer, interference. ("At all times I had about a dozen heads over my shoulder.") A slew of rough drawings marks his progress from the petite, fizzy, homely, broad-faced Karin, looking left, to the monumental, stern, public, Roman-nosed Britannia, looking right. Karin is five feet three and a half inches tall, whereas the stamp, she says, makes her look "almost like an eight-footer." "She's a very, *very* big girl," Barry agrees, almost awed by what he's drawn. Of course, pictorial icons are often far from the original truth: though the Duchess of Richmond was by all accounts a great beauty (and a great ninny), by the time she appeared on the coinage she had suffered a disfiguring attack of smallpox. In Marianne's case some of the adjustments might have been made at an even earlier stage, if the perennial rumors of Catherine Deneuve's face fixing are to be believed.

Britannia didn't just get bigger; her posture also improved. "As the design developed, she got taller and taller," Barry says. "In my first design, she was very reclined." A penciled note at the top of one preliminary drawing reads, THINGS DONE. REDUCED HELMET. NEW HAND. NEW BUSTLINE. NEW SHIELD, ETC. There were constant adjustments to her hips, her legs, and her torso. There was earnest and particular discussion of Britannia's bra size. "It was quite crucial," Barry recalls. Mike Denny of the Roundel Design Group explains: "Britannia must look powerful and imperial, but she also has to be feminine. When we started out, her chest was almost flat, which looked ridiculous. Then we went to the other extreme. Eventually, we settled for a 36B size." This was at least democratic: 36B is currently the standard bust size of this nation, having crept up, Gossard the bra manufacturers confirm, from 34B seven years ago. The pill and better nutrition are held to be two contributing factors; indeed, at this very moment the *femme moyenne sensuelle* is gently swelling toward a 36C. Barry Craddock remembers the moment when "a lady from the Post Office, Angela Reeves, took her pen and said it should be *that* big." He seems relieved that the final decision was not his: "A standard 36B–they told me."

Aside from Karin's Amazonian extension, there were stylistic and decorative accoutrements to be argued over. Britannia's first appearance on a coin–a brass sestertius issued under the Emperor Hadrian

(A.D. 117–138)—shows her in her original, subservient form, as a captive standing on a rocky crag with a spiked shield to hand. In modern times—that's to say, since the seventeenth century—she has been conqueror rather than conqueree, a resolute, imperial figure, who presents herself with mild paradox as the bringer of both war and peace. She has always carried a circular shield on which is emblazoned the national flag; she holds either a spear or (more recently) a Neptunian trident; and her two most familiar accessories are a warrior's helmet and an olive branch, which come and go according to the temper of the times. She is often portrayed vigilantly guarding the shoreline, and her maritime status may be emphasized by the addition of a ship or a lighthouse, sometimes both. Unusually, as on the fifty-pence coin in 1969, she is united with that other imperial beast, the lion.

Mr. Craddock's Britannia is a severe, imposing, and largely traditional icon. Shield, helmet, trident, olive branch, the familiar figurehead of Pax Britannica: first we conquer you, and then we call your state of submission peace. Barry made various attempts at softening the image, but he cannot be said to have succeeded. Karin recalls that at one point when she was posing "he asked me to hold the rake more gently," and there is perhaps something a touch limp-wristed about the way Britannia grasps her trident on the stamp. But Mr. Craddock's other initiatives met with committee resistance. "I suggested putting in doves," he recalls. "But they didn't like doves." Mike Denny agrees: "No, we didn't like doves. We wanted it to be symbolic, but we didn't want it to be a picture." Out, for the same reason, went a sailing ship Barry tried to introduce, as well as some vestigial White Cliffs of Dover. "What about these storm clouds in the background?" I ask, since it looks as if Hurricane Craig or Donna were blowing up over Britannia's shoulder. "Doesn't mean anything," Barry replies swiftly, and a little nervously, as if apprehensive that his weather might be taken for a subversive political subtext. Sometimes storm clouds are only storm clouds.

Then this adjusted, contested, examined, and agreed-on eight-foot, 36B Britannia was shoehorned into the space allotted to it by Roundel. Any presumption that the rest of the design paraphernalia would be fitted round the main image on the stamp is misconceived: before his six-week stint began, Craddock was handed a mock-up of the finished item, in which Britannia was the only discussable element. The layout had been fixed; so had the colors (an olivey green and a rather noisy purple); and so had the bossily modern typeface for the "£10" symbol. What looks to the untutored eye like a nasty clash of design elements is explained by Mike Denny as "trying to get across the sense of a contemporary nation with a heritage." In addition, there was a range of features to the stamp which had already been incorporated. The nine pustular uprisings beneath the Queen's head turn out to be Braille dots—the first time they have appeared on a British stamp. The four scallop-shaped bite marks that munch into the margins at top and bottom are there to discourage back-kitchen counterfeiters. "If you forge a stamp," Mr. Denny explains, "it's dead easy to do the perforations on a sewing machine." The new Britannia has found herself on what is termed a "high-security stamp." Mr. Denny says that it is "designed to be incredibly difficult to print"— and therefore, presumably, to reprint. Several different-colored inks are used as a deterrent; Mrs. Craddock is carpet bombed with a host of tiny marks in purple, red, green, and orange, which spell out "ten pounds"; even the thin lines of the sea which extend outward from Britannia's shin are revealed, on magnified inspection, to be murmuring "ten pounds ten pounds ten pounds ten pounds." Finally, there is a grid of twenty-five small silver-foil crosses overlaying the central figure: these outwit the criminal by turning black when photocopied. To the ordinary eye of the stamp-buying nonforger, however, the crosses shine rather disagreeably in the light, as if they were part of some connect-the-dots game. One of them falls directly below Britannia's right ear, like the centering mark in a sniper's sights. Mr. Craddock was even asked to move his figure sideways to avoid this conjunction, but he dug his heels in and declined. The general effect of all this overprinting is a little bizarre, and undoubtedly diminishes the visual impact of the stamp. It's like seeing a rather elegant house surrounded by mesh fencing and razor wire, with gaudy burglar-alarm boxes on every wall and throaty Alsatians on the front lawn. Which does, if unwittingly, add an extra symbolic resonance to the image.

As Barry Craddock discovered ("They didn't like doves"), tampering with the nation's iconography can be a tricky business. The design for the new ten-pound stamp was sent to the Queen for official approval (as all stamps must be), and duly received it on October 7; around the same time, in another part of Buckingham Palace a small storm in a silver-gilt epergne was brewing. Whereas with postage stamps the royal presence is lightly felt and only at the very end of the process, there is much closer involvement when it comes to coins of the realm. Prince Albert, consort to Queen Victoria and a zealot for the collaboration between Art and Industry, always took a close interest in coin design. In 1922 the Royal Mint Advisory Committee on the Design of Coins, Medals, Seals and Decorations was set up, and its president since 1952 has been His Royal Highness Prince Philip, Duke of Edinburgh, KG, KT, OM, GBE. The other committee members, a dozen or more, are drawn from numismatists, heralds, artists, designers, calligraphers, ornithologists, botanists, and wordsmiths, all bringing their cumulative expertise to bear on the complex, bureaucratic, delicate, and agreeable task of recommending to the Queen what the British circulating coinage should look like. Needless to say, they are not paid, though they do receive proof copies of the Maundy money–a set of tiny coins, no bigger than a child's fingernail, that are minted annually for distribution to an equally tiny section of the deserving poor on Maundy Thursday.

Most of the committee's members are men, with a good splatter of knights and professors among them, but there have occasionally been women, including the sculptor Elizabeth Frink and, currently, the Marchioness of Anglesey. Until recently, there was also the novelist and cultural historian Marina Warner. When I asked how she came to be appointed, she said, "Well, it was that very English thing. I was placed next to someone at dinner, and we started talking about the American dollar bill and its Masonic symbolism. He turned out to be John Porteous, the numismatist, and I told him about my book *Monuments and Maidens,* and he put me up for the committee." The appointment couldn't have appeared a more natural one: Ms. Warner, a woman of incandescent intelligence and Apulian beauty, is one of the country's most scholarly and perceptive writers on the significance and interpretation of cultural symbols. However, even before her appointment–to-succeed the late Poet Laureate Sir John Betjeman as "words representative"–it became clear to her that sitting among the numismatic great and good was not going to be a matter, or at least not *just* a matter, of discussing what should be couchant and what should be rampant. The committee lies at one of the many intersections of royalty and politics: while the Mint is naturally Royal, its official master is the Chancellor of the Exchequer. At the time of Warner's appointment in 1985, the Chancellor under Mrs. Thatcher was Nigel Lawson. Ms. Warner recalls, "I was rung up and asked, 'What have you been up to in your past? There's some trouble getting you on.' It turned out that Nigel Lawson didn't want me. He only let me go through with the protection of three Thatcherite sympathizers." And what had she done in her past? "I expect Lawson thought me a leftie." Since Ms. Warner is an impeccable liberal, he probably did. Perhaps she was rendered just capable of legitimacy in the eyes of the Tory establishment by the fact that her grandfather was P. F. "Plum" Warner, distinguished prewar captain of the England cricket team.

Asked about her numismatic preferences, Ms. Warner immediately cites the famous Greek coin minted in Syracuse which shows Arethusa as a girl with flowing locks and dolphins leaping round her head. "I wish we could go back to that. There doesn't have to be heavy nationalistic meaning–a coin can be something that gives *pleasure*," she says emphatically. "Pleasure" is not, however, a word that crops up too frequently in the deliberations of the Royal Mint Advisory Committee. More often than not, members will be discussing heraldic solecisms, symbolic minutiae, the fussiness of lettering, or the insoluble problem of Northern Ireland. It's a tiny reflection of the intractability of the Irish situation that it infects even these scholarly and largely dispassionate discussions in a wing of Buckingham Palace. The difficulty lies in the fact that, while each of the three other parts of the United Kingdom has a fair choice of uncontentious ancient emblems for public iconic use, Northern Ireland does not. How to represent the province on a coin? The Red Hand of Ulster would lie uneasily in a Catholic pocket, while the Protestant thumb might snag on a harp or a shamrock. The ancient crown of St. Edward is deemed acceptable, but crosses can stir trouble: the cross of St. Patrick, already familiar from flags and arms, is allowable, but the Celtic cross, which might be taken by some Protestants as an offensive religious symbol, is disbarred. One recent solution has been found in the torc— a ceremonial collar, often in heavy chiseled gold, worn by the old chieftains in Hibernia. Other safe options come from hedgerow and field: flax, the yellow pimpernel, the rowan. There was an attempt not long ago to put forward the elk as a symbol of the province: little did the wretched designer in question realize that it is heraldically questionable to place an elk upon a shield. This sort of impasse drives artists to ever greater ingenuity: one recent submission represented Northern Ireland as an adolescent girl innocently playing a tin flute while striding the Giant's Causeway.

Who actually delineated this tin-flute option would not have been known to the committee; the members would merely have been examining "Submission 1(d) from Designer No. 1 of Item 3: Regional Designs for £1 Coin." The anonymity of artists is scrupulously guarded, although over the years personal styles inevitably become recognizable. Sometimes—as with the commemorative crown piece to be issued later this year to mark the fortieth anniversary of the Queen's coronation—there is an open competition. More often, specific artists are invited to submit ideas. Such was the case with the new regional designs for the reverse of the one-pound coin. The coin itself was introduced in 1983, and it has been the practice to change the reverse design every year. In the first year of issue, there was a Royal Arms reverse, then a four-year cycle celebrating each of the constituent parts of the United Kingdom, then the Royal Arms again in 1988, followed by a different regional cycle. After the current buffer year, the next regional cycle will begin in 1994. A dozen artists were therefore asked to send in preliminary drawings to the Royal Mint by

December 31, 1991. They were requested to provide designs connected by a common theme or otherwise unified in style; they were
reminded of the Irish problem, and told of their reward. Those who
submitted one set of four drawings would be paid £250; those short-
listed and asked to supply plaster models of their designs (no larger
than seven inches in diameter) would be paid £500 per model; and
the winner would receive £2,500 for each of the four models given
the final royal approval, in return for which he or she would assign
full copyright to the Crown.

Nine of the twelve submitted work, and the Advisory Committee
met for its first appraisal on February 11, 1992, in the Chinese Dining
Room of Buckingham Palace. Committee members enter the building
by the Privy Purse Door on the right-hand side of the palace facade,
where they are met by military equerries. Here the men's coats are removed and, instead of being hung up, are folded in neat military fashion into fat cubes, which are placed on a table. (Fortunately, they
don't try this with the women's coats.) Then members go up to the
first floor, passing, until recently, an admonitory Landseer, a sort of
Victorian circus version of Daniel in the Lions' Den; they glimpse an
endless red-carpeted corridor lined with busts and urns, before being
ushered into the committee room. This is early-nineteenth-century
scarlet and gold chinoiserie–"the mantelpiece astir with a thousand
dragons spitting at you," Marina Warner recalls. All remain standing
and examine the designs to be discussed until the formal arrival of the
president, Prince Philip; then they take their places at a long table.
Asked to describe the meetings, Ms. Warner replies, "Well, it's rather
like the Mad Hatter's Tea Party. Everyone is a bit falling asleep.
There's a sense of pomp, and a feeling of being lulled by ceremony.
It's the culture of deference–an atmosphere which does tend to tie
people's tongues." At its first meeting, tongue-tied or not, the committee reduced the field for the one-pound coin reverse to a couple of
finalists: Designer 8, who had submitted a series of ploddingly traditional heraldic schemes, and Designer 9, whose elegant drawings, in
positive danger of producing pleasure, featured wild birds–the avocet
for England, osprey for Scotland, red kite for Wales, and roseate tern

for Northern Ireland. The thematic link among these four birds is that each had been close to extinction earlier in the century but had made a successful breeding return.

By the next meeting, on May 26, it was clear that both designs had their disadvantages. The heraldic series was criticized by both the Scottish and Welsh offices. The Scottish Office, having consulted Lord Lyon, King of Arms, pronounced the Scottish design in Series A of Designer 8 a confusing and incorrect marriage of emblems, while the Welsh Office pointed out the shocking heraldic solecism of imposing a Welsh dragon upon what looked to their eyes like the cross of St. George. The birds, meanwhile, were also running into trouble. Both the Scottish and Welsh offices, while finding them attractive, wondered if people would recognize the species as properly representative of their countries. The Duke of Edinburgh had an objection to the presence of vegetation: the avocet grasps an oak twig, the osprey a thistle, and so on. The design for Wales showed the red kite grasping a leek, rather as if it had swooped down on a greengrocer's stall and carried off the vegetable to feed its young. An ornithologically inclined member of the committee pointed out that red kites are not as yet known to eat leeks.

There were other criticisms, too: that the heraldic designs were heavy and dreary; that the Scottish lion should be made larger; that the birds be shown in flight rather than crouching; that the raven replace the avocet as the English symbol. A more menacing threat to the birds was voiced by the Deputy Master of the Mint and chairman of the committee, Mr. A. D. Garrett, who said that, since the pound was the premier circulating coin, the question of its design could not be approached with "complete flexibility." Also at this meeting was the Economic Secretary, Mr. Anthony Nelson, MP, representing the Chancellor of the Exchequer. His presence was a novelty: in the seven years of Ms. Warner's attendance, this was only the second time a Treasury Minister had turned up. Traditionally, the committee had done its work and reported to the Mint, which in turn reported to the Treasury. Now there was a minder sitting in. Mr. Nelson expressed the view that the adoption of the bird series might be seen as demoting coins to the status of mere stamps. Perhaps he was forgetting that one of the most popular British coins of the century, the now defunct farthing, featured a wren on its reverse side. It was a neat conjunction of image and value: the smallest British bird on the smallest circulating coin.

Still, it was agreed that both series should be "progressed." Designer 8 was to have all four designs redrawn by the College of Heralds to make them heraldically kosher, while Designer 9 was to amend the birds, first by showing them in flight, and, second, by adding the crowns of the four regions as extra identifying badges (though in truth the percentage of the British population likely to be able to tell one regional crown from another is wren-sized). The committee then met on November 3 to decide upon its final recommendation to the Mint. It first approved the minutes of the previous meeting and discussed the new two-pound coin to be minted for the tercentenary of the Bank of England in 1994. Then came "Item 3– New Series of Regional Designs for the Reverse of the £1 Coin." Scarcely had the topic been raised, however, than the Deputy Master of the Mint instructed the committee that it was not even to consider the bird designs. For an obedient while, members argued the pros and cons of the revamped heraldic series, which still had many faults and to some eyes had even been made worse, until Ms. Warner stirred up the Mad Hatter's Tea Party by demanding to know why they were not allowed to discuss the birds. "When we asked why," she recalls, "there was all this flanneling and red-faced puffing from this senior civil servant"–the Deputy Master. The reason, apparently, was that the office of the Chancellor of the Exchequer, Norman Lamont, had decided to preempt the decision. The birds, held to lack the gravitas the coinage demanded, had been shot from the sky, whatever the Royal Mint Advisory Committee on the Design of Coins, Medals, Seals and Decorations happened to think.

Of course, the committee is only advisory: in 1991 it had recommended a design for a Gulf War medal–coincidentally, by the same artist who drew the birds–only to have it rejected by the Queen and the Joint Chiefs of Staff. (This must have led to some interesting pillow talk at Buckingham Palace. "What did you do today, dear?" "Turned down your lousy medal, darling.") Still, for the Queen to interfere was one thing: annoying, but constitutional. To have the final decision-making process simply squelched from the agenda seemed positively irregular. Ms. Warner made her own inquiries and discovered "that Lamont had decided he wanted the heraldic series. The Economic Secretary was also heard to say, quite casually, 'It's just that the Chancellor doesn't like the birds.'"

Marina Warner waited until the next meeting, on February 10, 1993, to see if there was any chance of recycling the birds on a lower-denomination coin, and also to see how the whole kerfuffle had been minuted; then she resigned. "I really saw no point in turning up just to rubber-stamp Norman Lamont's taste in art," she crisply concludes. Then she passes me one of Charles Addams's last drawings, torn from *The New Yorker*. A medieval king is leaning from his castle battlements and addressing the assembled peasantry: "And now, as an experiment in democracy, I'm decreeing free elections to choose the national bird."

You could say that Lamont's short-circuiting of the committee was the sort of thing Ministers, whether of left or right, are often tempted to do, and perhaps the more tempted when relentlessly criticized for feebleness in their main sphere of activity. You could say that the natural condition of any committee is that of the Mad Hatter's Tea Party. You could say that Ms. Warner's experience was almost predictable: the Adventures and Misfortunes of a Female Liberal in a Male, Conservative, Royalist World. Even so, the question she left the committee with in her letter of resignation, about "the central problem of U.K. coinage today," is a proper, living one: "The political changes since the Middle Ages mean that the iconographic language of heraldry, rich and beautiful as it is, has to be pulled and pushed until it is out of shape in order to convey today's reality. Unicorns, dragons, etc., no longer meet the full needs of representation. . . . Some other image store has to be dug into in order to communicate the historical condition of the U.K." Or, as she put it more pungently to me: "It's a question of how we see ourselves.

Do we want to live in a Laura Ashley, potpourri, National Trust, olde-worlde land, or do we want to present ourselves as a forward-looking nation, on the threshold of a new world, a new Europe?" The answer is for the moment depressingly clear. Place your bets that the next time Britannia is refurbished, with her bust size rejigged to a 36C, she will appear swathed in Laura Ashley.

April 1993

■ 10 ■

The Deficit Millionaires

You don't often meet someone who has lost a million pounds. Even more rarely, someone who will mention the fact to a stranger–worse, a journalist–over the telephone. But this was almost the first thing Fernanda Herford said to me when I called her. "I hit a million this morning. They asked for another three hundred and nineteen thousand pounds. They are absolutely ruthless. Well, of course, they won't get it." This was all spoken in an even, slightly ironical tone of voice. The "they" of her complaint–East End mafia? specialty-drug doctors?–turn out to be the Lloyd's of London insurance market. Fernanda Herford is a Lloyd's investor, or Name, who despite the belief that her money was working at the low-risk end of the market, has been faced over three successive years with grotesque, parodic losses. The fact that she is so open about such losses–here in Britain, where furious secrecy and quasi-lavatorial shame still cling to money–is an indicator that for a small slice of society something has gone terribly, unprecedentedly wrong. One of the pillars of British society has turned out to be made of Styrofoam. Speaking out is a direct indicator of incredulity, betrayal, and rage.

A few days later, I met Mrs. Herford at her Chelsea house just off the Fulham Road. We sat in a sunlit backyard with a brimming Cafetière between us; her husband, an accountant, was working upstairs; in the kitchen, a student daughter was dragging a feed-the-village sack of Elephant chapati flour across the floor toward the stove. Amid this upper-middle-class English normality sat a woman in trim middle age who until two years ago was, by all outside criteria, somewhere between comfortably off and rich, who implicitly trusted what was held to be one of the world's great financial institutions, and who today is seriously insolvent. "Now they control every penny—and they will take it. They are *ruthless*," she repeats. And yet, compared with others, her case is not so bad: "I'm not a sob story in Lloyd's terms."

Asked to specify how and why she went into Lloyd's back in 1977, she insists that "I didn't do it for the money." This may seem an odd reply at first, yet money, after all, comes both to those who are fascinated by its working and to those who are not. She also didn't do it "to educate the children," that traditional explanation of the Lloyd's investor, who does not, of course, send his or her children to state schools. She did it "because my father was already a Name—I sort of slid into it." You "slide" into such things because of the assumptions of your social circle. Fernanda Herford had a brother and two sisters-in-law who were in Lloyd's; she also knew a Lloyd's agent named Anthony Gooda. "I did it because I knew the Gooda setup, because women were allowed into Lloyd's, and I thought it was a very English thing to do." Her first foray into the market—underwriting business up to £150,000—came the following year. Given the normal haggling time it takes to settle most insurance claims, the accounting period at Lloyd's is three years. So in 1981 Mrs. Herford received a check for £4,100, representing a 2.73 percent return for the year 1978. That may sound rather unimpressive but the point—one of the main points for those privileged enough to have been Lloyd's Names over the three centuries of its existence—is that the money invested is not actually handed over. The principle of the market is that a Name "shows" a certain amount of wealth, so that Lloyd's knows that if things go wrong—if, classically, the ship fails to reach port—it will have that wealth to call upon. The investor is free, while awaiting this postulated call, to invest his or her money, that same money, in something else. Lloyd's enables you, in this very precise way, to double your money. And it allowed Fernanda Herford to slightly more than double her money in a different sense, since the investor was allowed to underwrite business to a premium limit approximately two and a half times that of the wealth shown. In her first year, then, Mrs. Herford showed wealth of £75,000, insured business of £150,000, used her basic £75,000 elsewhere, and three years later received £4,100, which, though on one reading is a 2.73 percent return on investment, could also be seen as a 5.46 percent return on wealth shown; or, to put it another way, could be seen as money for jam.

This agreeable situation continued for eight more years. The traditional optimistic profit figure that is whispered enticingly to Lloyd's Names is a rather useful 10.00 percent on business insured. In nine years' trading, Fernanda Herford only once hit that figure. Her returns varied from a low of 0.78 percent for 1979 to a high of 11.18 percent for 1982. On the other hand, she was able to increase her wealth shown to £200,000 for 1984–1986. By 1989, when the results for 1986 came in, she had made a cumulative total profit of £82,665, or 5.51 percent on the amount of business underwritten. A way short of the fabled 10.0 percent, but then Mrs. Herford had been assured that she was not at the risky end of the market. This seemed logical. "I never had big gains, and never thought I was big risk." Indeed, her agent, Anthony Gooda, told her, in a phrase that not surprisingly lingered in her mind, that her investment was "so safe you could mortgage the cat."

In 1987, she increased her underwriting limit to £300,000, and in 1990 received news of her first loss: £13,391, which just about wiped out the previous year's gain of £14,199. Meanwhile, on the advice of her agent, she had increased her premium limit yet again: to £375,000 for the years 1988 and 1989, then to £500,000 for 1990. In late June of 1991, she received a letter from Anthony Gooda: "I am afraid you have sustained an overall loss [for 1988] of £219,985.27. I should be pleased if you would forward a cheque for this amount ... by the 12th July. We have been advised by Managing Agents any amounts outstanding after the 15th July will attract interest." Was she tempted to resign at this point, when the overall result of her eleven years in the market stood at a loss of £150,711? "In 1991, Anthony Gooda told me the worst was over. He told me another ninety thousand pounds was all I could lose. I still thought it was worth it." And in any case, she was already committed to the gains or losses on business she had underwritten for the years 1989 and 1990. When those results arrived, it was clear that cat-mortgaging time had come. In 1992 she got a call for £527,348.03 for 1989; and this year calls amounting to £319,000. There is now a new select breed of people in Britain who might be called deficit millionaires. Fernanda Herford, with an admirable lack of self-pity, reflects that "I have to say I was the sitting target—I trusted, which was my fault." By the time she became a deficit millionairess, her underwriting agents, Gooda Walker, had ceased trading, and Anthony Gooda, from being a sociable, wide-trawling agent, had become one of the most reviled figures in the market. There are three current options open to Mrs. Herford: file for bankruptcy, put herself into the hands of the Lloyd's Members' Hardship Committee, or sue those with whom she dealt for professional negligence. For the moment, she is suing. And one other thing as well: "We're now doing bed-and-breakfast."

THE MONTH OF JUNE 1993 was a good one for those who scrutinize the *faits divers* for clues to the nation's moral state. There was the luxury clifftop hotel in Scarborough which over a few much photographed days slowly collapsed into the sea; as a mud slide gobbled the building, prospectors lined the shore in the hope of plundering an intact bidet. Then there was the English soccer team's seismic defeat by the supposed ragamuffins of the USA, a result that provoked pert comparisons between team manager Graham Taylor and national manager John Major. And there was the survey of domestic consumer habits which concluded that Britons were Europe's scruffiest dressers. But who needed symbolic indicators of the state's welfare when the real indicators were so particular? On June 22, Lloyd's of London announced overall losses for 1990 of £2.91 billion, the worst losses in the market's history. The previous year, it had also announced the worst losses in its history. And the year before that it had done the same. Almost £5.50 billion over those three years, and with losses of more than a billion already anticipated for 1991. Nor was the monstrous figure of £2.91 billion necessarily the final low point: two-fifths of the insurance syndicates (157 out of a total of 385) had left 1990 "open"—that is to say, with their accounts unfinalized, since the full extent of the damage could not yet be properly judged. To view it historically: since 1955 the market's many felicitous years have brought cumulative profits of £3.7487 billion, while its few woeful years have brought cumulative losses of £5.3243 billion. Or to put it at the crudest, individual level: if the losses for the four years 1988–1991 were spread evenly among all the Names, each would be asked to fork out roughly a quarter of a million pounds.

The estimated £2.1991 billion was the biggest annual loss achieved by a single British institution since the Coal Board set the national record at £3.90 billion in 1984. But the resonance of Lloyd's cumulative catastrophe is wider than that comparison implies. Most citizens of this country don't know what goes on in the City of London but have a loyal idea of it as "the financial capital of the world." Asked to specify, the Briton might mention as its most famous institutions first the Bank of England and secondly Lloyd's. "As safe as the Bank of England," we like to quote, though after the Bank's inept failure to regulate BCCI in the time up to its collapse the catchphrase should perhaps be altered to "as sleepy as the Bank of England." As for Lloyd's of London, the popular perception of it has always been as a rather mysterious, Masonic place that began in a Coffee House, that nobody outside understands, but that is obviously very good at whatever it is it might do. And what might it do? Oh, something sui generis, and therefore inexplicable to the unwashed; something very English, rather upper-class, and poshly efficient—say, the financial equivalent of Savile Row or Rolls-Royce. (Savile Row, of course, is not as flush as it used to be, while Rolls-Royce had to be rescued from receivership in the early seventies.) Furthermore, Lloyd's has managed to present itself as an institution that is both very old and very modern: established before the Bank of England, yet capable of flourishing athletically in Mrs. Thatcher's world; richly enshrining all manner of quaint traditions, yet working out of a spanking modern building at No. 1 Lime Street designed by Richard Rogers, architect of the Beaubourg in Paris.

Lloyd's is different from other insurers in two key respects. First, membership is individual; and second, the liability of that membership is unlimited: in other words, you risk not just your agreed investment but everything you own. You do not buy shares in Lloyd's; you are elected to it on the basis of your wealth, and the accumulated wealth of the individual members makes up the funds that allow Lloyd's to trade. This nexus of exclusivity and money meant that until recent years the identity of the few thousand Names was unknown to the wider public; membership in Lloyd's was a badge of status murmured about rather than confirmed. But TOP PEOPLE LOSE MONEY is always a page-filling story, and nowadays high-profile Names are widely named: the Duchess of Kent, Prince and Princess Michael of Kent, Princess Alexandra and her husband, Sir Angus Ogilvy; Maj. Ronald Ferguson, father of the Duchess of York, and Maj. Peter Phillips, father of Princess Anne's first husband; Camilla Parker Bowles, the confidante of Prince Charles; forty-seven Tory MPs, including former Prime Minister Edward Heath, Scottish Secretary Ian Lang, Heritage Minister Peter Brooke, Party Chairman Sir Norman Fowler, and Attorney General Sir Nicholas Lyell; various peers, such as Lord Wakeham, the Leader of the Lords, and Lord Hailsham of St. Marylebone; eleven judges and at least fifty-four Queen's Counsel; Sir Peter de la Billière, commander of the British forces in the Gulf War, and Nick Mason, of Pink Floyd; writers Frederick Forsyth, Melvyn Bragg, Edward de Bono, and Jeffrey Archer; the publisher Lord Weidenfeld and the champion jockey John Francome; former British tennis No. 1s Virginia Wade, Mark Cox, and Buster Mottram; various earls and viscounts, marquesses and baronesses, lords and ladies, squires and squiresses. Recently deceased members include Robert Maxwell;

recently resigned members include boxer Henry Cooper, golfer Tony Jacklin, actress Susan Hampshire, jockey Lester Piggott. James Hunt, the former world motor-racing champion, known on the track in his early days as Hunt the Shunt, had a series of terrible shunts at Lloyd's; he died of a heart attack as the news was still emerging that he was on many of the worst-performing syndicates.

The presence of so many Tory MPs in the catalog of Names briefly raised a merry scenario of political destabilization. A bankrupt MP is automatically disqualified from sitting in the House of Commons, and loses his or her seat after six months. According to *The Times*, "at least thirteen" of the forty-seven Tories might be forced into bankruptcy by their losses. With John Major's Parliamentary majority in the trembly midteens and dropping with each by-election, an ironic denouement looked possible: that of Lloyd's inadvertently bringing down the party under whose aegis the City and Lloyd's itself had boomed in the eighties. But a "scenario"– that's to say, a piece of fictional hoping or fearing–is probably all this will be. In the first place, MPs, like other burnt Names, could put themselves in the hands of the Hardship Committee, a process that, even if humiliating, is specifically designed to avoid bankruptcy. And second, the Tory Party, of all parties, is famously skilled at looking after its own. Well-wishers unbuckle their money belts and secret funds disgorge their guineas. If Mr. Norman Lamont, the erstwhile Chancellor of the Exchequer, could be slipped £23,114.64 to prevent embarrassment when suing to rid his house of the tenancy of a flagellant prostitute, how much more readily would generous contributors come forth if it were a matter of the Government falling?

But the crisis at Lloyd's has had some unexpected side effects. I wasn't sure how flip Fernanda Herford was being in her reference to bed-and-breakfast until I read a story in *The Times* at the beginning of August: a company called Discover Britain, based in Worcester, has been enlisting cash-bothered Names to offer their homes as tony B and Bs. (Its managing director reported, "We have Names in the Cotswolds and in the Home Counties on our books. It gives foreign guests a chance to meet the more comfortably off British people and stay in some of the nicer houses in Britain.") Elsewhere, the property market and the auction houses have received some tasty bits of business. Henry Cooper sold his three Lonsdale belts (each awarded for three successful defenses of his heavyweight-boxing title) at Sotheby's for £42,000. The wine trade has felt the benefit of Lloyd's. Stephen Browett, a director of Farr Vintners, confirms that a number of private cellars have unexpectedly become available. "No one says, 'I'm selling because I've fucked up, I've lost money.' But, on the other hand, often—excuse the pun—the most liquid asset they have is their wine. It's more immediately salable than works of art or cars, or whatever." So Farr Vintners now advertises for stock in the pages of the *Financial Times*. In Browett's opinion, the recent collapse of the port market is partly attributable to events at Lloyd's. This is confirmed in a back-to-front way by an offer of the 1991 port vintage sent out at the beginning of August by Messrs. Berry Bros. & Rudd of St. James's, the most rampantly traditional of London vintners, with a bowfronted clientele to match. Among the various reasons proposed for buying a few cases of Churchill, Dow, Warre, Graham, or Quinta do Vesuvio was the following: "Alternatively, purchasing 1991 port would also make a decent investment should—heaven forbid—it need to be sold years hence either due to hitherto unnoticed teetotalism in one's offspring, or unforeseen future losses at Lloyd's."

LLOYD'S IS CURRENTLY enduring its longest and least welcome spell of scrutiny, but its misfortunes receive only the minutest salve of public sympathy. This commodity, so freely bestowed on any three-legged dog that happens to cross the tabloid press, is vehemently, puritanically, even laughingly withheld from Lloyd's Names. Partly, this is because there are more deserving cases out there; for instance, the pensioners of Mirror Group Newspapers, whose fund was systematically plundered by Lloyd's Name Robert Maxwell for his own private financial purposes. Partly, and mainly, it is a question of class, envy, prim-lipped glee, and wise-virgin huzzahing. What an unimprovable chance for social gloating and below-stairs schadenfreude when the Master is forced to hock his christening mug. Weren't we told at our mother's knee that there's always a price to be paid, no such thing as money for nothing, let alone a free lunch, and all the other clichés of the prudent? Those a long way from Lloyd's and its social circles can afford an even broader view, and reflect that in the strange and erratic trickle-down of the world's wealth there might well be some social, even moral, justice in the transfer of money from a comfortable upper-middle-class golfing Englishman to, say, an elderly American seaman suffering from terminal asbestosis. As long as it was as simple as that—which of course it turns out not to be.

The Names are well aware that, outside their exclusive stockade, they are pretty much on their own. "You don't get any sympathy," one businesswoman in her thirties told me. "People look at you and think, Well, she must be a rich bitch anyway." Rich, but not *rich* rich; moreover, for a girl of twenty-five, as she was when she signed up with Lloyd's, almost dismayingly careful. A third-generation Name who had worked in the City for several years after graduating, she had all the insider's advantages: she joined her father's agents, who put her on good syndicates; she was warned away from the danger-ous areas of the market, knew about taking out stop-loss policies to limit her possible liabilities, and consequently felt she had done her best to safeguard the money her grandfather left her. She started un-derwriting in 1986, made a small profit in the first two years, and then in the next three lost the whole of the trust fund she had come in with. Now she has resigned, not just because she hasn't any money to underwrite with anymore but also because "I can't bear the tension. I have to come to terms with the fact that I am going to lose all my money. Now I wish I'd spent it all on having some fun." She doesn't blame her agents in any way (indeed, her father has stayed with them and is trading through), but in a wider context is more rueful. "When I was growing up, the thickest men I knew went into Lloyd's. I should have thought at the time. At school, I had a friend who couldn't even get into the Navy. He took his maths O level five times and failed it five times. *He* joined Lloyd's. I should have thought then and there."

One who did think along these lines was Max Hastings, editor of the *Daily Telegraph* since 1986; he once said to a fellow board member of the newspaper, "Rupert, I never joined Lloyd's, because all the stupidest boys I was at school with seemed to go into it . . . and that worried me." (Hastings was at Charterhouse.) But historically, thickness was no especial handicap in Lloyd's—or, at least, not one that led inevitably to the impoverishment of the members whose interests you supposedly represented. The current chairman of Lloyd's, David Rowland, put it like this in a television interview last October: "Back in the sixties, early seventies, Lloyd's had a cost advantage over the rest of the world of maybe five to seven percentage points. Now, expressed in a different way, you could be quite thick and be a Lloyd's underwriter and make money because, whether you knew it or not, you had that advantage to play with and you could use it by having lower rates, higher commissions, any competitive tool." And now? By the end of the eighties, in Rowland's view, Lloyd's was operating at a cost disadvantage as other insurers had caught up: "You had to be quite seriously clever to be a Lloyd's underwriter and to make money."

But Lloyd's didn't reach its present crisis, where insiders and outsiders talk equally about the possibility of meltdown, merely because it was overstocked with Old Carthusians owning long names and short brain cells. The 1980s were particularly rich in bad things happening throughout the world, with the bill for them ending up at Lloyd's. Of course, to a certain extent insurers not only like but depend upon catastrophes. The businesswoman recalled to me the quietly sinister professional satisfaction with which an underwriter friend of hers had greeted the Japan Air Lines jumbo-jet crash of 1985. This is, after all, the logic of the business: if there weren't any burglars, no one would need house insurance against theft. But catastrophes, in a perfect insurance world, should come at the right intervals—just often enough to scare policyholders, harden rates, and make as much profit as possible before the next payout. The European storms of 1987 were said to be the worst for two hundred years; and so they may have been, except that this didn't prevent Nature's coming back for a second bite, and with just as much gourmandizing destructiveness, only three years later. Bad for business. Then there were the various hurricanes—notably Alicia, Gilbert, and Hugo; the destruction of the Piper Alpha oil rig in the North Sea; the *Exxon Valdez* oil spill; and the 1989 San Francisco earthquake.

These well-publicized losses were not in themselves threatening to Lloyd's; indeed, there is something sexy about being associated with famous disasters. Lloyd's insured the *Titanic*, paid out a hundred million dollars for the 1906 San Francisco earthquake, covered Hitler's private Junkers airplane, made a fortune out of "death and spare parts" policies during the V-1 and V-2 raids on London, underwrote the San Francisco–Oakland Bay Bridge, did well out of the Gulf War. Far less glamorous, and far more damaging to Lloyd's Names, was the increasing realization through the seventies and eighties of the magnitude of present and future claims in two particular areas: pollution and asbestosis. This was "long-tail" business, in which a policy might be activated many years after it was written. Sometimes the policies had started off at Lloyd's; sometimes they had started off in the States and been reinsured at Lloyd's; sometimes they had started off at Lloyd's, been reinsured in the States, and then reinsured back again at Lloyd's. Whichever way, once the claims began coming in, once American lawyers started getting busy and American courts generous, the bill became enormous and continuing.

Another, more self-inflicted piece of damage was a practice of reinsurance popular at Lloyd's in the 1980s. Just as bookmakers faced with money pouring in on the Kentucky Derby favorite minimize their potential losses by laying off the bets elsewhere, so insurers do the same. But whereas among the wise gentlemen of the turf one firm of bookmakers will devolve its liability onto another firm, at Lloyd's the risk was kept within the same market. The original insurers of a big risk would take out reinsurance in case claims exceeded a certain figure; the reinsurers would then seek to lay off their risk with a new layer of reinsurance, and so on along the chain. The advantage to Lloyd's was that with each reinsurance the underwriter took a premium and the broker a commission; often the same piece of business might go through the same syndicates and companies several times, to everyone's short-term advantage. The system became known as

London Market Excess, or LMX, and the chain of reinsurance was known colloquially as "the spiral." The thinking behind it was based on the belief—or the hope—that there was little likelihood of a claim going up beyond a certain point: a thousand roofs might blow off in a tempest, but not ten thousand; an oil rig might experience a small explosion but not a big one. Therefore, as you got to the top end of the spiral the premiums got smaller, and the final reinsurers were increasingly ill-equipped to pay a claim when a big disaster occurred. It is like pass the parcel: good fun until the music stops. Then it becomes very expensive. In the case of the Piper Alpha oil rig, for instance, which blew up in July 1988, the basic sum for which it was insured was $700 million. But that amount was reinsured and reinsured—to the great profit of brokers and underwriters—so that by the end of the spiral of reinsurance a total of $15 billion was sloshing through the system: "which means," as one underwriter commented, "that in some syndicates it must have passed through that syndicate fifty times." The losers, at the end of the day, were the Lloyd's Names: in 1989, a mere fourteen LMX syndicates lost £952 million, or nearly half the market's total losses.

LONDON MARKET EXCESS developed for a series of interlocking reasons: greed, of course; the ease with which it could be done ("Making a turn"—in the spiral—"was the easiest way to make money," one underwriter said); plus the presence of spare capacity in the market. Unreal business like LMX was written because there wasn't enough real business out there to write. And the reason for this was that during the 1980s Lloyd's participating membership—and hence its underwriting capacity—expanded faster than the market did.

It may have been noticed that on the list of high-profile Lloyd's Names given earlier some were extremely posh, but others were—well, less than extremely posh. Starting in the mid-1970s, the graph of membership went Himalayan. Between 1955 and 1975, the numbers had gently doubled, from 3,917 to 7,710; by 1978, they had virtually doubled again, to 14,134; then they jumped greedily through the eighties to an all-time peak of 34,218 in 1989. In the single year of

1977, 3,636 new Names were admitted; back in 1953, the entire membership had amounted to only 3,399. Both the nature of the members and the nature of the recruitment had changed. No longer was it a case of the tweedy third baronet, having slaughtered a bucketful of grouse, deciding over the crusted port that it was time to put young Marmaduke up for Lloyd's. Now it was a matter of active recruiters scouring for business: the accountant suggesting to the widow that Lloyd's was a safe place for her inheritance; the commission tout working the dinner tables; the members' agent specializing in one particular slice of high earners. In some cases, it was still a matter of the lowered voice and the "I could probably get you into Lloyd's, old boy"; but often the approach was much more blatant, or, if you prefer, businesslike. In June of 1988, Nicholas Lander sold his successful Soho restaurant L'Escargot, a piece of news that made the papers. Shortly afterward an accountant he had never even met phoned him up and began lauding the tax advantages to be had from joining Lloyd's. Lander declined the approach partly out of caution—"I don't understand the world of insurance and reinsurance"—but mainly for a more forthright reason: "I wasn't going to hand my money over to a bunch of upper-class twits to play with."

Others were more flattered. A recruiter in Hamilton, Ontario, signed up forty or more Canadian doctors and dentists. In England, a members' agent named Robin Kingsley, whose father had played Davis Cup tennis for Britain, used the Wimbledon connection to sign up a locker room of Names for his Lime Street Underwriting Agencies: Virginia Wade, Buster Mottram and his father, Mark Cox, and the wife of former British No. 1 Roger Taylor. Mottram was approached by a Kingsley representative in 1983 while he was in the bath after losing a doubles match at Wimbledon. Ten years later, he was talking a much more serious bath: many Lime Street Names had been put on LMX syndicates and were heading toward losses of £2 million each. At the time, the come-on from Lloyd's to groups like tennis stars was plausible enough: Here you are, still young but quite possibly at the peak of your earning power, why not think about making your pile work for you after your racquet has been laid to rest in its press? Besides, this was the 1980s, Mrs. Thatcher's eighties; new money was as good as old, and Lloyd's was in this respect becoming more democratic. The financial conditions for joining were now less stringent and the rules more laxly monitored. (In theory, you were not allowed to put up your principal residence as part of the wealth you showed, but Lloyd's happily accepted a bank guarantee instead, and since the bank guarantee was based on a charge upon your house the effect was exactly the same.) New money rushed to join Lloyd's. But one of the differences between old money and new money is that new money tends to be more fragile. Old money tends to have more money than new money—an advantage when you come to the concept of unlimited liability. Moreover, old money, having been at Lloyd's for longer, was more likely to find itself on the safer and more profitable syndicates. New money tended to be less wise, or more easily led. In the early 1980s, during an exchange about moral accountability at Lloyd's, one underwriter brutally—or realistically—dismissed the new intake in the following way: "If God had not meant them to be sheared, He would not have made them sheep."

But to most outside observers Lloyd's in the 1980s looked like a success story: rising membership, continuing profits, an old institution adapting to the modern world, with symbolic proof of that adaptation in the market's new premises. Richard Rogers's building, which opened in 1986, is spectacular and luxurious: an elegant financial factory with what was at the time the largest atrium in Europe. Built on principles of high tech, energy saving, and maximum space flexibility, it is—like the Beaubourg—an inside-out construction, with all the ductwork, service piping, and elevators on the outside, allowing a free, uncluttered interior without any central supporting core. It deliberately lacks the Beaubourg's spirited bursts of color: apart from a dull yellow on the stylish German escalators, a splash of red for the fire bells, and green for the floor numbers, the hues are muted, with a soft light seeming to allow maximum concentration on the business of making money. As one of the Richard Rogers Partnership put it to me, "Basically, they said we could have any color we liked as long as it was gray." The result led, predictably, to what is called a "row," which, just as predictably, seemed to consist of a few nonspecialist journalists moaning on about modern architecture and second-guessing the Prince of Wales. It also led to one or two rather good jokes. Lloyd's, it was said, had started in a Coffee House and ended up in a percolator. Lloyd's, it was said, was the only building in London that had all the guts on the outside and all the assholes on the inside.

Within the gray money shed sit sober-suited underwriters, who breach the nothing-but-gray rule only with their stripy golf umbrellas. Brokers bustle among the underwriters' "boxes," as their desks are known, with fat leather document cases; they loiter attentively, like sixth formers near a schoolmaster, until the underwriter is ready for them. There is none of that yelping and high-fiving which make trading in futures resemble a contact sport. Here there are computer screens, intense but discreet conversation, the penciled exchange of hieroglyphs, and the muted seep of testosterone: out of the 3,593 current "working members"—agents, underwriters, and brokers—only 118 are female. The liveried underlings, known as "waiters," are male too, and are among the intermittent reminders of the Lloyd's tradition. The most famous of these is the Lutine Bell, which occupies a central position on the main trading floor, and is housed in a curious mahogany edifice halfway between a cathedral baldachin and the sort of raised desk occupied by Madame in an old-fashioned French restaurant. The Bell was rescued in 1857 from the Lloyd's-insured HMS *Lutine*, and has been ritually rung ever since, once for disaster and twice for good news. A dozen yards away, on a broad mahogany lectern, are a pair of marine loss books, displayed side by side. The left-hand one, written out in stately quill pen, shows the week's disasters from a hundred years ago; the right-hand one, in slightly less stately quilling, shows the current week's. On July 19, the contemporary loss book revealed a quiet time on the Lloyd's-protected oceans. Nothing to report for a week, not since Monday the twelfth, when the following events were recorded: "Zam Zam St Vincent and Grenadines motor 1588 tons gross built 1966 abandoned in sinking condition lat 12.00 N., long 49.45 E July 9 Bahrein Radio." And, beneath it, a less routine anecdote: "Ham 308 Dutch motor suction dredger had explosion in engine room, extensively damaged after picking up bomb near Tsing Yi Island, Hong Kong, Feb 25. Settled as a War constructive total loss. 5613 tons gross, built 1968."

Upstairs, on the eleventh floor, is another part of the Lloyd's tradition: the Adam Room, removed from Bowood House, Wiltshire, and installed in successive Lloyd's buildings as the Committee Room. It comes complete with wall moldings, chandeliers, pictures, committee table, and armchairs, all in a nongray color combination, and is surrounded by a walkway that permits you to stroll round it and peer in. You could make a pretty symbol out of the Adam Room: here the Lloyd's Committee meets in period surroundings, in an architectural cocoon, shut off from the outside world. To be fair, though, you could just as easily reverse the symbol. Here is a room that appears antique but discloses hidden modernity: the chandeliers, for instance, are controlled by dimmer switches; at one end, the floor disgorges a huge screen, while at the other a painting swivels away to reveal the projection room. Looked at like this, it is less a room mired in the past than one wired for Goldfinger.

I PASSED THE SIGN to Bowood House on my way to visit a widow in the West Country who cannot be named because she is with The Hardship, as the Lloyd's Members' Hardship Committee is known, and part of the deal with The Hardship is that you don't talk about it. Our meeting is initially shadowed by the morning's news of a fifty-one-year-old North London solicitor who had hanged himself in despair after incurring losses on the Lloyd's market. His widow gave evidence to the Hornsey Coroner's Court: "He was told he might have to go bankrupt and would not be able to practice as a solicitor. He said they asked for more and more money." It is hard to estimate the number of "Lloyd's suicides," since troubles always compound one another and are rarely separable out as pure causes. Besides, there is no central clearing house for such statistics. One well-positioned Name gave me the figure of "seven, to my personal knowledge."

Those not ground down or appallingly depressed by their experiences with Lloyd's are likely to be feistily skeptical about the whole market. Certainly this is the case with the West Country Widow, now in her seventies, who lives with a vivacious, not to say deeply neurotic, pug dog. Around her village lies flat, rather overmanicured pasturage riddled with bed-and-breakfast cottages; Arabella's pony frolics in the paddock; the passing double-decker bus has a recruitment ad for the British Army on the back; and every other dwelling is called The Coach House or Ye Olde Forge. The Widow, on the other hand, lives in an undistinguished cul-de-sac, in a modest semidetached house of the sort it would seem pretentious to give a name to. But the Widow has defiantly baptized her house, and the nameplate, in brown wood with sunken black lettering, is the first thing you see as you enter her inside porch. This dwelling, it tells you, is called SDYOLLKCUF, which has a Celtic, perhaps a Cornish, feel to it; though if you read it backward you find it altogether more Anglo-Saxon.

"Have you seen this?" she asks as her pug welcomingly assaults my shoelaces. She hands me a cutting from the *Daily Mail* women's page. It shows a photograph of Dr. Mary Archer, head of the Hardship Committee, modeling a cocktail dress by the French designer Nicole Manier: a flouncy, black, above-the-knee number, with diaphanous sleeves and shoulder bits, topped off by a provoking headdress of ostrich feathers, or whatever are used nowadays in their stead. "Probably costs more than she's going to give me to live on for a year," grumps the Widow. Across the bottom of the picture she has written, "This woman is unfit to be Chairman of the Hardship Committee." I do not answer her question as to whether or not I have seen the cutting; in fact, I was shown it only two days earlier, in Chelsea, at the house of the Deficit Millionairess. It is clearly a much-circulated and efficient inducer of rage.

The Widow's story goes like this. Her husband died in the midsixties, at a time when death duties between spouses were heavier than they are now, and the house in which they had lived became harder for her to manage. "My accountant suggested I become a member of Lloyd's, and, most unfortunately, I had a cousin working at Lloyd's for Anthony Gooda." She began underwriting in 1978. Her initial premium limit was £100,000; subsequently, it was raised to

£135,000 and then to £188,000, on both occasions, she said, "without explaining." Over the first twelve years of membership, she received £39,000 and concluded from the size of her checks that she was on low-risk syndicates. Her accountant agreed, telling her, "Your lot must be safe, because they pay so little." Then the bills started. The first was for £120,000, of which she managed to pay £80,000. Then more and more. Like Fernanda Herford, she had the hazy illusion that some rough equity guided her dealings at Lloyd's, and that you wouldn't—couldn't, shouldn't—lose a larger sum than the one you underwrote. But unlimited liability, pedantically, grindingly, means what it says: "They say now I owe them three hundred and fifty thousand pounds." How did she react? "I walked about shaking and empty. I only got through with gin and arnica—it's a homeopathic remedy for shock—God, and a lot of friends."

Rather than face a writ for debt, she went to The Hardship. "It took us three weeks to fill up the form." She complains of "arrogant letters" from The Hardship and great silences. She feels in limbo, waiting for The Hardship to propose its terms of settlement: "They say, 'You will exist on our guidelines,' but they don't tell you what they are." She knows the process, however: "They take all the Lloyd's funds, and this house when I'm dead, and I pay all the capital gains on my funds and they take them as well." From being someone who worked twelve hours a day with horses and let Lloyd's quietly make her a little bit extra, she has become someone who spends several hours of most days dealing with forms, demands, action groups, and so on. "The worst part is the post. You literally shake for half an hour when it comes." From being someone who believed that Lloyd's was "the highest name of honesty," she has become someone who views it as "a cesspit of dishonesty." From being a Lloyd's investor, she has become a Lloyd's pensioner.

The Widow is exactly the sort of person who should never have been made a Name, and she knows it: "They took in so many little people like me to spread the risk." Later that day, I talked to a Name at the other end of the spectrum, much more the classic Lloyd's investor. Peter Dewe-Mathews was a chartered accountant for ten years, then began setting up health-care businesses and selling them on. We shuffle uneasily around the word "entrepreneur," and agree to use it only in quotation marks. He started underwriting in 1987, when he found he had a large number of shares locked into a public company he had built up, and wanted to use them to raise more than the 3 percent or so they yielded; he hoped, through Lloyd's, to raise that 3 percent to more like 5 percent. "It seemed like a reasonable thing to do," he remembers. In fact, 1987, the year after the new building opened, was probably the worst time to join Lloyd's. In that last of the boom recruiting years, 2,572 new members were elected, just before the wallet-scorching started.

Dewe-Mathews, unlike the Widow, was professional enough to protect himself at every turn. He sacked his first firm of agents, because he found them "a bunch of spivs"; he took out stop-loss insurance; he had himself taken off one syndicate when he saw that they didn't know how to write accounts, and reckoned that if they couldn't write accounts they probably couldn't write insurance; and he got the right advice when he asked about LMX syndicates, being told to keep off them "for a few years." He knew his way around, could read a balance sheet in the way that most "external" Names couldn't, and went in, as he says, "with my eyes open." So how much money has he made? He laughs. "I haven't made a pfennig." He broke even the first year, and since then . . . He tells me a figure in confidence. He has lost not just pfennigs but marks. So is he getting out? Not for the moment. "Insurance runs on an eight-to-ten-year cycle. So '93, '94, '95 are theoretically going to be the top. If Lloyd's doesn't have the capacity to make a profit then, where's its future?"

A CONSERVATIVE MP, speaking in the House of Commons, referred to the epidemic of money loss among Lloyd's Names as "the HIV of the upper-middle classes." Tasteless, if you wish, but there are apt points of comparison. First, there is a moment, a key and usually insouciant moment, when the Name has unprotected financial intercourse with Lloyd's, when he or she acknowledges the principle of unlimited liability. Second, there is a time gap when things are hunky-dory, when you really do seem to be getting something for nothing. Third, there is a calamitous realization that you are lost, that your life has changed forever, and that others will unsympathetically point the finger at you and seek to use you in a moral argument. *That's* what comes of wanting too much out of life/being greedy/not thinking about the consequences of your actions/listening to the siren voices of financial voluptuaries.

Seduction and betrayal. The first approach comes when you are most relaxed: on the golf course, in your bath after Wimbledon, around the dinner table. "The entertaining is prodigious," Fernanda Herford confirmed. Clive Francis, a former Royal Air Force squadron leader, told me, "I was hooked by flattery and greed." I talked to one woman who had joined because her marriage was on the rocks and a banker friend suggested that membership would give her financial security. (She is now "bust four or five times," a deficit millionairess twice over.) The atavistic appeal of Lloyd's was just as big, if not bigger, for new money as for old money. Buster Mottram describes himself as being "mesmerized by the Lloyd's myth." The daughter of a trade unionist, herself a woman of manifest common sense, told me, "I grew up on a council estate, and there is a sense of achievement in becoming part of an establishment." This normal human vanity was played upon with brutal success in the eighties.

The moment of unprotected financial intercourse with Lloyd's occurs at their place, not yours. First, the agent talks the prospective member through the terms on which he or she is joining. Memories of the agent's counseling vary directly with the Name's subsequent experience at Lloyd's. Those I talked to who had traded well–or, at least, not disastrously–remembered things being explained with due gravity; those who had gone down most heavily remember only a jollity that in retrospect seems insulting. Fernanda Herford said, "Certainly I understood [the concept of unlimited liability], but there was a great deal of ho-ho-ho." Buster Mottram was told that unlimited liability was theoretical, "like a meteor hitting London–an act of God, nothing more serious than that." A successful musician was told, "If you have twenty thousand pounds in the bank, you'll never need more than that. And if you're a person who can't sleep at night, take out a stop-loss policy." (She and her husband took out twenty-nine stop-loss policies over the years and are down four million between the two of them.) The West Country Widow recalls the softening up she received in the offices of the agent Anthony Gooda: "They said, 'You realize you will be warned about unlimited liability?' and I said should I back out, and they roared with laughter and said, 'Absolute nonsense, it's never happened and it never will. We took a shaker on Hurricane Betsy, but we soon made up for that.'"

Thus prepared, the Name is then brought before the Rota Committee of Lloyd's, where matters are explained again. The Rota Committee consists of two senior members of the market and a protocol secretary—or, if you prefer the words of the West Country Widow, three "bumbling shaking old fools." Sir Peter Miller, chairman of Lloyd's from 1984 to 1987, recalled in 1991 the way he used to induct new members: "I think the example I usually used was that you were absolutely liable for your last penny farthing, right down to the cuff links in your shirt, and if it was a lady, I usually said, well, down to the earrings in your ear, my dear." That phrase "down to your last cuff link" is a famous Lloyd's tag, part of the mystique, part of the sexiness of theoretical loss set against the much greater sexiness of almost certain gain. Most Names I talked to remembered those words, or something similar. No one suggested that the concept of unlimited liability was in any way concealed from them by the Rota Committee. On the other hand, few remember the occasion as being more than merely ceremonial. The businesswoman in her thirties, who had been inducted at twenty-five in honored solitariness, recalled, "That stupid thing in front of the table. You sit outside with your agent, having been given a good lunch. It's built up as a great thing and an honor, but then you go up there and everyone's dressed up to the nines and it's over in seconds." Other Names were dubbed in groups of anything from two or three up to a score and more. Clive Francis, the ex–squadron leader, remembered the moment when the sacred words *unlimited liability* were used. He remembered it because his agent nudged him and whispered, "They have to say that." They do indeed. Fifteen years on, he owes over £2 million.

What few of those Names signed up in the eighties realized was that their recruiter was often paid a fee. Surely the chap who drank at your table and admired your pictures and murmured, "I could get you into Lloyd's, old boy," wasn't in it for a kickback? After all, you were being asked to join an honorable club in which members were all on the same side, weren't you? But Francis later found out that the dinner acquaintance who sweet-talked him got a thank-you check for three thousand pounds. Other commission touts might receive an annual bounty: say, five hundred pounds for each year the Name stayed with the members' agent for whom he had been snaffled. And fees are, of course, negotiable: I heard of a recruiter who would go to the agent and say, "I've got a prospective member–what terms?"

As for who was on whose side, this was the key question for Names joining Lloyd's over the last fifteen years or so, and one they did not normally think of posing until it was far too late. The deal, as proposed, seemed magical, unmissable. "You send no money, we just send you a check every year" is how it was characterized to Francis. "I mean," he went on reflectively, "looking back, what a tit!" Lloyd's and its agents had a good way of talking money and yet not talking money. For instance, as long as you got your check you probably didn't look too closely at the way your winnings were computed. You might think it fine that your agent, who was responsible for placing you on the best underwriting syndicates he was able to, would take 20 percent of your profits. (This "agent" might be split into two–a members' agent, who dealt directly with you, and a managing agent, who dealt with the underwriters–in which case the former might take 8 percent and the latter 12 percent.) Twenty percent of profits, however, worked like this: Assume you were placed on fifteen syndicates, ten of which made money and five of which didn't. The former made, say, ten thousand pounds and the latter lost five thousand pounds. Balance in your favor, five thousand pounds. But the agent took his 20 percent on your ten thousand pounds of raw profit, leaving you with a net profit of three thousand.

The Lloyd's market is divided into working and external members, in a traditional ratio of about 20 percent to 80 percent. (As of August 4, 1993, there were 3,593 working members and 15,853 external members.) The working members underwrite insurance, just as you do; and they, too, want to be on the best syndicates, just as you do. But if you were an underwriter putting together a syndicate, whom would you rather have on it: a Widow from the West Country or an influential broker who, if he did well out of your syndicate, might repay the favor by bringing you some of his best business? That the market was heavily weighted toward insiders and against outsiders seems with hindsight obvious, logical, and consistent with human nature; that it didn't seem so at the time is a tribute partly to Lloyd's effective mystique and also to its effective secrecy. The figures simply weren't available. In the last year or so, however, computer analysis has been used to prove what many suspected: that external Names tended to be dumped on duff, high-risk syndicates, while working Names creamed off the best business. A breakdown on all the Gooda Walker members for the years 1983 to 1989 (when the dangers of the LMX spiral were being run) shows that only 10 percent were insider Names–half what you might expect if the market dealt fairly between the two segments of its membership. On Syndicate 387, a key location of financial horror, only 3 percent of the Names were insiders. Analysis was also made of the most profitable syndicates in all the four main insurance categories for 1991–1992. Twenty Names appeared on three of those four syndicates and were therefore likely to be the highest earners in the market; of those twenty, eleven were insiders, and, of those eleven, four are or have been on the Council of Lloyd's. Finally, there was a particularly nice computer breakdown on the correlation between geographical distance from No. 1 Lime Street and chances of being put on the better syndicates. This confirmed that Australia was a very bad place to live if you were a Lloyd's Name.

When I asked Peter Middleton, the chief executive of Lloyd's, about the weighting of the market, he replied, "In any activity, the professionals will know more than the others." He offered car maintenance as an analogy: you would not expect the mechanic at your local garage to lavish as much care on your vehicle as he did on his own; rather, you would expect him to do a good job on your car in return for a proper fee. This is all true, of course, though what happened to many external Names who sent their car to the Lloyd's Servicing Center in the 1980s was that they got it back with four bald tires and somebody else's radio, while the only gear that would engage was reverse.

THE FIRST QUOTATION in the Oxford English Dictionary for the word *Lloyd's* has a prophetic aptness. Here is Maria Edgeworth writing to her mother on March 4, 1819:

> Mr. Busk Blair's son in law was as great a gamester as Mr. Blair. Once he won £30,000 by a bit of gambling insurance on 2 missing East India ships. The ships re-appeared. The underwriters were obliged to pay him but it was suspected that he had some private intelligence—in short that there was some foul play. He could never shew his face at Lloyd's afterwards.

Much of Lloyd's in the 1980s is here: the value of raw intelligence, the gambling aspect, the tickle of fraud. When a famous institution is making money, the occasional tweak of criminality can usually be covered up (and Lloyd's has always been a successfully closed society: the first photograph of the Committee, for instance, did not appear until 1960). Just a case of one rotten apple in the barrel, bung it out, mum's the word, more profits next year, punters happy. This was the theme song, and through most of the eighties it charmed the ear. What had to be kept quiet, or talked down, or minimized, was a tangy succession of upsets, rogueries, and scandals. Or, as Peter Middleton, referring to those times, put it—and, yes, we are back on motoring again—"what we had in Lloyd's was a speed limit of seventy miles per hour on the motorway and no patrol cars, so some people were doing a hundred and thirty miles per hour and most about ninety-five."

Chief among the motorway violations were the following: the Sasse affair of the late 1970s, in which syndicate members for the first time refused en masse to pay their bills, were sued by Lloyd's, and sued Lloyd's in return; the Howden scandal, in which the American insurance brokers Alexander & Alexander bought a firm of Lloyd's brokers for $300 million and discovered on subsequent auditing a financial hole of anything up to $55 million; the Cameron-Webb affair, the biggest fraud in Lloyd's history, whose two chief villains were allowed to slip unprosecuted into foreign retirement; the flourishing of "baby syndicates," devoted to skimming off the best business for Lloyd's insiders; the case of Sir Peter Green, the very chairman of Lloyd's, who was found guilty of "discreditable conduct," fined £33,000, and kicked out of Lloyd's after channeling his Names' money into a Cayman Islands company he'd forgotten to tell them about; and the Outhwaite affair, in which counsel for Outhwaite Names suing their agent recently told the court that "it is probably the case that never in the commercial history of the City of London has so much of other people's money been lost by the single-handed negligence of one man." Ian Posgate, one of the chief underwriting barons of the time (who was himself banned from being a working Name), spoke of that period as the insider: "If you are making a good living, if you have self-regulation, if you are outside exchange control, it's human nature to get greedier and greedier and greedier." Ian Hay Davison, the chief executive of Lloyd's from 1983 to 1986, spoke as the motorway patrolman: he thought it was a question of sorting out a few rotten apples but discovered that "the barrel itself . . . was in some danger of being tainted." Christopher Hird, a financial journalist, spoke as the outside observer: Lloyd's in the 1980s "resembled a garden in which the rabbits were in charge of the lettuce."

As long as the "rotten apple" theory could be maintained, as long as the extent of insider weighting was kept largely secret (and as long as profits continued), investors gave their trust as well as their money. What has happened in the last few years is that the element of trust has very largely broken down. By April of this year, there were thirty-three groups of Names and ex-Names organized for defensive and offensive purposes, and by June the number of such members suing their professional advisers had reached the astonishing figure of

17,000. Seventeen thousand out of a membership of 34,000: deduct 20 percent for working Names, and you get something over 60 percent. Imagine a school in which 60 percent of parents were suing the teachers for badly educating their children. Imagine a restaurant in which 60 percent of customers were suing the management over food poisoning. Such a school, such a restaurant would not survive for long, however impressive the number of people it might have educated or fed in the past. Nor is such legal action going to be speedily concluded. According to the Lloyd's Names Associations Working Party, a body made up of the leaders of individual action groups, "the scene is set fair for five to ten years of litigation which will involve Members' Agents, Managing Agents, Directors of Agencies, individual underwriters, auditors, brokers, errors and omissions underwriters and the Corporation of Lloyd's itself."

Out there, the revolt of the shires is in earnest. The Names have witnessed negligence, fraud, complacency, and sardonic uncaringness; they have discovered the realities of money, how it works, and how those who live off it work. But they have also experienced something beyond this, something that at first sounds decidedly quaint: the offense against honor. What they were sold when they joined Lloyd's was the concept of an honorable society, operating on trust, on shared values, on everyone being "one of us." Instead, they have discovered that honor is a one-way street. Lloyd's called on them the first year, and they paid; it called on them the second year, and they paid, while being promised that things would be better in the third year; the third year came, and it was much, much worse, while forecasts for the next year were bad too. Even the Mafia supposedly looks after the little boot mender who falls on stony times; Lloyd's sent in Dr. Archer and The Hardship. The Names felt mocked and abandoned, used and abused. Fernanda Herford quoted to me a dictum from the portable philosophy of Lloyd's: "See a mug, use a mug." Hence the members who decline to pay with a strained cheerfulness born of desperation. Hence the frequently heard comment that if it weren't for this, or if it weren't for that, the Name would hide what money remained, or give it away, or go abroad and let Lloyd's get stuffed. I heard of elderly relatives being asked to change their wills to avoid leaving money to a beloved burnt Name, because otherwise Lloyd's would purloin it: leave it to the spouse, the child, the non-Name instead. I heard of ingenious money-distancing schemes. I heard of a couple planning to divorce under Scottish law, then have the wife go bankrupt, then marry again, all in order to obtain some obscure benefit and somehow tinily defeat Lloyd's. As one Name put it to me in a winky, nose-tapping way, "We've got far more time to think about it than the Hardship Committee."

Lloyd's itself is currently behaving like an old career criminal finally going straight. Shining morning faces are being presented to the world. There is much talk of a "transparent society," of healthiness, efficiency, cost reductions. Peter Middleton points to the introduction of "simple management practice that passes for normal everywhere else." Joint Deputy Chairman Robert Hiscox bullishly asserts that "we're now lean, keen, and our overheads are bloody low." A new business plan has been announced, radically reforming the investment base of the market. Insurance rates are hardening, there is work to be done, business to be written, a great institution to be saved; and in the meantime there is this bunch of dismissed peasants still whining at the gate about things that happened years ago. Lloyd's insiders occasionally seem baffled at the way journalists and burnt Names willfully ignore what they see as the main story—how the market is to be saved—and ghoulishly concentrate on the past. In this respect, Lloyd's is like a dowager wearing a necklace of herring. Her frock is new, her seams are straight, her makeup freshly applied: so why do people go on and on about the smell of herring?

As far as the Names are concerned, many offenses still rankle. For instance, when the burnt Names first started to organize, Lloyd's was deliberately obstructive; until Peter Middleton changed the rules, action groups simply couldn't discover who else was out there suffering in silence, assuming there was nothing to do except splint the upper lip. And each day seems to bring a new offense. Thus, the rescue plan for Lloyd's depends upon getting corporate capital into the market for the first time, and it seductively offers this new money terms that seem to taunt the burnt Names: limited liability, plus protection from earlier market losses. It is as if the old Names, with their unlimited liability and open years, were being shunted off into a financial isolation ward for infectious cases. Another offense is the discovery that eleven years ago, after an auditors' report stressing the unquantifiable losses likely to arise from asbestosis claims, the deputy chairman of Lloyd's wrote to agents that they were "strongly advised to inform their Names of their involvement with asbestosis claims and the manner in which their syndicates' current and potential liabilities have been covered." Yet few Names, let alone those brought in after 1982, seem to have been warned about asbestosis. There is the discovery, all too late in the day, of who is for you and who against you. "I always thought my agent was on my side," a farmer complained to me. "But they're acting very like debt collectors. I suppose they're afraid of Lloyd's going bust and them losing their jobs." Then there is the survey of company directors' pay in the August 1993 issue of the magazine *Labour Research*: deficit millionaires (there are perhaps 400 or so owing over a million pounds, and 150 or more owing £2 million plus) might look askance at the salaries of some well-known Lloyd's brokers. William Brown, chairman of Walsham Brothers, who made a fortune out of LMX reinsurance, last year was paid £3,653,346, a shocking 50.3 percent drop from what he had been paid the previous year. On the other hand, Matthew Harding, chairman of Benfield reinsurance brokers, got a 53 percent pay rise, taking him to £2,275,523. (Two other Benfield directors each earned more than £1,245,000.) In the face of such offense, and such market realities, expressions of anger such as that from the investor Alan Price, after a June 22 meeting at the Royal Festival Hall, are hardly surprising. "These underwriters should count themselves lucky that Lloyd's is not based in the Middle East," he said. "If it were, a large number of these wretches would now be walking around minus one hand. Some would be missing an arm and a leg." A grim English humor survives even in these circumstances, an arm and a leg being exactly what many Lloyd's Names have lost.

WHAT IS CURRENTLY going on is a face-off between Lloyd's and its seventeen thousand rebellious Names. The argument has run roughly like this. Lloyd's: Here's your bill. Names: Can't pay, won't pay. Lloyd's: You signed a legally binding contract to pay, so pay. Names: We're suing for negligent handling of our affairs. Lloyd's: Pay now, sue later. Names: No, sue now, pay later, and then only if the judgment goes against us. Lloyd's: If you don't pay now, Lloyd's might collapse. Names: Don't care. Lloyd's: If we collapse, the policy-holders will have to be paid first, so you won't get any money; the only way you can benefit is if Lloyd's keeps going, so pay. Names: Well, we might pay in October. Lloyd's: But in September Lloyd's has to satisfy the solvency requirement of the Department of Trade and Industry if it wants to keep trading. Names: Tough. Lloyd's: You're bluffing. Names: No, you're bluffing.

One of those Names who would happily see Lloyd's go into meltdown is ex–Squadron Leader Francis, whose bill of £972,000 for the year 1990 took him comfortably over the £2 million mark. He left the RAF in 1967 with a £1,500 gratuity, used it to buy a small apartment, and within a decade had become a property millionaire. Then he joined Lloyd's. The obvious question to ask is: Given that he was such a successful businessman, how come he didn't examine the deal he was being offered more closely? "Good point. The answer is: One's normal critical faculties were completely dulled." Now his coffee table is stacked with documents, press cuttings, and colored charts, while his phone overheats with Lime Street business. He seems not in the least ground down by it: a bronzed and energetic sixty-five-year-old, he reckons that "it's probably put ten years on my life, all this extra activity." Though now being forced by Lloyd's to sell his handsome terraced house near Holland Park, he is at least self-sufficient. "I'm entirely responsible for myself. No weeping wives in the corner, none of that. I've got no one I'm letting down by having perpetrated this. I'm pissed off about this house, quite frankly. But try being a Bosnian Muslim."

Francis takes a reasonably philosophical view of his fate: "I have to admit, at the end of the day, who's the fool who's lost my money? Me." But he is much less philosophical about the process by which the fool and his money were parted. In Francis's analysis, there was a "tacit understanding among the top brass" about the potential losses from asbestosis claims. He doesn't go so far as some who theorize about active conspiracy, a mafia, or the nefarious influence of the three Masonic lodges that exist inside Lloyd's: "I don't believe they all climbed into their aprons and said, 'Let's shaft the Names.'" On the other hand, he asserts that "the first eleven" in Lloyd's knew about the dangers by 1980. He points to a 1979 meeting in America between eleven Lloyd's underwriters and Citibank, at which upcoming claims were mooted. (This is a key Chinese-whispers moment in recent Lloyd's history. Several people I spoke to knew someone who knew someone who was present at this meeting, when a Citibank official allegedly said that Lloyd's would have to get in 10,000 or 50,000 or [fill in your number here up to 250,000] "little men who can be broken" to pay for what was coming down the track; but the speaker has never been identified or traced.) Francis points out that during the period between 1980 and 1989 not a single chairman of Lloyd's mentioned the word *asbestosis* in his annual report. "I spent twenty years in the RAF," he concludes. "You know, trust, honor—and then to find in such an august body a bunch of craven crooks."

Francis, like all the burnt Names I talked to, had a few words of special dispraise for the Lloyd's Hardship Committee, which exists, according to your point of view, either to protect Names from bankruptcy, draw a line under their liabilities, and make sure they can continue to live in modest comfort, or else to see that every last Irish sixpence is wrung out of them before depositing them like dishrags on the shores of destitution. There is something peculiarly infuriating for a Name who has seen one department of Lloyd's devastate his or her capital having to come to another department to have the financial last rites read, and to be awarded a pittance on which to live. There is also something grimly piquant about the Hardship Committee's address: Gun Wharf, Chatham. This, after all, is the Medway town where Dickens had his first experience of impoverishment and its attendant shames. He was five when his father moved the family here in 1817; John Dickens, already in severe financial difficulty, had been offered a job in the Chatham dockyard. But the family's fortunes didn't prosper: they moved to a cheaper house in 1822, and left the town later that year, selling all their furniture before departure (and a year after that John Dickens was imprisoned for debt in the Marshalsea). Dickens's first work *Sketches by Boz*, has a comic portrait of Mrs. Newnham, one of the family's Chatham neighbors back in the 1820s: "Her name always heads the list of any benevolent subscriptions, and hers are always the most liberal donations to the Winter Coal and Soup Distribution Society. She subscribed twenty pounds towards the erection of an organ in our parish church, and was so overcome the first Sunday the children sang to it, that she was obliged to be carried out by the pew-opener." Mrs. Newnham's modern-day equivalent on the Chatham Winter Coal and Soup Distribution Society is Dr. Mary Archer, who chairs the Hardship Committee. She is also the wife of the airport novelist Jeffrey Archer, a preposterous and comic figure whom Thackeray would sketch better than Dickens, and who currently bustles around under the title Baron Archer of Weston-super-Mare. Lady Archer ("She prefers to be called Dr. Archer," a voice at The Hardship advised) lists among her recreations in *Who's Who* "picking up litter"—a pastime that Mrs. Thatcher once urged upon the nation in the course of a grotesque photo call—and perhaps there is an element of tidying the trash in Dr. Archer's residency at Gun Wharf.

If Peter Middleton, the chief executive of Lloyd's, is the one figure of whom the burnt Names uniformly speak well—praising his sympathy and his straightforwardness—then Dr. Archer is the one who catches the flak. Abuse, from casual to deeply considered, was all I heard from Names in the weeks before I met her: "Unctuous, holier-than-thou, and aren't-we-doing-well?"; "That evil old bat" (this from a woman who was probably no younger); "Even a member of the Council said, 'You could crack eggs on her.'" In part, this is normal rage at the figurehead of a money-squeezing department; in part, the sort of comment that high-achieving and good-looking women frequently attract in British society. Lloyd's probably thought it a canny PR move to put Dr. Archer in charge of The Hardship: not just a woman (therefore assumed to be abundantly sympathetic) and a

Name herself since 1977, but also the wife of a Name who earlier in his career had known spectacular debt; she could be billed, therefore, as someone who had herself taken the medicine she was now dishing out. However, there is something about Dr. Archer that gets up people's noses like a gigantic dose of snuff, and I have to admit that as I munched my sandwich lunch across a desk from her at Gun Wharf, while sunlit yachts cruised the Medway in the background, at least part of my mind was occupied with this issue. She is small, dark, pretty, poised, groomed, and very, very precise. She appears utterly in control (though a friend of mine once danced with her and claimed she was "a helpless child" in his arms). Perhaps it is the voice, which is pure bone china, or Cheltenham Ladies' College. When my plastic thimble of near milk failed to turn my coffee much more than one shade away from ebony, she asked, attentively, "Would you like a second milk?" But it sounded, to my ears, more like "Are you sure that thumbscrew isn't uncomfortable?" However, the only moment when I got any true handle on the reaction she provokes was when I mentioned that there was a good deal of resentment out there among her current constituency. "Resentment, anger, distress," she replied. "All that is very understandable." But she listed the nouns as if identifying base metals rather than volcanic emotions.

Her committee has a staff of twenty-eight (twenty case officers and eight administrators) and by August 3, 1993, had received 2,327 applications from Lloyd's Names. Of these, 906 had subsequently withdrawn their applications. This seems a remarkably high percentage. Two main factors explain it. First, a distaste for the process often sets in once its details are revealed (one sticking point is that a Name's spouse must also make a full financial declaration to Lloyd's). Second, going to The Hardship was initially seen as a very useful time-wasting exercise: once you had applied, your funds at Lloyd's were frozen and could not be drawn down. This led also to various picturesque excuses for tardiness, of the sort not needed since schooldays: one Name claimed that he had run over his toes with his lawnmower, as if this would obviously affect the form-filling phalanges at the other end of the body. The Hardship has since tightened its procedures, but even so progress is slow. Of the 1,421 cases currently active, 361 have been examined and 328 Names have had a proposal made to them. Of these, 108 have accepted the settlement offered, though by August 3 a mere 7 cases had actually been signed and sealed.

"We are about avoiding bankruptcy and leaving the Name in an ongoing financial situation," Dr. Archer says. Plights vary (especially when there is spouse wealth), but what this effectively means in the case of a single person is that the Name will have to hand over to Lloyd's all his or her assets, assign any windfall money—inheritances, lucky days at the lottery—received over a three-year period, and sell anything other than "a modest and only home." This is roughly estimated as one worth between £100,000 and £150,000, depending on region. Lloyd's will take a charge on the Name's house, which will be claimed after death. The Name will be allowed, again if single, something between £7,000 and £12,000 per year for the three-year period of the deal: anything earned above this figure is to be handed over. Finally, the settlement insists that Lloyd's can claim money from the Name after the three years are over if it is Lloyd's-related money: profit from open years, profit from stop-loss policies, or money received after Lloyd's has been successfully sued. This last clause is especially unpalatable for some members: first, Lloyd's loses your pot of gold through incompetence, then you go bust, then the Hardship Committee goes through your pockets, then your court case wins you back some of the money you shouldn't have lost to begin with, whereupon The Hardship reappears and snatches that back off you too. I told Dr. Archer that the newspaper photograph of her in a Nicole Manier frock was being satirically circulated among the burnt Names, and she responded, with a mid-November smile, "I don't blame them."

What happens, I asked her, if you smell a rat? "If we smell a rat, we sniff around." Business accounts might disclose complicated loans, or the Name might prove reluctant to let the committee talk to his bank. "But most of our Names are very straight," she insists. "They are mostly modest people in distressed circumstances. They say,

'Give me finality.' " A caseworker I talked to confirmed this: instances of attempted deceit seem rather minor and incompetent—a zero missing from an interest payment, or "putting down under expenses three television licenses on one property" (under British law you need only one license per property). Though the caseworker confirmed that "we still get a certain amount of bitterness creeping in, especially among the older Names who've lost their life savings," the process, as described at Gun Wharf, is necessarily painful but comparatively untroubled: honorable Names seeking to have a line drawn under their troubles, trusting Lloyd's even in their financial extinction, sheep coming docilely to the final shearing. This may indeed be the case—so far. It may be that the committee has only seen the smaller fry, a likelihood endorsed by the fact that half the Names coming to The Hardship have a bank guarantee on their house (the rule-bending way of showing wealth in the eighties). It may also be that only those least tempted by dishonesty have come forward as yet, or that feelings of rage weaken and fiendish plans seem less plausible when faced with the bureaucracy of Gun Wharf. There did, even so, seem a huge disparity between the view from the banks of the Medway and the opinions I heard among the burnt.

BUT THEN THE FURTHER you go into the Lloyd's story, the deeper the incompatibility of views you meet. Names coming honorably to settlement, or Names doing their utmost to get off the hook? A decade of high-level Masonic conspiracy against the external Names, or just a decade of lolloping incompetence? A linked series of individual tragedies blasting its way like HIV through the upper-middle class, or merely a moral-free demonstration of "one lot of rich people stealing from another lot of rich people" (as a carbonized Name put it to me)? Assessing the true extent of the social and financial trauma is tricky. As you talk to Lloyd's Names and those close to them, you frequently hear of depression, marital breakdown, even suicide; of estates being sold, children taken out of school, and vertiginous downward mobility. Occasionally, the stories have a comic edge: I was told of one Name whose vivid taste for serial marriage was finally quenched when, anticipating possible losses, he put all his assets in his wife's name; now he lives in fretful dependence on a woman who would normally have passed her sell-by date. But mostly the tales are painful ones, often terminating in a statement like "an entire swath of English society has been wiped out." If Lloyd's melted down, and every member went bankrupt, such a statement would certainly be true: the membership still embroiled in one way or another is about thirty thousand, which happens to be roughly the number of entrants in the current edition of *Who's Who*. But we are far from this figure at the moment. It must seem like "an entire swath" to Lloyd's sufferers because Names tend to know other Names (that is, after all, how they became Names in the first place). "Wiped out" also has its gradations: sometimes a husband will have put his wife up as a member and stayed out of Lloyd's himself, thereby limiting the family's potential loss; while the "losses" are usually of those things—private education, second homes, skiing holidays—which seem to others gross and unwarranted social privileges in the first place. Finally, it's hard to quantify loss after you factor in stiff-upper-lipdom. One Name who had been obliged to sell part of his prized book collection sanguinely quoted to me the dictum "Don't cry over things that can't cry for you." And an underwriting agent told me of the following quintessential exchange he had overheard between two City gents as he was leaving his luncheon club. "How are you, old chap?" asked the first gent, to which the second, with a sad shake of the head, merely replied, "Lloyd's, I'm afraid."

The final incompatibility of view, and the final choice to be made, is this: Is Lloyd's, under a new management team, with a sparkling business plan and with Mr. Middleton's patrol cars seeing that the motorway speed limit is observed, getting itself lean and keen, keeping its overheads bloody low, and about to embark on a historic phase of regeneration in the midnineties, or is this all blarney and bluff, since the capital base has been disastrously eroded, Names are leaving not like sheep but like lemmings, corporate capital has much better things to do than rescue Lloyd's, and the whole boiling is going into meltdown very soon?

Truths normally lie in the middle, but one thing is certain. Lloyd's might survive the rage of its Names and the spate of legal actions; it might turn into a decent, well-regulated market; it might endure the losses still to come. What won't survive, what Lloyd's has lost forever, is a certain sort of Englishness on which it once prided itself, and which was coincidentally good for business. In the first place, it will have lost its money base in Arabella's-pony land, that world of second homes, private incomes, and private education: Peter Middleton anticipates that, if the business plan succeeds, within seven or eight years no more than 15 percent of the membership will be opting for unlimited liability—a 15 percent that will be "decreasingly English," with a fresh intake of buccaneering souls from the Pacific Basin. Beyond this, Lloyd's will have lost—has already lost—its peculiar, arcane, mystical, sexy status among that segment of British society it once did so well by; for want of a better word, it has lost its honor. It was the assumption of honor—beyond, or at least beside, such motives as snobbery, greed, and supposed canniness—that brought in the rush of new Names in the eighties; and in the dishonoring of Lloyd's they have lost their shirts. Of course, loss of honor may be no bad thing: see Falstaff. The irony is that those rendered insolvent by Lloyd's seem to feel this dishonoring more than those who caused it. The suicides are heavily on one side.

It's hardly a surprise that very few people are currently joining Lloyd's. The participating membership has fallen from 32,433 in 1988 to 19,681. From 1989 to 1992, 10,661 Names resigned and a mere 735 new members were elected. For all the received wisdom about going in at the bottom of a market, for all the statistics to prove that the best syndicates continued to make money through the worst years, these 735 must have nerve. Peter Middleton, among others, quoted to me the Lloyd's maxim "If you don't want any risk, go to the Post Office," but in late 1993 the Post Office looks a most attractive place. More than once, I heard the ultimate Doomsday scenario from the burnt Names. It goes like this. Leave aside the question of corporate capital, since, if it comes in, it will be largely protected from assuming earlier losses in the market. Names are going bust all over the place, the capital base has dwindled, many of this year's bills are unpaid, more losses are predicted for next year (and, if previous forecasts are a model, the reality will turn out to be grimmer): where is the money going to come from? If a member is bust four or five times over, even a visit to the Hardship Committee doesn't make the bills go away, so whom do they devolve onto? Onto the members who are still solvent. "We're all connected via the Central Fund," Clive Francis points out. So far, in order to pay these wider debts, there have been three annual 1.5 percent levies on the amount every single member underwrites. ("You do rather grudge it," an Irish Name told me. His already painful cash call for the year 1990 had been augmented by six thousand pounds to help out the losers.) But, as more Names go under, the pressure on the remainder mounts. Here is the bottom line of the Doomsday scenario as expressed by one professional Lloyd's watcher: "I take the view that every Name at Lloyd's is bust—it's just that they don't know it."

One of those who don't know it—or, to put it another way, who are trading through the current difficulties—is one of the more unexpected Names among the Lloyd's Great and Good. Melvyn Bragg, novelist and TV arts presenter, is from the Cumbrian working class, the son of a publican who later kept a sweetshop. One of Bragg's first memories is of sitting in the fourth row of the Temperance Hall in Wigton and listening to his mother read the treasurer's report of the local Labour Party meeting. Throughout his high-profile TV career, he has been a loyal and equally high-profile member of the Labour Party. Indeed, at the time he went into Lloyd's—"about 1980"—he was also seriously tempted by a career in Parliament. Had this taken off, he would today have found himself the only Name on the Labour benches, opposite the forty-seven Tory Names. He admits that he "didn't think through" the potential conflict between membership of what is seen as one of the true bastions of the Tory upper-middle class and membership of what was then a comparatively left-wing Labour Party.

So why did he join? At the time, he had a house in Hampstead worth £150,000, a cottage in Cumbria, £20,000 in the bank, and "the income was beginning to build." He didn't fancy the stock market, and a financial adviser suggested Lloyd's. "It seemed a fair punt. That sort of thing suits my temperament and financial needs. I quite liked the gambling element." What was his response to the concept of un-limited liability? "I quite liked the punt. My father, on a small income, gambled all the time, though he never left my mother short." The odd thing is that, apart from Lloyd's, Bragg doesn't gamble at all. "I don't even have a bet on the Grand National. I always thought it was a mug's game, but, well, there you go." The few artsy Names there are in Lloyd's tend to be–like Baron Archer of Weston-super-Mare–as openly right-wing as Bragg is left. When I put the rarity of artsiness, leftiness, and Namedom to Bragg, he pauses and wonders, "Is John Mortimer a Name?" This is the same response I get whenever I put the question elsewhere: "Is John Mortimer a Name?" I ring the benign Rumpole creator to check. "Certainly not," he replies, sounding slightly indignant at the suggestion. Why not? "I think it's a totally idiotic way of losing your money. I don't see how anyone goes in unless they're insane."

Bragg, though at times puzzled, seems untroubled by his mem-bership. "I honestly think it's an honorable way to make your money work for you." But he could have put his money–while avoiding the stock market–into, say, a regular insurance company: was there an el-ement of snobbery in his decision? "One hesitates not to claim vices," he replies, and we leave it at that. Bragg has also given his profes-sional advice to Lloyd's. A year or so ago, he was informally con-sulted about the unhelpful publicity the market was getting. He was shocked to discover that "they had a press office as big as Border Television's"–i.e., roughly one man, a boy, and a grouse. This side of things is now handled in a more assured and glossy way, as part of the "transparent society" Lloyd's now claims itself to be.

The novelist admits that at the time he was "appallingly lack-adaisical" about the consequences of joining Lloyd's. But he was also fortunate in the advice he received. The easily made comparison be-tween Namedom and gambling on the horses has some validity, though not in one basic respect: if you walk off the street into a bookmaker's, you are likely to get more or less the same odds from any firm; if you walk off the street into Lloyd's, the first and probably the biggest gamble you take lies in which agent you are introduced to. Bragg followed "very, very lightly" the syndicates he was put on; he never took out stop-loss insurance ("When I worked out the figures, it wasn't worth it"); and, though he's lost money in the last couple of years, "I think I'm quite a bit ahead in a crude sense." He is currently on twenty-eight syndicates, he says, four losing and twenty-four doing "very well." Do the losses of the last years make him think about getting out? "The equation is insane," he replies. By which he means that resignation does not exempt you from future losses on the syndicates left open; so in effect you would only be resigning from your winning syndicates. Leaving doesn't cross his mind. "I think Lloyd's is a better bet now. If I could get off the open syndicates, I'd pour it in now. There's masses of syndicates making money. It's a good time to join."

Both the English novelist and an Irish businessman I'd talked to took the same line. If they'd known at the time of joining what was to happen, they would never have gone in ("The sort of punter I was in 1980 wouldn't touch it with a barge pole now," says Bragg); on the other hand, given that they are in, and have survived the losses of the last three years, they think it's a fine time to stay in. The comparison with gambling seems truest when you get down to gut psychological response. If you've lost and been burnt, you know it's a mug's game—that the horses are nobbled, the jockeys bribed, and the stewards corrupt. If you've won, or broken even, you feel yourself a squire of the turf next to the poor saps who've lost their cuff links—you're the one who gets hot tips from the stables, who can sniff a dodgy fetlock at a hundred paces, who knows a chap who knows a chap.

The chap whom Melvyn Bragg knows is the Lloyd's joint deputy chairman Robert Hiscox, who is also his agent. As the son of a former chairman, Hiscox is very much a Lloyd's insider, he has been a working Name since 1967, spent twenty years "on the box," insuring art at the high end of the market, and is currently the chairman of the underwriting agents Roberts & Hiscox. A dapper fifty-year-old, whose words are quiet in tone yet combative in content, he has been arguing in favor of limited liability for twenty-five years. This was always resisted, partly because of a general misreading of the Lloyd's Acts of 1871 and later, which seemed to forbid it (in fact, they did so only for individuals), but mainly on the ground of "If it ain't broke, don't fix it." "To which I used to reply, 'Most things cannot be fixed once they're broken.'" Now he is in charge of raising corporate capital and saving Lloyd's neck: the biggest fixing job there is.

Hiscox is a plainspoken man and a market realist. He was also the author, a dozen years ago, of that notorious phrase "If God had not meant them to be sheared, He would not have made them sheep." Faced with that quotation in a TV interview in June of this year, by which time quite a number of sheep had been not just sheared but also butchered and scoffed with mint sauce and all the trimmings, Hiscox correctly pointed out that the true author of the line was Eli Wallach in his favorite film *The Magnificent Seven*. But still, what did he mean by it? "There are people," he replied, "who unerringly choose the wrong accountant in life, they choose the wrong wife or husband, they choose the wrong solicitor, they choose the wrong stockbroker, and they have unerring bad judgment, and, unfortunately, if one's trying to regulate a market so that these people cannot lose money the trouble comes when they meet the wrong Lloyd's underwriting agent, and it has been a very bad experience for them." This sounds pretty much like blaming the victims (in any case, shouldn't one be quoting Yul Brynner rather than Eli Wallach?); and when our conversation turns to "all this grief and misery" of the last few years Hiscox observes that the events of the eighties were always liable to happen "if you have very undemanding capital." This seems a strange and most chilling way to describe the people I'd been talking to over the last weeks. Besides, wasn't that what he, as an agent, wanted? He disagreed: "We turned them"–such applicants–"away in droves. So they ran out of this door and into Gooda Walker, unfortunately, and they didn't go into it with great depth. They trusted a three-hundred-and-five-year-old institution, part of Britain and the Empire, and they didn't really look into it."

The new business that Lloyd's is seeking to attract is unlikely to have many ovine characteristics, and will certainly "look into" things. When I asked Peter Middleton why corporate capital should be attracted to a market that had so dramatically favored the insider in recent years, he pointed out that such institutions are perfectly capable of identifying the syndicates they want to be put on (and will presumably use their muscle to get there). The market will begin accepting corporate Names in January 1994. They will need a capital of £1,500,000 and will have to deposit 50 percent of the amount they underwrite with Lloyd's (as opposed to 30 percent for individual Names); their liability will be limited; and previous Lloyd's losses will be "ring-fenced." This last aspect has attracted criticism from current Names who see themselves as bearing the burden of earlier Lloyd's failings while corporate capital waltzes in and enjoys all the juicy new business. Hiscox forcefully argues the market necessity of this two-tier system: "You won't get a new investor coming in and paying a penny for the past." Besides, he says, in this respect Lloyd's is no different from the stock market: if a share price falls to a low level, an investor buying it at, say, 24 pence would not–and would not expect to–help out those who had earlier bought the stock at 124 pence.

Hiscox admits that the revolt of the shires has given the action groups a certain whammy over Lloyd's for the moment. Time is not on his side when it comes to attracting corporate capital, and the sight of a mass revolt by previous investors, not to mention the referral of one case to the Serious Fraud Office for possible criminal prosecution, constitutes bad PR. What if Lloyd's Names refuse to pay? What if no corporate money comes forward? "With no corporate capital, we can survive into 1994." He finds it ironic that, having seen off various enemies in the past, and having even got the Labour Party on its side in some recent bits of House of Commons business, the market is now "fighting our own Names." But then, he wryly observes, "England can only perish but by Englishmen." This strikes me as peculiarly rich and cheeky, since Lloyd's has for many a long century lived off being English to the core. I remember the Deficit Millionairess saying, "I thought it was a very English thing to do." I also remember the West Country Widow's sharp observation when I mentioned the advent of corporate capital: "I wouldn't invest in a company that invested in Lloyd's."

If the new business plan works and Lloyd's survives, the market will substantially change its nature. The days of dinner-party trawling, the Wimbledon connection, the amateur investor–the days of sheep and "undemanding capital"–will go. The individual Name will be a rarity; most Names will band together to achieve some corporate status and operate with limited liability, or else they will invest through a larger institution. Of course, the money would come from some of the same people as before, though this time it would be filtered through pension-fund managers rather than arriving like a bag of silver fish forks in the back of a Range Rover. When I ask what Lloyd's–assuming it survives–will be like in ten years' time, Hiscox looks misty, if it is possible to look dynamically misty. "My dream is of it as it was at its peak, a pocket of excellence, creating and innovating." When was that peak? Surprisingly, "about 1790." Hiscox then talks of "three fundamental things Lloyd's hasn't had for twenty years." These are "One, a rich, sophisticated capital. Two, total integrity. Three, strong government." At which point, Hiscox makes another cinematic reference: not Eli Wallach this time but Tyrone Power. In 1936, in one of his lesser-known roles, Power played the part of an underwriter in Darryl F. Zanuck's *Lloyd's of London*. The time is around 1790, the "three fundamental things" hold sway at Lloyd's, and the underwriting hero, according to Hiscox, is a man of "total integrity, doing his thing for his country." Hiscox kindly lent me a tape of the film.

Lloyd's of London is a thoroughly jolly piece of tosh, and if you believe that Freddie Bartholomew can grow up into Tyrone Power you will happily believe the rest of it as well. Young Freddie is a childhood friend of a rather posher boy called Horatio Nelson, until destiny separates their paths. Nelson goes into the Navy, and Freddie runs away to London, where he is adopted by the famous Coffee House. He is reminded at the knee of John Julius Angerstein, a famous underwriting baron of the time, that "Lloyd's is founded on two great pillars: news and honest dealing. If either fails, we fail, and with us the whole of the British merchant marine." Freddie grows suddenly into Tyrone and falls in love with Madeleine Carroll. The Napoleonic Wars break out. Business is written. The Lutine Bell is rung (anachronistically). Power proudly quotes Angerstein's dictum that "Lloyd's is not a collection of moneygrubbing brokers but an organization linked with the destiny of England." For most of the film poor Nelson is an offstage figure; it is the underwriter who is the visible man of action. Thus he audaciously continues to insure the British merchant fleet at prewar rates, even though it lacks the protection of the British Navy. The Lutine Bell is rung like a dinner gong. Napoleon is finally defeated, and a swooning admirer congratulates the heroic underwriter with the line "Nelson's won, England's saved, and Lloyd's is saved."

Interesting, and proleptic, and perhaps judiciously forgotten in Mr. Hiscox's description of the underwriter as a man of "total integrity," is the route by which the protagonist saves England, Nelson, Lloyd's, his underwriting capacity, and his love for Madeleine Carroll (and *her* money too, for that matter, since she has, sheeplike, delivered her inheritance into his arms). He does it by perpetrating a gross deception on Lloyd's, on his investors and his friends, on the British Admiralty and the British nation, and by repeating and defending that lie for several days, until his old pal Horatio wins the Battle of Trafalgar. For this deceit (and other complicated reasons), he is shot in the back by George Sanders at exactly the same moment as Nelson is being shot by the French at Trafalgar. The admiral, as we all know, dies, but the underwriter survives. Perhaps there is some lesson here, for England and for the burnt Names of Lloyd's.

September 1993

The losses for 1991, announced in May 1994, were twice what Lloyd's had predicted twelve months earlier: £2.5 billion (or, if you prefer the newly introduced and more agreeable system, which strips out the "double count" when two syndicates reserve for the same claim, a mere £2.048 billion). Apart from asbestosis and pollution claims, there is now a new long-tail threat: claims against manufacturers of silicone breast implants. Tom Benyon, chairman of the Society of Names, estimated that up to 9,000 Names would be ruined by the 1991 results. In October 1994 there was some apparent good news for the deficit millionaires: a group of 3,096 Names successfully sued the underwriters of the Gooda Walker syndicates for negligence. Solicitors for the plaintiffs estimated that the award would be worth more than £500 million. However, nothing is straightforward at Lloyd's. Where were the policies covering the Gooda Walker underwriters against "errors and omissions" written? Mostly at Lloyd's, of course. Even those which were reinsured outside Lloyd's may well turn out, such is the vortical nature of the business, to end up back in the London market. So Names may find that they have won money from their negligent underwriters, who in turn claim on their professional insurers, who in turn call in the money from the same Names who are owed it elsewhere. Bankrupt already? Now you can make yourself even more bankrupt!

■ II ■

Mrs. Thatcher Remembers

A few years ago, an elderly friend of mine was being examined in a British hospital for possible brain damage. A psychiatrist catechized her patronizingly. "Can you tell me what day of the week it is?" "That's not important to me" came the cagey reply. "Well, can you tell me what season of the year it is?" "Of course I can." The doctor plodded on to his next tester. "And can you tell me who is the Prime Minister?" "Everyone knows *that*," my friend answered, half triumphant, half derisive. "It's Thatch."

Everyone did indeed know, for more than eleven long years, that it was Thatch. No other Prime Minister in my lifetime has been always *there* to the extent that Margaret Thatcher was, in terms not just of longevity but also of intensity. She trained herself to sleep only four hours a night, and most mornings the nation awoke to a parade-ground snarl, to the news that it was an 'orrible shower, and the instruction to double round the barracks again in full pack or else. Those who met her in private confirmed that she was just as powerful an eyeballer as on the parade ground. The poet Philip Larkin wrote of the moment when "I got the blue flash," going on to moan appreciatively to another correspondent, "What a blade of steel!" Alan Clark, a minor Tory minister and rakehell nob diarist, treasured a moment when "her blue eyes flashed" and "I got a full dose of personality compulsion, something of the *Führer Kontakt.*" (He also noted her "very small feet and attractive—not bony—ankles in the 1940 style.") Even President Mitterrand, whom one might expect to be immune on both national and political grounds, can be heard succumbing to La Thatch in Jacques Attali's "Verbatim." "The eyes of Stalin, the voice of Marilyn Monroe," he muses in tranced paradox.

When she came to the Tory leadership in 1975, it seemed as if she might be a brief and token phenomenon. She was of the Tory right, and British politics had for years shuffled between governments of the Tory left and the Labour right: little bits of tax lowering and denationalization on the one hand, little bits of tax raising and renationalization on the other. Worse, she was a woman: though both major parties had pachyderm prejudices against the species, it had always been assumed that the officially progressive Labour Party was the more likely party to put a woman at its head. Tory women, it was known, preferred men; and so did Tory men. Finally, there was Mrs. Thatcher's apparent suburban Englishness: it was confidently asserted that she would get no votes north of the Watford Gap (a motorway service area in the South Midlands). So her first election victory was put down to the temporary weakness of the Labour Party; her second to the knock-on effect of the Falklands War; her third to renewed Opposition fissuring. That she was deprived of the chance of winning a fourth was due not to the Labour Party, still less to the Tory faithful in the country at large, but to a disgruntled Parliamentary Party, which decided (and only by a whisker) that she had passed her vote-by date.

Those who opposed her, who felt each day of her rule as a sort of political migraine, tended to make two fundamental miscalculations. The first was to treat her as some kind of political weirdo. This was understandable, since she was a Tory ideologue, and when had the Conservatives last been a party of ideology, of inflexible programs, of Holy Grail beliefs? What took years to sink in was the nasty truth that Mrs. Thatcher represented and successfully appealed to a strong and politically disregarded form of Englishness. To the liberal, the snobbish, the metropolitan, the cosmopolitan, she displayed a parochial, small-shopkeeper mentality, puritanical and Poujadiste, self-interested and xenophobic, half sceptered-isle nostalgia and half count-your-change bookkeeping. But to those who supported her she was a plain speaker, a clear and visionary thinker who embodied no-nonsense, stand-on-your-own-two-feet virtue, a patriot who saw that we had been living on borrowed time and borrowed money for far too long. If socialism's gut appeal lies in the argument from science (which implies inevitability), Thatcherism's gut appeal lay in the argument from nature (which also implies inevitability). But arguments from nature should always remind us of one of nature's commoner sights: that of large animals devouring smaller ones.

The second miscalculation was the assumption, made until quite late in the day, that what she was doing to the country could, and would, eventually be undone. This had always more or less happened in postwar politics: little pendulum swings to the left and then to the right along the years. Now, post-Thatcher, the pendulum continues to swing, but inside a clock that has been rehung on the wall at a completely different angle. Like many, I used to think that the official saturation of the country with market values was a reversible phenomenon; a little skin cancer perhaps, but no irradiation of the soul. I abandoned this belief–or hope–a few Christmases ago, and when I want an image of what Mrs. Thatcher has done to Britain I think of the carol singers. At the time she came to power, they would, as they always had, stand outside your house, sing a carol or two, then ring the bell, and if you answered, sing some more. Halfway through the rule of Thatch, I began noticing that they wouldn't bother to start singing until they had first rung the bell and checked that you were there to listen and pay up. After she had been in power for about ten years, I opened the door one Christmas and peered out. There were two small boys some distance from the house already, unwilling to waste their time if they got a negative response. "Carols?" one of them asked, spreading his hands in a businesslike gesture, as if he had just acquired a job lot of tunes off the back of a lorry and could perhaps be persuaded to cut me in.

Mrs. Thatcher's achievements were, in political terms, remarkable. She showed that you could disregard the old pieties about consensus, whether intraparty or cross-party. You could govern the United Kingdom while effectively shrinking your MP base to a purely English party. You could survive while allowing unemployment to rise to levels previously thought politically untenable. You could politicize hitherto unpolitical public bodies, and force the holy principles of the market into areas of society presumed sacrosanct. You could sharply diminish union power and increase employer power. You could weaken the independence of local government by limiting its ability to raise money, and then, if it still bugged you, you could simply abolish it: London is now the only great city in the world without an elected metropolitan authority. You could make the rich richer and the poor poorer until you had restored the gap that existed at the end of the last century. You could do all this and in the process traumatize the Opposition: the presence since 1979 of a Tory Government that has been frequently unpopular yet ineluctably reelected has driven the Labour Party steadily to the right, until it has abandoned much of what it believed in the seventies and presents itself now as the party of nice, caring capitalists, as distinct from nasty, uncaring ones. Even the unemployed have been traumatized, to the extent that at the last election (Thatcher-free but still fought around Thatcherism) they actually ended up voting in slightly higher proportion for the Tories than the previous time round.

From the start, the prime appeal of Margaret Thatcher was her granitic certainty. Her "great virtue," Philip Larkin told an interviewer in 1979, "is saying that two and two makes four, which is as unpopular nowadays as it always has been." Later the same year, the poet elaborated: "I adore Mrs. Thatcher. At last politics makes sense to me, which it hasn't done since Stafford Cripps (I was very fond of him too). Recognizing that if you haven't got the money for something you can't have it—this is a concept that's vanished for many years." Politics, of course, is a matter of decimals, logarithms, and long division, but Mrs. Thatcher, by making parts of it appear simple, not only infuriated those who knew it to be more complicated but also cemented her support among the two-plus-two brigade. Thus, she loved to explain the nation's economic policy in terms of the domestic shopping basket. Budgetary squabbles with the EC were a matter of getting "them" to give "us" "our" money back. She loved polarizations into them and us. Also into good and evil: like Superman, the Iron Lady made the world easier to understand. She and Reagan took readings from the same moral graph. One of the few genuinely comic moments in *Margaret Thatcher: The Downing Street Years* is a color photograph taken during a banquet at No. 10. The Prime Minister is banging out a speech while the President looks up at her with an expression of goofy awe. Underneath this official souvenir he has written, "Dear Margaret—As you can see, I agree with every word you are saying. I always do. Warmest friendship. Sincerely, Ron." During the Reagan-Thatcher years, local dreamers could imagine a reverse of the Kennedy-Macmillan era. Macmillan liked to portray the Atlantic alliance as the relationship of wise old Greece (Britain, in case you were wondering) to vigorous young Rome. For a while, at least, during Reagan's sleepy-senior-citizen act, Thatcher could pose as the dynamic ideas merchant.

"Personally dominant, supremely self-confident, infuriatingly stubborn," Mrs. Thatcher "held a strange mixture of broad views and narrow prejudices." This is the summing up not of some vexed Labourite but of the normally unctuous Kenneth Baker, one of her Party chairmen. (Baker was once tipped for the succession, and his oiliness provoked the comment "I have seen the future and it smirks.") She made up her mind, kept to it, spoke it, and repeated it verbatim for as long as necessary. In *The Downing Street Years* she dismisses the hapless John Nott, Defense Minister during the Falklands War, with the neutering line "His vice was second thoughts." None of them for Maggie. Larkin was once invited to a dinner party at the house of the historian Hugh Thomas, and recorded her combative and unself-questioning manner: "Watching her was like watching a top class tennis-player; no 'uh-huh, well, what do other people think about that,' just bang back over the net." Since the other guests included Isaiah Berlin, V. S. Naipaul, Tom Stoppard, Mario Vargas Llosa, J. H. Plumb, V. S. Pritchett, Anthony Powell, Stephen Spender, Anthony Quinton, and A. Alvarez, this was quite tony company to play tennis in. But then Mrs. Thatcher was no more snob-struck by "vain intellectuals," as she characterizes the breed in her book, than by Tory toffs. There was an early move in her Premiership to present her as a PM who liked a workout on the ideas mat with a few top brains—the historian Paul Johnson was one such scrimmager—but it does not seem to have lasted long. Certainly none of the above names even makes it into the index of *The Downing Street Years*: you can have "Berlin disco bomb" but not "Berlin, Isaiah."

Indeed, the subject of the arts occupies a whole two pages here, and one of those is spent describing Mrs. Thatcher's heroic but thwarted attempt to bring the Thyssen art collection to Britain. ("It was not only a great treasure but a good investment," she typically notes.) Where other Prime Ministers—however truly or hypocritically—like to maintain that the arts are at least a decoration, if not actually an additive, to life, with Mrs. Thatcher they do not enter the equation: if you have that sort of spare time, you aren't doing your job as PM. She remembers Macmillan telling a group of young MPs that "prime ministers (not having a department of their own) have plenty of spare time for reading. He recommended Disraeli and Trollope. I have sometimes wondered if he was joking." He almost certainly wasn't, and it's significant that John Major, who has gone back to the Macmillan "easy-listening" style of Premiership, also claims Trollope as his favorite writer—indeed, is a member of the Trollope Society. (The fact that the novelist was scathing about politicians, and especially about Tories, doesn't seem to bother modern Conservatives.) Mrs. Thatcher, by contrast, cites as her favorite reading "thrillers by Frederick Forsyth and John le Carré." This is probably just as well. The sight of Mrs. Thatcher pretending to like art would not be for the squeamish.

Far better is her unfeigned response on the occasion when Kingsley Amis presented her at No. 10 with an autographed copy of his novel *Russian Hide-and-Seek*. "What's it about?" she asked him. "Well," he explained, "in a way it's about a future Britain under Russian occupation." "Huh!" she cried. "Can't you do any better than that? Get yourself another crystal ball!" This put-down ("unfair as well as unanswerable," Amis noted) failed to decrease the novelist's devotion to the Prime Minister. In his memoirs he calls her "one of the best-looking women I had ever met" and adds this recherché compliment to her allure: "This quality is so extreme that, allied to her well-known photogenic quality, it can trap me for split seconds into thinking I am looking at a science-fiction illustration of some time ago showing the beautiful girl who has become President of the Solar Federation in the year 2220." More routinely, Amis admits that Mrs. Thatcher has replaced the Queen as the woman he dreams about most; once, she even drew him close and murmured lovingly, "You've got such an *interesting* face." Well, she may make his dreams, but, no, he doesn't make her index, either. Nor, for that matter, does the name of a British subject sentenced to death by a foreign power during her Premiership. You would think this might have caused some offense to the notions of British sovereignty, honor, and independence that bray out like trumpet cadenzas from these pages. Bad luck, Citizen Rushdie.

Those high concepts are, by contrast, regularly involved when it comes to one of the central events of Mrs. Thatcher's Premiership: the Falklands War of 1982. Her account of it has a novel clarity: history with little nuance or complication, whether political or moral. The Argentine invasion of the islands was completely unforeseeable (she set up a royal commission afterward which confirmed it, so that's that); the British were defending "our honour as a nation"; while our wider duty was to ensure that Aggression did not Succeed, and that international law be not flouted. But the war also sprang from—and celebrated—Mrs. Thatcher's nature, and her resolution. When the Argentine fleet set off to invade the Falklands, the second-thoughting Defense Minister gave her the feeble official view that, once seized, the islands could not be retaken. "This was terrible, and totally unacceptable. I could not believe it: these were our people, our islands. I said instantly: 'if they are invaded, we have got to get them back.'" What was the alternative? "That a common or garden dictator should rule over the Queen's subjects and prevail by fraud and violence? Not while I was Prime Minister." She has to kick a few peaceniks into line, including her Foreign Secretary, Francis Pym, who shows wobbliness and a disproportionate interest in diplomatic solutions; and she is willing to threaten resignation to get her way with the War Cabinet. Staunch support comes from Caspar Weinberger, Laurens van der Post, and François Mitterrand (who had, of course, his own postcolonial aggravations); but it is, essentially, Maggie versus the Argies. At one point, she is down on her knees at Chequers measuring territorial waters on naval charts with the Attorney General. Eventually, "the freedom, justice and democracy which the Falkland Islanders had enjoyed for so long" are returned to them. "I do not think I have ever lived so tensely or intensely as during the whole of that time," she writes.

Much of this is comic-strip simplification. The Falklands, with its depressed company-store economy, tiny population, and militarily insufficient runway, held no interest for the British except perhaps among philatelists. We had been trying to unload the islands for decades, efforts which culminated in Nicholas Ridley's "leaseback" proposal of 1980. This was thrown out by the House of Commons; but still, in classic schoolyard fashion, we did not really want, or think about wanting, the islands until someone else did. Hence the war sweetly characterized by Borges–a "vain intellectual" living under a "common or garden dictator"–as "two bald men fighting over a comb." Nor was Mrs. Thatcher at all in the valiant isolation she now chooses to describe. The House of Commons fell immediately and noisily behind the Prime Minister, not least after a key intervention she fails to acknowledge: that of Michael Foot, old-socialist leader of the Labour Party and, in his own words, an "inveterate peacemonger," who came out for war. So did most of the nation: the British are still a bellicose race, and they rather like fighting, preferably by themselves and in a good-versus-evil struggle as sketched by the Prime Minister. For once, something was happening out there, the TV pictures were good, and xenophobia could be indulged.

Mrs. Thatcher, with her shopping-basket view of the world, likes to assure us that she does her sums. But it's odd that she doesn't mention the basic statistic of the war. One thousand eight hundred islanders were liberated from the Argentines (who brought not torture and death but color TV sets to cheer the crofters' firesides), at a cost of just over 1,000 deaths, 255 of them British, plus countless modern maimings. Try doing the sum on a different war: imagine that the reinvasion of France in 1944 had cost 23 million lives, 6 million of them Allied. Would we rejoice so much and praise our leaders? Freedom is indivisible, politicians like to say, but of course it isn't; on the contrary, it falls into strict categories. It was lucky for the islanders that they were white, just as it was lucky for the Kuwaitis that they exported oil rather than Turkish delight. Nor was the aftermath of liberation much like Paris in 1944. The British soldiers who reoccupied the islands were unimpressed by the Falklanders, whom they nicknamed "Bennies," after a notoriously dim character in a TV soap. An official order had to be put out instructing the troops not to use this insulting term. Shortly afterward, they took to referring to the locals as "Stills." A mystified officer asked a soldier to explain this new sobriquet. "Because they're still Bennies, sir," came the magnificent reply. Today, the Falkland Islanders are no nearer the hearts of the British than before; a political solution has been endlessly deferred; and the enlarged airstrip, which we once couldn't afford, has now been built, to the ultimate benefit of the Argentines. Were the islands worth a single death, or even the money the expedition cost? Before hostilities began, Macmillan advised Mrs. Thatcher to keep the Treasury out of things (ironic counsel, since it was Macmillan as Chancellor of the Exchequer at the time of Suez who helped pull the plug on that campaign). So this was to be a No Expense Spared War. And what did it cost? All we find in *The Downing Street Years* is bland mumblings: "It was a remarkable testament to the soundness of public finances by this stage that we managed to pay for the Falklands War out of the Contingency Reserve without a penny of extra taxation and with barely a tremor in the financial markets." Another example of good housekeeping, then. In fact, the cost of the campaign, plus that of securing the Falklands to the end of the eighties, was upwards of £2 million per islander. High price for a comb.

All this, though, is politically irrelevant. However impressive the feat of arms, its true and lasting significance for the British was as a domestic metaphor. Politics has a presiding rhetoric of "fighting and winning," which we citizens are rarely able to compute when it comes to matters of trade balance and interest rates. And when we can compute it—as with "the battle against unemployment" or "the fight against crime"—we always seem to be losing. So a clear and televised success in war (especially when for years your soldiers have not been getting a result in Northern Ireland) encourages the belief that other problems are equally soluble, other victories assured, and that Mrs. Thatcher is "a winner." Hence subsequent chapters of *The Downing Street Years* are called "Disarming the Left" and "Mr Scargill's Insurrection." (Mr. Scargill was not a guerrilla leader in the Yorkshire Dales but a trade-union leader.) And hence the explicit linkage Mrs. Thatcher made immediately after the war in a speech in Cheltenham: "We have ceased to be a nation in retreat. We have instead a newfound confidence—born in the economic battles at home and tested and found true 8000 miles away." In her view, "without any prompting from us, people saw the connection between the resolution we had shown in economic policy and that demonstrated in the handling of the Falklands crisis." "People," here, as elsewhere in the book, is not a generic term referring to the British but a specific term denoting those who supported Mrs. Thatcher. Her vision is ruthlessly monocular.

She can see, for instance, that she was the most feted and fetishized of modern Prime Ministers but not that she was also the most loathed. She was loathed in a personal as well as in a political way, since her perceived character—domineering, mean-spirited, divisive, unheeding—seemed to inform and infect her policies. That character is amply on display here. She is contemptuous of Tory wets and Tory grandees. She is contemptuous of the Tory tradition that she supplanted, referring at one point to the "thirty-year experiment" of "socialism" in postwar Britain: as far as one can follow her chronology, this clearly includes the Conservative governments of Heath, Douglas-Home, Macmillan, and Eden, and possibly that of Churchill. Special spite is reserved for two of her main adjutants, Nigel Lawson and Geoffrey Howe, neither of whom could finally stomach her. Howe's resignation speech prompted a challenge to her leadership, ensuring, to her eyes, that "from this point on [he] would be remembered not for his staunchness as Chancellor, nor for his skillful diplomacy as Foreign Secretary, but for this final act of bile and treachery. The very brilliance with which he wielded the dagger ensured that the character he assassinated was in the end his own." As for the real Opposition, try this for superciliousness: "Mr. Kinnock, in all his years as Opposition leader, never let me down. Right to the end, he struck every wrong note."

Monocularity at home, cecity abroad. Alan Clark reports a comment that Mrs. Thatcher made to the civil servant Frank Cooper two years after she had been made leader of the Opposition. "Must I do all this international stuff?" she asked, and when he replied, "You can't avoid it," she pulled a face. Cooper also recalled that "during that period she and [Cooper] had met Reagan and Carter, and she was *astonished* at how stupid they were. 'Can they really dispose of all that power?' etc." She grew to enjoy motorcade acclaim, of course, and the banquets chez Mitterrand, while never seeming to suspect that when you are applauded in Eastern Europe it does not necessarily mean more than a public snub to the local leaders. She is sure that "the beliefs and policies which I . . . pioneered in Britain" have helped "to remould world affairs." She cannot conceive that the Falklands expedition might be viewed elsewhere not as an early start on the new world order but as the last twitch of an imperial past. She is much happier with distant sheikhs than with European democrats. She imagines that her obstructive, nagging, bullying attitude to Europe was taken as a sign that Britain was walking tall once more. She thinks that if you insult people you gain their respect.

In a TV series made to coincide with the publication of *The*

Downing Street Years, she came up with the following subtly graded observation: "There's a great strand of equity and fairness in the British people: this is our characteristic. There's not a great strand of equity or fairness in Europe—they're out to get as much as they can. That's one of those enormous differences." For the bicentennial of the French Revolution—whose "abstract ideas," she notes, were "formulated by vain intellectuals"—she gave an interview to *Le Monde* from which she proudly quotes: "Human rights did not begin with the French Revolution . . . [they] really stem from a mixture of Judaism and Christianity . . . [we English] had 1688, our quiet revolution, where Parliament exerted its will over the King . . . it was not the sort of Revolution that France's was. . . . 'Liberty, equality, fraternity'—they forgot obligations and duties I think. And then of course the fraternity went missing for a long time." How strange that all those poor benighted foreigners still harp on 1789, rather than 1688, as their symbolic date. But how equally strange that the English revolution Mrs. Thatcher chooses to cite is that of 1688 rather than the much more famous one earlier in the century, which also led to Parliament's exerting its will over the King, though in a somewhat different way—by cutting off his head, just as they were to do in France. *Le Monde,* as if humoring the deranged, headlined its interview "LES DROITS DE L'HOMME N'ONT PAS COMMENCÉ EN FRANCE," NOUS DÉCLARE MME. THATCHER.

The Downing Street Years is not, of course, a "book" in the normal sense of the word. Top politicians generally have an arm's-length acquaintance with their own language: they only truly mean what other people help them say. A speech needs speechwriters (Mrs. Thatcher used the dramatist Ronald Millar and the novelist Ferdinand Mount, thereby perhaps according "vain intellectuals" their true employment); and a book needs book writers—ghosts, researchers, anecdote trufflers, document sifters, prose scrubbers. This shouldn't strike us as either shocking or dishonest. Mrs. Thatcher's book is authentic in its public pomposities, its regurgitated speeches and documents, its bulging acronyms. It is authentic, too, in its coy sartorial annotations—"I had worn a simple cotton dress and flat shoes to visit the refugee camp"—and glutinous domestic dues paying: "Being prime minister is a lonely job. In a sense, it ought to be: you cannot lead from the crowd. But with Denis there I was never alone. What a man. What a husband. What a friend."

Finally, it is authentic in being a work of colossal, if unsurprising, vanity. Over the decade or more of her rule, Mrs. Thatcher went from Prime Ministerial to Presidential to regal—a progression that was marked both in her language (growing use of the royal plural) and in her frocks. Her later official garments, for such outings as the Lord Mayor's banquet, increasingly conjured up references to Queen Elizabeth—the First, that is, the powerful one, not the mere Second. Yet while settling the great affairs of state for us she also had an unsleeping eye for the dandruff on our collar, the soup stain on our tie: "Every time I came back from some spotlessly maintained foreign city my staff and the then Secretary of State for the Environment knew that they could expect a stiff lecture on the litter-strewn streets of parts of London." Reality does not always break in (otherwise, a connection between the state of the streets and the abolition of the Greater London Council might have occurred), but the performance in the book is of a piece with Mrs. Thatcher's performance in real life. It is a justification and a continuation of her rule, as well as a means of making various jolly millions. It also has the sort of relentless presence that her Premiership had. Every so often, you have to shake your head and remind yourself that just because a book is heavy this doesn't make it history. Indeed, even among ardent Thatcherites there are different gospels. When the Prime Minister is taking advice from her colleagues during the leadership election of 1990, the procession of traitors and hypocrites is momentarily enlivened by the arrival of Alan Clark. Mrs. Thatcher records:

> Even melodramas have intervals, even *Macbeth* has the porter's scene. I now had a short talk with Alan Clark, Minister of State at the Ministry of Defence, and a gallant friend, who came round to lift my spirits with the encouraging advice that I should fight on at all costs. Unfortunately he went on to argue that I should fight on even though I was bound

to lose because it was better to go out in a blaze of glorious defeat than to go gentle into that good night. Since I had no particular fondness for Wagnerian endings, this lifted my spirits only briefly. But I was glad to have someone unambiguously on my side even in defeat.

Here is Alan Clark's account of the meeting, from his *Diaries*:

I went down the stairs and rejoined the group outside her door. After a bit Peter said, "I can just fit you in now—but only for a split second, mind."

She looked calm, almost beautiful. "Ah, Alan . . . "

"You're in a jam."

"I know that."

"They're all telling you not to stand, aren't they?"

"I'm going to stand. I have issued a statement."

"That's wonderful. That's heroic. But the Party will let you down."

"I am a fighter."

"Fight, then. Fight right to the end, a third ballot if you need to. But you lose."

There was quite a little pause.

"It'd be so terrible if Michael [Heseltine] won. He would undo everything I have fought for."

"But what a way to go! Unbeaten in three elections, never rejected by the people. Brought down by nonentities!"

"But Michael . . . as *Prime Minister*."

"Who the fuck's Michael? No one. Nothing. He won't last six months. I doubt if he'd even win the Election. Your place in history is towering . . ."

Outside, people were doing that maddening trick of opening and shutting the door, at shorter and shorter intervals.

"Alan, it's been so good of you to come in and see me. . . ."

Mrs. Thatcher creates a comic interlude, ponderously narrated, in which she demonstrates statesmanlike gravitas. Clark sketches a tragic episode, lightly told, in which he is the passionate truth teller. It's hard not to prefer Clark's version, even if it is just as self-serving. (Look, I'm the sort of chap who isn't afraid to say "fuck" in front of Maggie.) Future historians will not be able to avoid the Thatcher memoirs, any more than those who lived under her for so long could avoid her glowering, lowering presence. Had she been more of a Trollopian, she might have known to give the *The Downing Street Years* its rightful, inescapable subtitle: "She Knew She Was Right."

November 1993

■ 12 ■

TDF: The World Chess Championship

*I*t is a most curious form of theater: austere, minimalist, post-Beckettian. Two neatly dressed men crouch attentively over a small table against an elegant gray and beige set. One, tall, gangly, pallid, and bespectacled, occupies a high-backed, fat-armed oxblood club chair; the other, shorter, compacter, and browner, has a low-backed black-leather number with chrome base and legs, of a design you might call Moscow Bauhaus. Each is fiercely possessive of his chair. They are happy enough to change costume, and on alternate matinees they swap sides of the table; but they always take their chairs with them.

The only other visible characters are a pair of older gentlemen who sit at the rear right of the stage, observing their juniors like some mirroring subplot. None of the four speaks; nevertheless, the theater-goer's ears are filled with dialogue. A third pair of actors, unseen, high up in a glazed box at the back of the upper circle, guess at the thoughts of the characters onstage. This earphone-filling game of hazard and prediction provides the main interest, since the visible action is limited and repetitive. Occasionally, the two protagonists will make slight movements with their hands, then immediately scribble notes to themselves. Otherwise, there are only exits and entrances during these four- to six-hour matinees: one character will suddenly stand up as if offended and depart stage left, the gangly one tiptoeing away ganglily, the compact one bustling away compactly. Every so often, in an audacious device, both may be offstage at the same time. But always the disembodied voices continue in the ear, assessing, theorizing, imagining; anxious, confident, exultant, apologetic.

Skeptics maintain that live chess is as much fun as watching paint dry. Ultraskeptics reply: Unfair to paint. Yet for three months the cheapest seats at the Savoy Theatre were, by a long way, the most expensive cheap seats in London. Twenty pounds to watch the Times World Chess Championship from the stalls, £35 from the upper circle, £55 from the dress circle. This wasn't entirely greed, or desperation on the part of Times Newspapers to recoup some of their estimated £4 to £5 million investment. It was also a genuine anticipation of domestic interest. For the first time in the modern history of the championship—deemed to have started with the 1886 match between Steinitz and Zukertort—a Briton had emerged as title contender. Nigel Short was also the first Westerner to contest the final since Bobby Fischer in 1972. Pre-Fischer, you had to go back to 1937 to find another Westerner, the Dutchman Max Euwe; post-Fischer, the only way to get into any of the next seven World Championship matches was to be a Russian whose name began with *K*: Karpov, Korchnoi, Kasparov. Now, at last, there was a local boy to root for, and a serious underdog as well. Kasparov is constantly described as the strongest player in the history of the game; Short wasn't in the top ten. The size of his task could be estimated by the fact that even one of Kasparov's seconds, the Georgian grandmaster Zurab Azmaiparashvali, was ranked above him.

Gary Kasparov was, or was thought to be, a known quantity. He was the dynamic, aggressive, and moody champion, much photographed lifting weights, thumping a punch bag, playing football, and swimming on his "Croatian island retreat." He was the new-style Russian, from "war-torn Baku," the chum of Gorbachev, then of

Yeltsin; easily packageable, and with the zippy if secondhand nick-name of Gazza. Nigel Short was the harder case for packaging, since, like many chess players, what he had mostly done in his twenty-eight years was play chess. Only two things seemed generally known about him: that he had once played in a teenage rock band called the Urge (originally titled Pelvic Thrust), and that he was now married to a Greek drama therapist seven years his senior. But then the phrase *chess biography* is—as Truffaut once cattily remarked of the expression *British film*—a contradiction in terms. Chess is, famously, an activity entirely unrelated to the rest of life: from this springs its fragile pro-fundity. Biography theoretically links the private to the public in such a way that the former illuminates the latter. But in chess no such con-nection, or reductiveness, applies. Does grandmaster X prefer the French defense because his mother forsook his father when he was as yet a small child? Does bed-wetting lead to the Grunfeld? And so on. Freudians may see chess as Oedipal: an activity whose ultimate aim is to kill the king, and in which the sexy queen is dominant. But at-tempted matchups between on-board and off-board character pro-duce as many counterindicators as corroborations.

Ruthless gutting of Cathy Forbes's *Nigel Short: Quest for the Crown* therefore added only a few embellishments of dubious pertinence. Nigel had fallen into an Amsterdam canal as a child; Nigel had been mugged in his home city of Manchester at the age of twenty; Nigel's parents had separated when he was thirteen; Nigel's frequently stated ambition was to become a Tory MP. As an indicator of how scarily scant the record is, Ms. Forbes is driven at one point to record that, as a teenager, Nigel "alarmed acquaintances by threatening to dye his hair blue." An unfulfilled threat, as it turned out, though perhaps help-ful to the imaginative psychobiographer, given that blue is the em-blematic color of the Conservative Party.

These exiguous and banal details were widely reproduced. Since chess players are on the whole neither charismatic nor polymor-phous, it was comic to see the varying journalistic templates into which Short was excitedly fitted. For *Hello!* magazine, that tinned rice pudding of the newsstand, it was Nigel the family man posing happily in his Greek retreat with wife Rea and little daughter Kyveli. For *The Sun*, it was Nigel as modern British hero, who "loves rock music and a pint with his mates. . . . He stormed up the ranks but he didn't ignore his other passions–women and music." Short dutifully posed for a laddish photo, hoof to plume in black leather, strutting his stuff among knee-high chess pieces while toting an electric guitar. Headline? IT'S ONLY ROOK AND ROLL BUT I LIKE IT. Harmless fun and all that, but at the same time, seriously unconvincing. Nigel has a nickname too, by the way. If Gary is Gazza, Nigel is Nosher. Etymology? "Nigel Short" anagrams out schoolboyishly into Nosher L. Git.

Short is twenty-eight, Kasparov thirty, but judging from their prematch press conferences you would guess at a much wider age differential. Short, a boyish figure in a bottle green suit, with boffinish specs and cropped hair, cut a nervous, adolescent, halting figure, and spoke with the slightly strangulated vowels of one who has had speech therapy. He was accompanied on the podium by his manager and accountant, grandmaster Michael Stean (of whom it was once said that he thought about chess all the time except when actually playing it); Stean would occasionally lean over and deflect the trickier questions. There is, of course, no reason at all why a chess player should be good at PR; even so, the difference between Short and Kasparov was remarkable. For a start, the Russian has much better English than Nigel. He handled the conference by himself and with presidential ease; was just as much at home with geopolitics as with chess; attended courteously to questions he was mightily familiar with; and generally came across as a highly intelligent, worldly, rounded human being. In his many interviews and appearances, Short, by contrast, gave the impression of being thoughtful, considered, wise, and precise when talking about chess, and barely adult when talking about anything other than chess. He brought to mind the remark of the great world champion Emanuel Lasker in his *Manual of Chess*: "In life we are all duffers."

The talking up and coloring in of the match entailed a certain halfhearted attempt at demonizing Kasparov. It has been a feature of all world championship matches since Fischer vs. Spassky that there has to be some goody–baddy, them-or-us aspect for the non-aficionado to get a handle on. In that epochal match in Reykjavik, Fischer was held to represent the triumph of Western individualism against a nominal figure thrown up by the Soviet chess "machine." (Linguistic note: we may occasionally have had a "program," they always had a "machine.") When Kasparov emerged to play the first of his five wearying bouts against Karpov, he was portrayed in the West as the admirably uppity young pup, the half-Jewish outsider taking on Moscow Center; later, he was the symbol of Gorbachev's Russia, of openness and renewal, warding off the ex-chum of Brezhnev. Now that Kasparov was taking on a Westerner, he had to be restyled into "the last great beneficiary of the Soviet machine," while the fact that he had assembled a strong team of ex-Soviet seconds was put down not just to the sinister continuance of "the machine" but also to the money Kasparov had amassed during his reign. Short could therefore be depicted as the cash-bothered Western individualist (though he was paying his coach Lubomir Kavalek $125,000 for twenty weeks of work, with a promised victory bonus of the same amount). The political angle was also rejigged. The fact that Kasparov had moved on from being a Gorbachevian to a Yeltsinite prompted Short, the Tory hopeful, to denounce his opponent's politics as "a fake"; he also talked knowingly in prematch interviews of "the KGB connection." By which was meant, first, that Kasparov had enjoyed the friendship and protection of a local KGB boss back in Azerbaijan; and second, that he had received special training from the master manipulators in how to unsettle opponents. "The story may be nonsense," Short said of the latter claim, while blithely rebroadcasting it to *The Times*, "but it would be absolutely consistent."

Nor was this all. Short and his camp deliberately promoted their man's personal dislike of Kasparov as a factor in the encounter. "I find it hard to pinpoint the exact moment when Nigel Short first began to loathe Gary Kasparov," wrote Dominic Lawson, editor of the *Spectator* and a close friend of Short. He made a pretty good job of it nonetheless, identifying an incident during a tournament in Andalucía in 1991, when Short had played a certain move against Kasparov and the world champion had responded by laughing. The Russian, Lawson revealed, also "glares" at opponents and, according to Nigel, walks up and down in their line of vision "deliberately . . . like a baboon." Not that Short needed his friend as a mouthpiece. He was already on record as calling the champion an "Asiatic despot," complaining that Kasparov "wasn't spanked enough as a child," labeling his seconds "lackeys and slaves" and pugilistically lamenting that when it came to the World Championship final, "I don't want to sink to the level of the animal to beat the animal." At the prematch press conference, Short was asked about his characterization of Kasparov as an "ape." Although the journalist gave him an out by admitting that it was an "old quote," Short replied with schoolboy jauntiness: "Anyone who has seen Kasparov by the swimming-pool will know that he is very hairy." When this drew a chuckle, Short backed up his "old quote" by pointing out that "the Norwegian women's team refer to Kasparov as 'the Rug.'"

But whether calculated or ingenuous, the Englishman's remarks were the equivalent of a wild pawn push. The attack was easily refuted. Kasparov and the KGB? "I think," the champion responded suavely, "I met some KGB officials in my life. I don't think anyone can take seriously the accusations of the English boy who did not live in the Soviet Union." Kasparov as ape? Perhaps those girls round the swimming pool had been more taken with the Russian than with Nigel's "pale English beauty." Kasparov played the urbane ambassador, the imperturbable champion, which made Short's comments seem not just prattish but also an offense against hospitality. If a world champion comes to your country to display his skills, you do not greet him by chortling about his body hair.

Kasparov himself had made only a single prematch verbal strike, just before Short played the Dutchman Jan Timman for the right to challenge for the title. Asked whom he expected to meet, and how he expected the final to go, the champion had replied, "It will be Short, and it will be short." But Kasparov's serious—and scary—response to Nigel's taunts came, quite properly, across the chessboard at the Savoy. Watched closely in the early games, he failed to glower, he failed to smirk at Nigel's moves, failed to pace up and down like a baboon. He behaved impeccably. And at the same time he played cruel and destructive chess.

The first four games of the twenty-four-game match were catastrophic for Short. Setting off for the Strand in a state of rather wan patriotism that first Tuesday in September, I thought, 2–2 after the first four, we'll settle for that. No, we'd be *thrilled* with that. Short is a notoriously bad starter in big matches. So (this was my modest plan) Short should attempt to slow the champion down, blanket him, frustrate him, not let him play the way he wants to. Eight days later, Short had made almost the worst possible beginning, with three losses and a draw. It was bad not just because of the brute score but for various and cumulative reasons. Short lost the first game after running out of time in a frenetic scramble and ignoring the offer of a draw. He drew the second after missing a chance to create a passed pawn, which some said might have given him winning chances. He lost the third despite a furious, flamboyant attack on Kasparov's king. And he lost the fourth despite laying out a lengthy and impressive opening preparation. The preliminary conclusion seemed to be this: that Short was showing he could set Kasparov problems, but the champion was showing he could answer them in style.

The Grandmasters' Analysis Room is located a couple of doors away from the Savoy at Simpson's-in-the-Strand. This is one of those venerable British restaurants where the roast beef arrives in a silver-gilt armored personnel carrier, and a guinea to the carver helps you dodge the gristle. But it is also a place with historic chess associations. During the last century, patzers and pros met upstairs at Simpson's Divan to drink coffee, play chess, and gamble for shillings; here in 1851 Anderssen played his so-called immortal game, a classic of sacrificial attack, against Kieseritzky. This location no longer exists, but a curved brass plaque reading SIMPSON'S DIVAN TAVERN hangs like an armorial shield on the wall of the downstairs smoking bar, now commandeered for grandmasters and their hangers-on. The atmosphere is part senior common room, part sweaty-socks rumpus area. Here, away from the formality and actuality of play, are the basic necessities for following the game: two large display boards flashing out the moves as they happen, a television link with a fixed long shot of the players at work, another set disgorging live commentary on the first hour's play, an array of chessboards on which to thump out possible continuations, power points for databases and the *Official Bulletin* laptop, ashtrays, and a half-price bar. Here also are the luxuries: space to roar and burble, chunter and chatter, rage and wail. A roomful of grandmasters in a state of busy analysis recalls some wildlife clip of lion cubs furiously scuffling. There are snarls and spats and ear-chewing expressions of territoriality; only when the camera pulls back do we realize that the lion and lioness themselves are lolling higher up the hill.

By the end of the third game there were sympathetic murmurings around the Analysis Room about "luck." Short had been "unlucky" to lose on time in Game 1 when a pawn up; "unlucky" to miss that passed-pawn opportunity in Game 2; "unlucky" when Kasparov found himself with a crucial defensive rook in the right place to thwart black's powerful attack in Game 3. Kasparov, not surprisingly, didn't think he'd won the third game for this reason: "I always felt that truth was on my side." Short snorted at this: "It's total nonsense. Chess is not a science." On the other hand, he wasn't going to fall back on "luck" to explain things. "Luck does exist in chess, but that is not the reason for my failure to take my chances. I haven't played well enough, that's all. You make your own luck." My own experience of the vertiginous joys and sorrows of the sixty-four squares has always led me to the conclusion that chess is a luck-free zone, even more luck-free than, say, tennis (where you might get a somnolent line judge, or a bad bounce on a worn court) or pool (where you might get a nasty contact if the cue ball has dirt on it). Surely in chess there is just you, your opponent, the pieces, and—in Kasparovian terms—an examination of the truth of the position. I put the matter to Colin Crouch, a bearded and amiable international master who holds one of the strangest records in the book: playing black in a tournament in London nine years ago, he made the highest-ever number of consecutive checks in a documented game—forty-three in all—as he methodically chugged to victory. Crouch maintains that luck does exist, and of two kinds: the first is when your opponent misses something, or messes up his position to your benefit (though this might seem an imbalance of skill rather than the operation of hazard); and the second is when a position develops of enormous complication, which neither player properly understands or can see the advantage in but which they are nevertheless both obliged to play. Kasparov rather confirms this when he says, in Fred Waitzkin's *Mortal Games,* "People think of chess as a logical game, and yes, there is logic, but at the highest level the logic is often hidden. In some positions where calculation is almost impossible, you are navigating by your imagination and your feelings, playing with your fingers." Even so, when you are in the Land Beyond Analysis, are you not discovering the superiority of one player's imagination, feelings, and fingers, rather than submitting to the mute operation of fortune? Perhaps, at some final level, chess players wish to decline absolute responsibility for all that happens.

Still, however "luck" might be defined and however generously interpreted by chess patriots over the first three games, no one was impertinent enough to reach for this explanation after Game 4. This was the noisiest afternoon so far in the Analysis Room, full of grandmasterly bustle and anticipation. Short had the white pieces for the second time, needed to go for a win, and came out with a lengthy prepared opening. Kasparov, who would have been forgiven for playing quietly with the black pieces, sitting on his lead and inviting Short to do his damnedest, instead responded with the aggressive Poisoned Pawn variation. In this, black accepts the gift of a pawn on the white Queen's Knight file, the disadvantage of which is that his queen gets marginalized and has to spend awhile working its way back to the center of things. White in theory neutralizes the black queen, chivvying it around the board while at the same time developing his own pieces in an attacking formation. Chess games, even at patzer level, are arguments over structure and activity, development and material; in the higher strata, a single interruption to the tempo of your play can be most damaging. This is what Short was doing: yielding up a pawn to speed his own attack.

Then came something even more unexpected: Short offered Kasparov a second pawn for his hungry queen. The assembled grandmasters were puzzled: surely Kasparov wouldn't dare take this pawn as well? It may not be as notoriously poisoned as the first one; even so it must be fairly toxic. But the black queen was boasting an iron stomach that afternoon, and gobbled up the second pawn; whereupon Short drove it back again into its lonely hutch on the inactive side of the board. This time, it seemed even more tied down than before. Kasparov was two pawns up, but Short at move 20 could easily have forced a draw by repetition of moves if he was in any doubt about his advantage in the position.

When the monitor flashed out Short's next move as Rae1, declining the tacit draw, there were whoops and claps around the Analysis Room "He's going for the win—he's turned down the draw!" Better still, "After Nc4 Kasparov will have to sac." Indeed he did, sacrificing rook for knight in order to prevent his queen being trussed up and carried off like a spidered bluebottle. Short pressed on with his attack, while Kasparov seemed merely to give his position a loosening shrug, part readjustment of his defenses, part quiet counterthrust. They reached a point where a Kasparov pawn capture would inevitably provoke an exchange. The champion duly played 27 . . . dxc4, whereupon the room clearly expected Short to recapture a black pawn with his bishop. When he didn't, there was a sweaty, fearful hush. "Look, Nigel's thinking again. That's a very bad sign. He does not look like a man who's going down a route he planned." Nigel thought on. "The body language is looking bad." The Englishman, it later turned out, had miscalculated the result of a long forced exchange and was now obliged to play an inferior move.

From then on, the room watched a fierce demonstration of Kasparov proving a win. Short was reduced to doing what inferior players with crumbling positions are all too familiar with: throwing pieces forward in a Western Front attack on the opponent's king, while acknowledging the probability that you will be machine-gunned to bits before you get to his trenches. "What do I say about that move?" Eric Schiller, American National Master and editor of that day's *Official Bulletin* asked. He paused over his laptop at the main grandmasters' table and waited for advice. "It's crap," one expert replied. "Complete crap," a second added. The mood was gloomy, with that extra tinge of bitterness which comes when the homeboy seems to be letting you down. "Is it crap or complete crap?" Schiller asked, trying to lighten things up. "It's necessary crap," came a third opinion. "Is it crap, complete crap, or necessary crap?" But no one had the heart to respond, and on move 39, just before the time control, Short capitulated. This oral exchange, not surprisingly, didn't make its way into the printed *Bulletin*, although opinion there is not particularly coded. Short's reply to 27 . . . dxc4 is dismissed as "frankly, absurd," while the American grandmaster Patrick Wolff (who had declared a win for Short on move 14 and a win for Kasparov on move 20) announced laconically of Short's position after move 34, "This is a dead parrot."

WHEN YOU EAVESDROP on the chatter of chess, you discover that it reproduces and confirms the game's compelling mixture of violence and intellectuality. As pieces are finger-flipped around demonstration boards in swift refutation of some other grandmaster's naive proposition, half the language has a street-fighting quality to it. You don't just attack a piece, you *hit* it. You don't merely take a piece when you can *chop it off, hack it off,* or *snap it off.* Pawns may advance, but they prefer to *stomp* down the board like storm troopers. Getting your opponent into time trouble, you try to *flag* him; playing a sacrifice, you *sack* a piece, as you might sack a city. And since violent verbs require victims, your opponent's bits of wood are personified into living matter: "I want to hit *this guy* and *this guy.*"

Aggression involves contempt. So an opponent's strategy which seems passive or unadventurous is dismissed as *vegetarian.* (Hitler was a vegetarian, of course, but no matter.) Here is Nigel Short reflecting before the title match on whether to recycle some of the offbeat lines he had played against Karpov: "Kasparov could destroy such openings at the board, and then I'd be fucked. I must play a real man's opening. No quiche.'" Real men don't let themselves be fucked; they fuck. Here are some other Shortian prematch reflections, taken from Dominic Lawson's *The Inner Game*. "I'm going to give it to him good and hard." "I'm going to give the guy a good rogering." "I'm going to give it to him good and hard, right up him." "I want to rape and mate him." Lawson recalls the moment in Barcelona in 1987 when he first heard Short use the acronym *TDF*, which he assumed to be short-hand for some complex tactical ploy. At first he didn't want to confess his chessic ignorance, but after Short and the American grandmaster Yasser Seirawan had used the expression several times, he finally cracked and inquired. "Trap. Dominate. Fuck," the two grandmasters chanted back at him.

Interwoven with all this is a more polysyllabic language of theory and aspiration. A move may be *natural* or *artificial, positional* or *antipositional, intuitive* or *anti-intuitive, thematic* or *dysfunctional*. If its aim is to inhibit the opponent rather than strike menace on its own be-half, it is said to be *prophylactic*. And what are the two players seek-ing? The *truth of the position;* or sometimes, the *absolute truth of the position*. They are struggling to *prove* something; though an outside observer might not *believe in* it. This makes each game a courtroom scene, and a world championship match a Day of Judgment. Another analogy is with the philosophical symposium: as in "The players are *continuing their discussion* of the Bc4 variation of the Najdorf." Thus high ambition combines with low brutality; there seems to be no middle vocabulary developed by the players.

Strategic verbal violence features in life off the board as well. The two terms of abuse I heard most often down among the chessists were *traitor* and *nutter*. Such epithets were widely deployed during the global institutional wrangling that preceded the London match. For decades the world championships had been run by FIDE, the In-ternational Chess Federation, but increasingly there were collisions between this entrenched bureaucracy and volatile egos with high fi-nancial expectations. Relations between FIDE and the top players had deteriorated sharply under the Presidency of Florencio Campo-manes. When I asked one English grandmaster his opinion of Campomanes, he replied that he found him charming, intelligent, and very likable; the only problem was that he should have been running a small Marxist state with a large military budget rather than a sports federation.

The qualifying cycle which produced Nigel Short as Kasparov's challenger was organized as usual by FIDE. They had got as far as awarding the final to Short's home city of Manchester when the two contenders hijacked the match for themselves, setting up their own rival organization, the Professional Chess Association. The PCA showed (partly of necessity) that you can successfully run a major championship with fewer officials and levels of bureaucracy; they introduced some spectator-friendly rules changes (thus, every single game was finished without adjournment); they earned more money for themselves; and they were naturally accused of being traitors. Kasparov had been fighting FIDE for years, while Short didn't like being taken for granted. "FIDE thought I was a little bunny rabbit because I smile a lot and look fairly inoffensive," the Englishman later recalled. "But I'm a bunny rabbit with sharp teeth, and they got bitten."

Long-term audacity plus a principled assertion of the individual's right to sell his services to the highest bidder, or short-term self-interest? No doubt a bit of both. The setting up of the PCA made for good prepublicity; but it also distracted the players in their final preparations. Short, as debutant at this level, was the more likely to suffer from this distraction; he also received the greater abuse of the two. A Manchester dignitary, seeing the match slip away from his city, called Nigel a "breadhead," while the British Chess Federation passed a motion declaring that Short had brought the game into disrepute and berated their most famous player in an oddly lachrymose press release: "You could have been a chess hero, a legend in your lifetime, but not like this." Campomanes meanwhile retaliated by relieving Kasparov of his title, stripping both players of their ELO ratings (the officially computed measure of strength), and setting up a parallel and contemporaneous FIDE world championship. The world of chess had become as fissured as that of boxing, and by the end of the year there would be three world champions: the PCA titleholder, the FIDE titleholder, plus Bobby Fischer, who down the years had continued to argue that since no one had ever beaten him and his title had been illegally removed by FIDE, he was still numero uno.

The PCA, a body so ad hoc that it consisted—and still consists, at the time of writing—only of Short, Kasparov, and Kasparov's lawyer, was formed, in Raymond Keene's oft-repeated words, "to bring chess into the modern world." This meant "giving fans maximum enjoyment and sponsors full value for money," according to one of the Association's rare public statements; it also meant "better-focused marketing." Nigel Short at his opening press conference spoke of the need "to professionalize and commercialize the sport, as has been done in the past with tennis and golf." This sounds fair enough, but there is also a certain amount of humbug in the Association's proclamations. Creeping bureaucratese, too. Try this for size: "The PCA is the first governing body to be cofounded by a world champion and to be vested by him with the ability to further confer the title through competitions organized by it. As a result, the PCA has an organic right to do so not enjoyed by any previous sanctioning body." In playground terms this means: I've got the biggest conker, come and get it, ya ya ya.

PROFESSIONALIZE AND COMMERCIALIZE . . . tennis and golf. This meant, in part, television, and the medium responded with enthusiasm. Channel 4 (as co-backer) put out three transmissions on every match day, and the BBC one. Television close-ups roundly emphasized the physiognomic and gestural differences between the two players: Kasparov fizzingly coiled, scowling, frowning, grimacing, lip scrunching, head scratching, nose pulling, chin rubbing, occasionally slumping down over his crossed paws like a melodramatically puzzled dog; Short more impassive, bland-faced, sharp-elbowed, and stiff-postured, as if he'd forgotten to take the coat hanger out of his jacket. But this repertoire of tics, plus the undifferentiated way of playing the moves (not much room for commentary on the back lift, pickup, or follow-through of the arm) generates few additions to the pantheon of sports images. Experts did their best with junior anthropology interpretations of body language ("Nigel's got his knuckles pressed up to his chin—he's really concentrating") but were too often reduced to valorous attempts to talk up the action. "We're actually seeing two people thinking in public!" enthused the aptly named Mr. Keene at one point. "Thinking incarnate on the TV screen!" The camera did provide one shot that gave a powerful idea of the force field of a chess game: an overhead view of both players straining forward across the board, with only two ranks separating them from a Maori nose rub or, more likely, a head butt. Still, when all is said and done, the basic and constant visuals in television chess are of two seated players pushing wood.

Or, too often for comfort, not pushing it. Channel 4 carried the first hour of each game live, and wandered into quasi-philosophical problems of being and nothingness. What invariably happened was that the players would in the first few minutes rattle out a familiar opening, until one produced a prepared variation from the known line. The player who had been varied against would then settle down for a long and slumberous ponder while the innovator went off and made himself a cup of tea. The high point of such on-air "thinking incarnate" came during Game 9, itself a facsimile of Game 5 in its opening moves. After the first eleven moves had been flicked out in a couple of minutes, Kasparov varied. Short thought. And thought. Commercial break. And thought. And thought. Second commercial break. And thought. Finally, after using up forty-five minutes of live television time, he castled. Tennis and golf? Forget it.

Another reason chess is unlikely to take off (and the support of the ignorant couch potato plus know-nothing stadium clogger are an important financial factor) is the variable charisma of those who play the game. If all players were as intelligent, voluble, and linguistically assured as Gary Kasparov, the game could print its own checkbooks. But the truth is that too many pawn pushers belong to the train-spotter tendency. Anoraks, plastic bags, old sandwiches, and an introverted excitement are some of their characteristics. Television did its chivvying best with the species: two of Channel 4's resident grandmasters were Daniel King, whose shoulder-length hair and colorful shirts looked positively *vie de Bohème* in the context, and the fluent, bankerish figure of Raymond Keene (nicknamed the Penguin for his well-lunched stomach and the rather Antarctic set of his head on his shoulders). The third, however, was the far more compelling—or, if you were a ratings-troubled television channel controller, uncompelling—figure of Jon Speelman.

Speelman is a very strong player indeed, who beat Short in the Candidates' cycle in 1988 and was currently acting as one of the Englishman's seconds. Some, indeed, take the view that Speelman's mazily unfathomable style might have given Kasparov more trouble than Short's more directly aggressive manner; though when I tentatively put this theory to Grandmaster James Plaskett in the bar of the Analysis Room he looked at me as if I had just played some nutter's opening (say, 1h4), and replied, "Gazza beats everyone, doesn't he?" To add my own penn'orth of tribute: I once played Speelman in a charity simultaneous, and he seemed to handle my attacking verve and prepared innovations pretty well, especially given that he was also taking on thirty-nine other opponents at the same time. (To come clean, what happens is this: you sit there trembling at the board, hideously alone, knowing that you are obliged to have your move ready the moment the grandmaster arrives before you. This is fine at the start, when the chance of going humiliatingly wrong is less, and you have some time to ponder as he strolls round the other thirty-nine boards; but as the game goes on, other players drop out, and the position complicates, your tormentor comes whizzing along with ever-increasing frequency. At moments like this you feel the tiniest inkling of what it must be like to be subjected to full-time, high-level pressure from across the board. The other humiliating aspect is the realization that the flurrying figure who gazes briefly at the position, bangs out a move, and flurries on, isn't really playing *you;* he's playing the board. You are not just one-fortieth of his thinking time; you are also merely the equivalent of some practice position set up by one of his trainers to get the sleep out of his eyes.)

But Speelman, for all his great savvy on the board, and the affectionate respect in which he is held, is never going to be the Agassi of the sixty-four squares. His name was once misprinted in *The Times* as Specimen, and the sobriquet is still remembered and apt. Tall, gawky, and shy, with downcast eyes, thick-lensed spectacles, and a circular shrubbery of comb-free hair, Specimen is the ultimate boffin version of the chess player. His other nickname, from the days when he had a wild beard as well, was Speelwolf. There exists rare TV footage of him on the dance floor after a chess Olympiad. Unwinding is what he seems almost literally to be doing: a sort of frenetic, uncoordinated whirling response to all the self-imposed discipline of the previous days. Boadicea with knives on her chariot wheels cleared less space around her than the grandmaster on the dance floor. Despite his regular appearances on television over a period of three months, it would be a fair bet that no clothing chain has subsequently approached him with the suggestion of a sponsoring deal. He is, in brief, a sports marketer's worst nightmare. This is, of course, all to the greater and more serious glory of the sport he takes part in. But the alarming and true presence of Specimen stands like an emblematic bar to the popularizer's dreams.

As Game 5 began, with Short already three clear points down, the bookmakers William Hill were declining to take any more money on Kasparov. Local cheerleaders ransacked the records for examples of bad starts heroically overcome (hadn't Steinitz been 1–4 down in a world championship, the great Fischer 0–2, Smyslov the same ½–3½?). By Game 9, however, Short was five clear points down, and his cause was lost. What the brute statistics failed to reveal was that the chess had been vivid and thrilling, as it would continue to be until almost the very end of the match. Both players favored sharp, open positions, which–apart from anything else–meant that the amateur observer could see much more clearly what was going on. Not all professional observers approved. U.S. Grandmaster Larry Evans was in the Savoy Theatre commentary box during Game 6, and through the earphones you could practically hear his neck crack from incredulous head shaking. "Looks like a position out of Hack Attack in *Kingpin* magazine. It doesn't look like a world championship game. It looks like a coffee-house game." Perhaps, but one thing was certain: there were none of those mean-spirited, glued-up positions of the older Soviet school, in which denial of space was the main ambition, with the eventual intention of a pawn exchange on about move 80, followed by a crafty bishop-for-knight swap on move 170, all leading to a mildly unbalanced opponent and a slight technical advantage on about move 235 of a grinding endgame. None of that: here were glamorous pouncing attacks, and escapes of Keatonesque vertiginousness.

Game 8, a street-fighting draw, was further enlivened by the news that Nigel Short had sacked his coach at the end of the first week's play. Lubomir Kavalek had been paid off after Game 3 and was now back in the States. The surprise was all the greater given the unremitting public praise of "Lubosh" right up to the opening pawn push. He was, we were told, Nigel's secret weapon; he had an unrivaled database of a million games; he was "the Czech who loved beating Russians" (having left Prague in 1968, he had resurfaced four years later in Reykjavik as Fischer's unofficial second). He had coached Short since the start of the Englishman's run at the title and was variously described as his mentor, guru, father figure, and Svengali. The extent of his influence may be judged from this delicate revelation from Cathy Forbes: that Kavalek "also pays attention to the regulation of his charge's bodily functions. After Short has let off steam by playing his guitar before a game, Kavalek will remind him to empty his bladder."

Kavalek was sacked, it later emerged, because he had stopped coming up with new ideas, was enjoying the free hotel life too much, and had become a "depressing influence" according to Short. Though the Short camp tried to make light of the event, with Dominic Lawson talking about Nigel finally getting "the team he wants," the same journalist's subsequent account of Short's anger and dismay is revealing: "Tomorrow I must kill Kasparov. But today I am killing my father. . . . He was my mentor. In the past year I have seen as much of him as I have of my wife. No, in fact I have spent more time with him than I have with Rea. . . . Don't you feel the brutality of this moment? It's parricide." Listening to this plaint, Lawson "began to feel like an extra in *Oedipus Rex*." It is, no doubt, never quite the right moment for parricide, but the timing of Kavalek's departure—and that of his much-lauded database—seemed inept: comforting to the enemy, dispiriting to the home supporters. Besides, who was now reminding Nigel to pee before each game?

BY THE FIRST SATURDAY in October, the match had reached its halfway point, Short had yet to win a game and was still trailing by five clear points. In one sense, the match was dead, and the bookmakers rated a Short victory as improbable an event as proof of the Loch Ness Monster's existence within the next year. Ambitions for Short were readjusted: he was aiming, as a starting point, to register a single victory; he was "learning to play" Kasparov with the longer-term ambition of doing better next time. A far cry from the apprehension that he might have to "sink to the level of the animal to beat the animal." But in terms of excitement things were far from dead, and Short had just had his best week of the match. In Game 10, he built his most powerful attack so far with white, then missed what the *Official Bulletin* called "four absolutely trivial instant wins" and had to settle for a draw. In Game 11, Kasparov cleverly played on the expected demoralization the missed win would have caused: he switched openings to the Scotch, with which he had crushed Short a couple of years ago, and thumped it out as if he knew exactly what he was after. Short's pawn structure soon looked a wreck, with doubled pawns on two files, but Short defended astutely and the game drifted away from white into another draw. (One of the match's revealing subplots concerned Short's readiness to accept doubling of his pawns. This usually traumatizes the amateur, whereas top players see it as usefully creating an open file.) Game 12 went in a sharp blast from opening to endgame, leaving a position that to the chess duffer looked awful for Short: he had a bishop for three pawns, but whereas his own three pawns on the queenside were blockaded by two of Kasparov's, the champion had four passed and interconnected pawns on the kingside, which looked all set to pile down the board like space invaders. Still, International Master Crouch at my elbow called a draw; duffers shouldn't underestimate the power of a sole bishop or the defensive usefulness of a mobile king. Short got his third half point of the week.

That afternoon the Analysis Room was bustling: grandmasters, hangers-on, journalists, drinkers, wives and children, traitors and nutters. Rea Short and Kyveli were in evidence; while Stephen Fry, the chessoholic actor, wandered in to unleash his own bit of literary home preparation about Short's plight (*Antony and Cleopatra* II.iii, Soothsayer to Antony: "If thou dost play with him at any game/ Thou art sure to lose, and, of that natural luck/He beats thee 'gainst the odds.") The atmosphere should have been genial, but there was a distinct edge of rattiness. The grandmasters' table was, as always, voluble, opinionated, and largely pro-Short. But those around it were also watching something which they themselves would certainly never achieve: a challenge for the world title. And, given that chess is a game of extreme competitiveness, a further edge may develop toward the person who is there instead of you—namely Nigel Short. Patriotism (or support for the underdog, or politeness to one's hosts) can therefore give way to "Christ, what did he do *that* for?" When Short blocked a long diagonal bishop attack with a knight, a roar of disbelief went up from the table; but in fact it proved the start of a solid defense. Throughout the match, experts, whether on television, over headphones at the Savoy, or in the Analysis Room, constantly mispredicted the two players' next moves. Only a few were prepared to say, "I don't understand what's going on," or, "We'll only know when we get the players' analysis of the position." But to those in the grandmasters' circle, tapping into their databases, flicking out possible continuations and then taking them back, freed from the stress of actual play, shuttling to the bar for drinks, fizzing with rivalry yet safe from the highest rivalry two doors away, there was often an exaggerated certainty about what was going on. "Well, there's *this*," snapped Tony Miles (the first-ever British grandmaster), bossing a couple of pawns around, "but it's a bailout." Not a bailout that was followed by Nigel Short, as it happened. At times I was reminded of a remark by the writer Clive James, who had once provided captions to a set of photographs in the *Observer* magazine. A helpful subeditor generously restyled them for him, accentuating the wit and taking out the longueurs. "Listen," James cruelly explained to the sub while making him restore the original text, "if I wrote like that, I'd be *you*."

Miles was one of those who were consistently severe on Short's play: "He's out of his depth. Having said that, most people would be against Kasparov." This is true: Kasparov was slaughtering Short. On the other hand, Short used to slaughter Miles. And Miles (a "traitor" for having apparently offered his services to Kasparov) would slaughter Dominic Lawson. And Lawson (a "nutter" according to one whispering international master) would doubtless slaughter me. Late in the twelfth game, I was pondering Short's position with another frowning patzer when Raymond Keene wandered past. "What do you think of this?" I asked, indicating a rook advance which seemed to me to lock up white's defenses and also offer sharp countereattacking chances: a move, I lightly fancied to myself, almost Shortesque in conception. "Disastrous," commented the Penguin, and waddled away. This remark stung for, oh, roughly a month or so, and the pain was only transformed into a guffaw during Game 18. Keene was commenting alongside Speelman on Channel Four and proposed a certain rook move. Speelman, who as Short's second was understandably inclined to diplomatic circumspection, replied, "Well, I think if Nigel plays it, I'll fall off my chair instantaneously."

In Game 13 violence was expected. Kasparov considers thirteen to be his lucky number—he was born on the thirteenth, achieved his grandmaster rating on the thirteenth, and is the thirteenth world champion. Gary, the whisper went, would really be going for it today with the white pieces: he'd want to put behind him the three-draw week and start the second half of the match with an explosion. Nigel had zilch chance of winning: he'd lost four games out of six with black, and you had to go back two years to find the last occasion Kasparov was beaten playing white. But there was no explosion. Kasparov looked weary, Short fresh, and they ground out a solid, dull, professional draw. This disappointed some but pleased others. "They're playing world championship chess now," said one international master.

There were good extraneous reasons for both players to be comparatively docile. Between the twelfth and thirteenth games, the attempted coup against Yeltsin had taken place; Kasparov had to sit and watch tanks blast his parliament building. "Frankly speaking," he admitted, "I spent more time looking at CNN than at the chess books." Short's worries were more parochial. While Kasparov contemplated the future of democracy in Russia, the Englishman consulted libel lawyers over a *Sunday Times* article alleging that he was "near to collapse," that there were "deep divisions" in his camp, and that after the departure of Kavalek, Dominic Lawson was exercising "too much influence." Most insultingly, if not most libelously, Short, hitherto compared to David taking on Goliath, was now held to resemble Eddie "the Eagle" Edwards, a British ski jumper who became a comic national mascot by cheerily finishing last—and usually a very long way last—in various major competitions up to and including the Winter Olympics.

Short's reaction had its ironic side. Here was someone who had breezily trashed the moral character, political integrity, and physical appearance of the world champion coming on all sensitive and writ-happy when offered a forkful of rough abuse himself. More to the point, he was finding out a little of the cost of "professionalizing and commercializing" the game, of putting it up there with tennis and golf. Marketing a sport involves changing it to suit the people who pay the bills. Marketing means making your sport more accessible to people who are only half-interested in it, and thus coarsening either it or the process by which it is described, or both. Marketing means getting written about by people who understand your sport even less than those who normally write about it do. Marketing means playing up inherent nationalism and chauvinism: witness Corey Pavin wearing a Desert Storm cap during the Ryder Cup. Marketing means betraying the subtlety of your sport, and the subtlety of human character; it means Heroes and Villains, and pratting around in black leather for the cameras. It means extravagant praise leading to extravagant blame: the tall-poppy syndrome, as it's known in Australia. Marketing can mean earning a lot more money, and marketing surely and finally means, unless you are very lucky, getting dumped on. The comparison between Nigel Short and Eddie "the Eagle" Edwards is, apart from anything else, severely inaccurate: Short–to take the Olympic analogy–was already assured of the silver medal when he met Kasparov. But you can't expect to be written about with fastidious accuracy once you "professionalize and commercialize" your sport. There had been an early warning of what might come when Short and Kasparov opened the bids for their match at Simpson's-in-the-Strand. The Englishman sat his daughter, Kyveli, on his lap. A harmless and unprovoking gesture, you might think, but one publicly derided by Dutch grandmaster Hans Ree as "Saddam Hussein–like." Short for once had the lightness of touch to respond: "It's a long time since I invaded Kuwait." Some might think being compared to Saddam *and* Eddie the Eagle is a bit tough. But that's marketing.

BETWEEN THE FOURTEENTH and fifteenth games, I lunched some observations out of the international master William Hartston. He had been at school with me back in the days when chess was a very amateur business in this country, and the notion of a British grandmaster was as speculative as the yeti. At our school, there were two reliable ways of getting out of the playground rain at lunchtime. The uncompetitive joined the stamp club, the competitive the chess club. (I joined the stamp club.) Thereafter I followed Hartston's progress from a distance: top board for England, chess correspondent of *The Independent*, resident BBC chess sage. The last time I had seen him he had arranged to have me slaughtered in a charity simultaneous by a fourteen-year-old (*much* more soul liquefying than being slaughtered by Speelman).

Hartston has a positive lifetime score against Nigel Short of 2–1, though he admits that both victories came before Nigel started shaving. As an industrial psychologist, he tends to take a broader and more amused view of proceedings, thereby attracting the "traitor" rather than "nutter" label. For instance, he was skeptical of the new official line about Short: that since he was not going to stage a miracle recovery, he was now "learning to play" Kasparov for the next time round. In Hartston's opinion, there won't be a next time: "If you put Short back into the ratings, he would be ninth, with five younger players above him."

This assumes that the Professional Chess Association will still be there next time round. Hartston was not as dismissive as I had expected about the marketing possibilities of chess. . . . But tennis and golf? Why not, he replied. He reckons that the players are just as promotable as golfers, and points out that the last game of the 1987 Karpov–Kasparov match in Seville drew an astonishing live television audience of 18 million Spaniards. When I asked him to assess the chances of other grandmasters abandoning FIDE and throwing in their lot with the Professional Chess Association, he replied, with a sort of benign cynicism, "The way to a chess player's heart is through his wallet." This doesn't, of course, make chess players much different from anybody else; indeed, in their case the cardio-economic link is all the more understandable. The very best players have always been able to make a living, but in few other professions (except perhaps poetry) does the earnings graph go so suddenly into free fall when set against the graph of ability. International Master Colin Crouch, who is around number 30 in the country, took nine days off from the Short–Kasparov match to play a tournament in the Isle of Man. The top prize was a mere £600, and despite a bright start Crouch came home with only his expenses. This is the reality of even a strong player's life: small tournaments, small money, local fame. A couple of years ago, Hartston did the following calculation during a grandmaster tournament in Spain: assuming that all the prize money on offer was divided simply between the grandmasters (and there were some powerful IMs scrapping for the loot as well), their average earnings worked out at between £2 and £3 an hour. The basic rate for the female industrial mushroom pickers in the North of England who demonstrated outside last year's Booker Prize ceremony was £3.74p an hour.

Hartston certainly thinks that the pursuit of money and the PCA politicking were serious distractions to Short's first-time title challenge. Indeed, he goes further, believing (as does Cathy Forbes) that at some level Short recognized he wasn't going to beat Kasparov and therefore put his energy into getting the best possible payday that he could. In Hartston's view, this fundamental self-disbelief had also leached into the Englishman's play: "I get the feeling that Short is trying to prove to himself that he isn't afraid of Kasparov—*but he is*." Hartston admires what he calls Short's "classical, correct chess style," and praised his tactics against Karpov, when he varied his openings in such a way as to provoke damagingly long periods of reflection in that Russian. This is a fundamental part of successful match play. "The history of the world chess championship," Hartston maintains, "shows that the way to beat a great player is to allow him to indulge his strengths in unfavorable circumstances." This is what Botvinnik famously did against Tal in 1960. I asked Hartston what strength-cum-weakness Short might play on against Kasparov, and he replied, "Impatience."

WITH APT TIMING, Game 15 arrived to annotate this theme. Short, with the black pieces for the eighth time, played the queen's gambit declined—a solid, traditional defense which he knew well and had used in all his candidate's matches but had not so far offered to Kasparov. Observing the opening moves, the international master Malcolm Pein praised "a sound, sensible Nigel Short not trying to strangle Gary Kasparov from the beginning." David Norwood, Hartston's co-commentator in the BBC studio and fellow critic of Short's Panzerism, enthused over what he saw as "normal chess." When the anchorman muttered that nothing much seemed to be happening, Norwood patiently explained that "normal chess is about fighting over half-squares." Hartston agreed: the game would turn, ultimately, on whether white's two central pawns were weak or strong, but the truth of the position would not be swiftly yielded up. Indeed it wasn't: Kasparov wheeled and probed, Short adjusted and secured. Kasparov had the choice—the eventual choice—of attacking either kingside or queenside; black's job was to stay patient, shore up the seawall, and wait to find out from which direction the waves would break. Short seemed to do this admirably: there were none of the wide open spaces and forced piece trading of earlier games. Then, fascinatingly, the game developed as "normal chess" sometimes does: that is to say, a rather closed, quiescent position, with no material gains and only a half-square or so advantage to either side, opens up into a thrilling, charging attack. The answer to Hartston's question as to whether white's central pawns were strong or weak was disclosed: they were strong, not least because they belonged to Kasparov. In ten brutal moves, the world champion jimmied his way into Short's position and ripped the place to bits. Short had not gone on a rash strangling trip, and Kasparov had been obliged to wait a long time for the right moment. Yet he had shown no signs of self-destructive "impatience." On the contrary, he had displayed exemplary patience, then perfectly calculated aggression.

Subsequent analysis of Game 15 showed, not surprisingly, that the above description is too neat, too thematic. Kasparov may have jimmied open Short's front door, but the householder had lifted the latch himself. Moments like this—when subsequent analysis acts like gravy thickener on the game you thought you knew—are part of chess's fascination. If you watch a video of an old Wimbledon final or Ryder Cup match, you aren't really reanalyzing; you are merely reminding yourself of what happened and suffusing yourself again with the emotions provoked by the original events. But a chess game, after it has happened, continues in organic life, changing and growing as it is examined. In Game 6, for instance, when Short opted for what he called "the most violent method of smashing Kasparov's defenses," sacrificing a bishop on move 26, it was generally thought that he had "missed a win." Analysis of the game continued, however, and by the time the players were hunched over Game 15 a defense to Qh7 had been found which would have given Kasparov a draw. On the other hand, at the time of playing no one had seen this possible defense, so in a sense it didn't exist. This is one of the aspects of chess that gives it a sense of high and oscillating peril: the tension between objectivity and subjectivity, between some coldly ascertainable, finally provable "truth of the position" and the clammy-handed actuality of play, with half a dozen different half-truths running through your head while the clock ticks, while the footlights and your opponent glare.

Eventually, some final truth about a position may emerge, months or years down the track, with the help of outside analysts and subsequent world champions. The immediate postmortems, while appearing to start this process, may in fact work more as a continuation of the struggle on the board, and thus be more psychologically freighted. What normally happens when a game finishes is that the players discuss between themselves the final position and the key moves that led to it. This is not just from sadistic or masochistic interest but also from lucid need. (Kasparov used to do this after games with Karpov, even though he loathed and despised him. "I am talking chess with the number two in the world," he explained. "I wouldn't go to a restaurant with him, but who else can I really talk to about these games? Spassky?") Such analysis continued for television and the press, with Short showing himself at his best: straight, rueful, likable, self-critical, still fretting about the truth of the position. Kasparov, by contrast, the supreme strategist and consummate psychological bruiser, seemed to treat the follow-up discussion as part of the match. Avuncular, dismissive, unfretted, he played the wise don to Nigel's anxious student. Yes, on the one hand there was this, this, and this; but then I have that, and maybe that, and then that; and if Rb8, then Nc5; and of course that move of Nigel's was a big blunder, so really I think the position is equal; perhaps I even have the better chances. Kasparov's analyses often seemed craftily to diminish Short's (and everybody else's) assessment of what had happened. "Nigel's problem was hesitation," Kasparov announced in a lordly way after the debacle of Game 4. "He has big psychological problems, and I am curious to see how he deals with them." After Game 15, Kasparov commented that Short's use of the queen's gambit declined "wasn't a very good choice by him" since it led to the sort of positions with which the champion was thoroughly familiar. "It wasn't that difficult," he summed up. "Probably the cleanest game of the match." Clean as in clean kill, that is.

ARRIVING FOR THE SIXTEENTH game, with Kasparov six points clear and needing only three draws to retain his title, I ran into one of the rumpus room's senior figures, Professor Nathan Divinsky. Benign and epigrammatic, he is President of the Canadian Chess Federation (and, among other achievements, was once married to Canada's prime minister Kim Campbell). I observed that the match might be over that week.

"It's been over for six weeks," he responded.

What about the idea that after the match was settled they might play a few exhibition games for fun?

"It's been an exhibition game since the beginning." As a transatlantic observer sitting day after day at the grandmasters' table, Divinsky confessed himself disappointed with the narrowly partisan attitude of the local analysts, with their "Nigel-this, Nigel-that" approach to the match. Here, after all, was a rare and privileged opportunity to watch in action the strongest player in the history of the game: "When Nijinsky danced, they didn't care who the ballerina was." He cited a knight move in Game 15 (21 Nf4), which Kasparov had identified as the key moment, but which the boys at the round table hadn't heeded. As general corroboration of this British insularity, Divinsky pointed out a news story in that morning's *Times*. An Englishman had just been awarded the Nobel Prize jointly with an American. The paper had printed the Englishman's photo, described his career, interviewed his gerbil—and not even mentioned the American's name.

The charge sticks (though British insularity is perhaps no stronger than, say, French chauvinism or American isolationism—each nation earns its own abstract noun). In defense, I could only plead the extreme rarity of a local challenge reaching this ultimate stage, and the deleterious effects of hype. Later, another explanation occurs. If you are a top player, one who in all likelihood has played against Short, it's probably not too difficult to imagine yourself in his position, challenging for the title, trying to assess the correct response to Kasparov's tormenting strategies. It's much harder—perhaps impossible—to put yourself into the champion's mind. The round table and the assembled commentators were frequently baffled by Gazza's ideas, awed by his chess brain. Two remarks from the Savoy Theatre commentary team that afternoon stressed the difference. The first was a reference to "Nigel's habit of having big thinks and then playing the natural move" (which on this occasion he duly did). The second was an honest and exasperated complaint about Kasparov: "It's depressing, he sees instantly more than we see in a quarter of an hour."

However, Game 16, to everyone's great surprise, turned out to be the moment of cheer for the Nigel-this, Nigel-that brigade. For once the ballerina jumped higher than Nijinsky. Even more surprising were the circumstances of the leap. Short had white, and played one of his least attacking games against Kasparov's habitual Sicilian. (It later emerged that the challenger had a cold and didn't feel up to more than a *piano* approach.) After eighteen or twenty moves, the Analysis Room was calling it as dull as it was equal: Speelman wandered past the board I was sitting at with Colin Crouch, whacked a few pieces about and declared the position moribund. For a change of scenery in the most tedious game so far, I went off to the Savoy. As I settled in, Short was offering an exchange of queens, and the headphones were groaning: "Oh, Nigel, that's *such* an unambitious move."

In the commentators' box a bored, end-of-term facetiousness reigned. Cathy Forbes began speculating on Short's awkward body position, wondering if it was because no one had told him to pee before the game. We were all waiting for queens to come off and glutinous drawdom to arrive. Short later gave two slightly different explanations of why this didn't happen. At his press conference, he said, "I was a little bit too ashamed to offer a draw and I think he was too ashamed, too." Later, he suggested, "I was too lazy to offer a draw and so was he." Given that the match had virtually been decided, and the two players were now business partners popularizing a sport, shame was the likelier motive. And there was also perhaps a familiar unspoken subtext as the rival queens stared at each other in a proposed suicide pact. Go on, *you* offer the draw. No, *you* offer it. After you, Claude. No, after you, Cecil. *I'm* not taking the blame. Well, you're six points down, it's up to you to do something. Kasparov appeared to be playing simply to stay equal, at one point rather futilely retreating his bishop to a8 rather than proffer a whisper of an attack. The commentary team interpreted Ba8 like this: " 'I'm not going to offer a draw, English swine'—that's what that move says."

The tournament director at Linares seeks to discourage quick, crowd-displeasing draws by making contestants play at least as far as the forty-move time control. One effect of this is that seemingly drawn positions may come to life again, like some bonfire you think you have terminally damped down by piling on a mound of sodden leaves. All of a sudden there is a thin spiral of smoke, and then, before you know it, a warning crackle. This is what happened in Game 16. Short called off the queen swap and fiddled around with a queenside knight, while Kasparov put his own queen imperiously in the center of the board. Things began to stir, not just on the queenside but also on the kingside *and* in the center. In just a few moves, a great woof of flame went through Kasparov's position, leaving it gutted. The champion shook hands, declined any on-board postmortem, and stalked off. It was his first defeat in eighteen months. Short acknowledged applause fit for a diva with an unoperatic, soft, semiclenched fist (oddly, or Englishly, a very similar salute to that of Glenda Jackson on being elected an MP), then disappeared. This being a theater, the audience worked to exact a second curtain call; but chess has not yet gone that thespian.

Afterward, at his victory press conference, Short was engagingly modest and thoughtful, keeping his result in perspective. What had been his strongest move? "I thought I played the middle game quite well." (This is the diminishing British-English "quite.") He admitted to having been "rather shaken" by his loss in the previous game and so "didn't want to do anything drastic." He acknowledged that after a seven-year gap he had almost "forgotten what it was like to beat Kasparov," and gently contrasted his own style with that of Karpov, who tended to play "like a vegetarian against the Sicilian." The visceral response to victory was time-delayed. Dominic Lawson later described Nigel's touching behavior over the dinner table that night: "He jumped up repeatedly from the table, almost between mouthfuls, and clenched his fists together in front of his chest, like a footballer after scoring a goal. 'Wurgh! Wurgh!'"

After this brief interruption to normal service, Kasparov drew the next four games without much inconvenience, to come out the winner by 12½–7½. Asked which was his favorite game, Kasparov replied,

"I don't know, because unfortunately I made mistakes in every game." This may be read as an indication either of modesty or of arrogance, or as an early strike at whoever emerges as his next contender. But beyond this, it reminds us that the best chess contains a striving not just for victory but for something beyond: for an ideal, harmonious state that produces a perfect mixture of creativity, beauty, and power. So it's not surprising if God comes into the chess player's equation at some point, even if only as a linguistic reference. "I'm looking for the best move. I'm not playing against Karpov, I'm playing against God," Kasparov said during his 1990 world-title match. Nigel Short, after winning *his* eighth game against Karpov, was even more hubristic: "I played like God."

However, the Englishman's relationship to the Almighty is not just one of emulation but also (as befits a prospective Tory MP) one of negotiation. Cathy Forbes has revealed that part of Short's buildup to important games was "to visit churches, even though he is an atheist." An odd habit, which seemed even odder when Short explained it during his match against Karpov in Linares: "At first I said, 'Please God let me win this game,' but I realized this was asking too much. So instead I asked, 'Please God give me the strength to beat this shithead.'" In the course of his subsequent match with Timman, Short elaborated on his atheistic prayers. Yes, he was an unbeliever, he admitted, but "I am also an opportunist." We shouldn't be too hard on him for this—it is only a rougher version of the Pascalian bet as to God's existence. After his sole and splendid victory in Game 16, amid a flurry of proper questions ("But what if f5 b6 cxd4 Nd8 Bc2 then can't he get a draw by perpetual check?" and the like), I asked Short if he had continued his churchgoing habit during the final. He gave the sort of strangulated, glottal pause that tends to precede his answers to nonchess questions, and replied, "No." But he had done so in earlier rounds? Short looked a little puzzled, as if some nutter had infiltrated the press corps and in his moment of incandescence was calling him a traitor to the Almighty. "Perhaps I should," he added politely.

Perhaps he should. Losing at sport releases a swarm of if-onlys, among which God is (as always) the most elusive. If only Short had saved a few more seconds on his clock in the opening game and/or accepted Kasparov's offer of a draw. If only there hadn't been that upsetting ruckus with his coach, which also led to the loss of his database. If only he'd clinched Game 10 when even a blindfold patzer might have secured it. If only he'd been able to hold his score with black to a reasonable percentage. If only he'd had a cold more often, as he did when winning Game 16. All of which boils down to the main, the cruelest if-only: if only he hadn't been playing the strongest, the most competitive, the most undermining, the most carnivorous chess player in the world. What happened to Nigel Short during his autumn season at the Savoy Theatre can best be left in his own words: trapped, dominated, fucked.

December 1993

> *Short's game has not yet recovered from this defeat: in the next world championship cycle, he was routed 5½–1½ by Gata Kamsky. Grandmaster Daniel King subsequently appeared in double-page adverts for the Audi A6: "Neither moves without thinking." But whereas a mere chess grandmaster "takes several minutes thinking of his next move, the Audi A6 takes just 0.006 seconds."*

■ 13 ■

Five Years of the Fatwa

*L*ast month, I took part in a fund-raiser for a cash-strapped Oxford college: two poets, two prose writers, and two musicians were the evening's entertainment. The six of us filed into the hall and sat unidentifiably in the front row. The organizer began by apologizing for the fact that my advertised fellow novelist was at the last minute unavoidably unable to make it (he had unavoidably gone skiing, but the fictioneers' freemasonry does not permit me to finger him). Instead, she announced, his place had been taken at short notice by Salman Rushdie. There was, at that point, an example of speaking applause. It wasn't cheerleader stuff (this was England), or even the standing ovation he frequently receives (this was Oxford). It was considered, thoughtful applause, extensive but not self-congratulatory. It simply said: Yes, good, and we are on your side; keep going.

Rushdie has kept going. On February 14, he celebrates the fifth anniversary of the Ayatollah Khomeini's *fatwa*. The verb in that sentence may seem uneasy, but it fits. It is a matter for celebration that he has survived five years with a million-dollar price on his head; equally, he has survived vilification, demonization, burning in effigy, attacks from a vengeful clerisy abroad, and shameful denunciations from fellow Britons at home. Better, he has continued to exist as a writer, and has been able to inject sporadic normality into his life. He has lost a little hair, put on a little weight, started to suffer from asthma, but is impressively much the same character who, five years ago, was setting off for the memorial service of his friend Bruce Chatwin when news came through from Teheran of his own planned funeral. The fortitude, intelligence, imagination, and humor that took him into trouble in the first place have helped sustain him so far. And at the political level there are now, perhaps for the first time, mild grounds for optimism: the inactivity and glacial indifference of the Bush and Thatcher administrations have been replaced by the comparatively more sympathetic presences of Clinton and Major.

On November 24, 1993, Rushdie met President Clinton at the White House for a few minutes. It was a rare historic moment: Presidents on the whole tend not to entertain foreign nationals condemned to death by the ecclesiastical authorities of yet a third country. Clinton's brief political blessing (which came in the context of Rushdie's hour-long meeting with Secretary of State Warren Christopher and others) was the culminating point of a two-year profile-raising campaign organized by the London-based International Rushdie Defence Committee. It also emblematically returned the case to the widest political arena, which is where it had begun. For this was never just a story of an elderly cleric's venture into literary criticism, or one in which America might intervene at some late stage as untainted peace broker. It has been universal business from the start, and Americans, in case they have forgotten, are World Devourers. Here are a few extracts from the Ayatollah Khomeini's follow-up speech of 3 Esfand 1367, or February 22, 1989:

> The issue of the book *The Satanic Verses* is that it is a calculated move aimed at rooting out religion and religiousness, aimed above all at Islam and its clergy. Certainly, if the World Devourers could, they would have burnt out the roots and the title of the clergy. But God has always been the guardian

of this sacred torch and, God willing, he will continue to be so—on condition that we recognize the tricks, ploys, and deceptions of the World Devourers. . . .

The issue for them [the Western powers] is not that of defending an individual, the issue for them is to support an anti-Islamic current, masterminded by those institutions—belonging to Zionism, Britain, and the USA—which, through their ignorance and haste, have placed themselves against the Islamic world. . . .

God wanted this blasphemous book, *The Satanic Verses*, to be published now, so that the world of conceit, of arrogance, and of barbarism, would bare its true face in its long-held enmity to Islam; to bring us out of our simplicity and to prevent us from attributing everything just to blunder, bad management, and lack of experience; to realize fully that this issue is not our mistake, but part of the effort of the World Devourers to annihilate Islam and Muslims. Otherwise, the issue of Salman Rushdie would not be so important to them as to put the whole of Zionism and arrogance behind it.

If the Rushdie case were a fiction, how would we judge it? Dark, melodramatic, remorseless, and distinctly lacking in jokes—though Vice President Quayle's venture into the world of Edmund Wilson and Lionel Trilling was a fine conceit. We should vote the story unput-downable; but we should also, if we prefer traditional narrative, complain about all the postmodern loops and digressions we have had to put up with. British readers have been particularly thrown by this, and over the past five years have often seemed to lose concentration on the central story. Elsewhere in the West, the main themes have always been clear: freedom of expression, and religious (or state) terrorism. In Britain, there have been too many subplots for the local taste: minority communities, their rights, vulnerability, and leadership; electoral votes, and MPs' fear of losing their seats; trade, and the potential loss of overseas customers; racism and antiracism; the intelligentsia's lack of political muscle; victim blaming (disguised as the academic thesis "Hero or Antihero?"); plus, finally, the eternal national quest for a quiet time. Every so often over the last five years, as the story has swirled and shimmied like a dust storm, the British reader has been obliged to give the head a good shake and say: Hang on—do you mind if we go back to the beginning? Can we go back to the single vicious plot hook: the idea that a man, a British subject, may publish a novel here in full freedom, committing no vestige of offense under British law, and yet be obliged to go into hiding, protected round the clock by the Special Branch, as the result of an extraterritorial decree of assassination from a far country? Can we get back to that, please?

And when we do, when we now flip to the start of the story, what seems astounding is the lack of outrage in government circles at this historically unparalleled event. When the *fatwa* was announced, the Foreign Office summoned the Iranian chargé d'affaires, had him pointedly received by "only an under-secretary," and told him that the death sentence was "totally unacceptable." As the columnist Simon Jenkins, no parlor pinko, wrote at the time, "I gather this is fairly strong stuff, well up on the Richter scale from 'regret' and leaving 'concern' far behind. Concern, you may recall, was what the Foreign Office said we felt about the Iraqis gassing the Kurds." Outrage was conceded to the Iranians from the beginning; so was principle.

The official British attitude was almost entirely reactive; and that reaction one of conciliatory passivity. Here, for instance, is the sheepish Foreign Secretary of the time, Geoffrey Howe, groveling on the BBC World Service: "I do emphasize that we are not upholding the right of freedom to speak because we like the book, because we agree with the book. The British Government, the British people, don't have any affection for the book. The book is extremely critical, rude about us. It compares Britain with Hitler's Germany." It doesn't, of course, do any such thing, and when I talked to Rushdie after the Oxford reading, he reckoned he might have a nice day out in the libel courts over that last remark, if he didn't have troubles enough already. Still, what sticks in the throat more is those words "the British Government, the British people." I can remember no referendum or even opinion poll on the literary merits of *The Satanic Verses* in early 1989, though it had by this time won the Whitbread Prize for the best novel of the year and been short-listed for the Booker Prize.

Geoffrey Howe went to Brussels shortly after the *fatwa* was issued for a meeting with his European colleagues, and was surprised to find himself briefly kicked into a semi-nonspineless stance. Britain, "diplomatic sources" admitted afterward, was unprepared for the zeal of France and West Germany in the matter, and Howe found himself carried along by a "spontaneous upsurge of feeling that something tough had to be agreed." This "something tough" was the recall of EC ambassadors from Teheran and the expulsion of the Iranian chargé d'affaires in London. Thereafter, for the next four years, official Britain lay like a sleeping hog in the sun, heedless of the potatoes regularly being thrown at it. There was the death sentence and the bounty; the frequent endorsing of the sentence; the raising of the bounty; the grotesque addition of expenses to go with the bounty (imagine the finance-department quibbles back in Eşfahān: "*Five* nights at the Dorchester? *Three* rocket launchers?"); the sight and sound of domestic Muslim leaders inciting Rushdie's murder; the own goal of a terrorist who sat on his bomb in a Paddington hotel; the deportation of Iranian students suspected of plotting murder; the expulsion of Iranian Embassy employees on the same ground; the diplomatic halting of the trial of an Iranian for arson and firebombing despite evidence the judge called "formidable"; and finally, almost comically, the 3,600 percent increase in the cost of a visa for a British citizen to enter Iran. In the last five years, diplomatic relations between the two countries have been officially broken off and officially restored—broken off by the Iranians, restored by the British.

Britain is a medium-ranked trading nation with memories of great wealth and a fear of future poverty: the latest European Commission survey placed us eighth among the twelve members of the Union in terms of average gross domestic product per capita (ahead of only Spain, Ireland, Portugal, and Greece). We also used to have a reputation as a libertarian haven: Voltaire and Zola each took refuge here when things were hotting up for them in France. But perhaps principles go best with either being rich or being poor. It would, of course, be extremely embarrassing to the British Government if Rushdie were assassinated; and he was awarded immediate Special Branch protection. But, beyond this, for the first four of the last five years the Government snoozed. They did initially have one very good excuse, or at least something that could be played as an excuse: the fact that there were British hostages in Lebanon. The Iranians themselves never made any official linkage between the two cases (and, had they wanted to, it wouldn't have been difficult to think one up: hand over Rushdie or we'll have the hostages topped). But this didn't affect the argument: it was nod-and-wink time, and if-you-knew-what-we-knew. Rushdie was told to pipe down: don't rock the boat or you might kill Terry Waite. This blackmail, or wise diplomatic inducement, worked: for instance, a planned mass vigil at Westminster's Central Hall on the thousandth day of the *fatwa* was deemed potentially provocative by the Foreign Office and forcibly dwindled into a bookshop reading. As Rushdie himself put it: "Until the day Terry Waite was released, I was a sort of hostage to the hostages." Then, one fine day, the last of the captives was free. So, presumably, I asked Rushdie, it was at this point that the Foreign Office approached you with thanks and fresh plans? "No, we approached them." "But did you," I pressed pedantically, "give them time to approach you?" "Well, yes," he replied, with a still disbelieving chuckle. "I mean, they knew where I was."

And so it has continued. There has been one major and continuing success to the story, and it is one that Rushdie, not surprisingly, appreciates: "What the British have had to do is the bottom line–which is keep me alive. The security forces around the world are really impressed by what the British security forces have done. The Americans said, 'We couldn't have done it.'" But more often the latest plot wrinkle has tended to be dismaying. Last September, for instance, it emerged that British Airways had banned Rushdie from all its flights, arguing, inter alia, that staff would walk off any plane he walked onto. Unfortunately for the airline, Rushdie had managed to evade the ban on one occasion, flying BA from Paris to London: the staff, far from walking off, asked him for his autograph. British Airways happily—indeed, proudly—flies politicians and royals with a similarly high level of threat against them. And what is the Government's position in all this? According to Rushdie, the Government has on three occasions asked its national carrier to fly this particular endangered citizen, and on three occasions BA has refused. A government that can't even get tough with its own airline is hardly likely to make Teheran break into a sweat.

Novels often torment us with if-onlies, and the Rushdie affair constantly invites us to consider alternative narratives. It might seem, at first assessment, one of Rushdie's extra misfortunes that his five years of internal exile have been spent with a Conservative government in charge And, in a sense, vice versa: for what could be less appealing to the average Thatcherite MP as a test of your principles than a brown-skinned left-wing novelist who in an essay at the time of the 1983 election had described the beloved leader as "unusually cruel, incompetent, unscrupulous and violent," and the nation as "nanny-Britain, straight-laced Victoria-reborn Britain, class-ridden know-your-place Britain, thin-lipped, jingoist Britain"? What's more, didn't he in the very damn book that was causing such a hoo-ha down among the natives refer to the PM as "Mrs. Torture"? (He didn't, actually: he had a satirized Thatcherite briefly and affectionately so refer to her; but that, of course, is being literary.) Pity the poor Tory MP faced with such a hard case—though pity Rushdie more for having to plead his cause before Tory torpor.

Yet the hypothesis, the alternative narrative, that suggests he might have done better with the Labour Party in power is unconvincing. Though historically more libertarian and arts-favoring than the Tories, Labour hardly fell over itself to support one of its well-known supporters. The Party's former leader Michael Foot (one of the Booker Prize judges who had short-listed *The Satanic Verses*) was a staunch public advocate, but his two successors, Neil Kinnock and John Smith, have been more than ultracautious. Kinnock was hindered by the fact that his chief home and foreign-affairs spokesmen, Roy Hattersley and Gerald Kaufman, seemed keen to cause the Government the least possible embarrassment on this issue. Hattersley, then Deputy Leader, is a sort of novelist himself (he writes chubby sagas full of characters called Hattersley), and took the twin line that Rushdie had the right to publish his novel but ought to suppress the paperback: some might spot a plump contradiction slopping around in there. Two Labour MPs called for withdrawal of the book, arguing that Labour "ambivalence" on the matter (i.e., pro-Rushdie squeaks) might cost the Party as many as ten seats at the next election. Labour MPs might be sympathetic in private, but publicly the Party didn't want to know.

Politicians can be very crude and noisy when they sniff votes; the truth in the Rushdie case–or, at least, the truth as most British politicians saw it–was that there was little to gain and much to lose by openly supporting him. The ignoble reasoning presumably was that, while pro-Rushdieites would tend to vote on wider issues, anti-Rushdieites in the Muslim community were likely to be single-issue voters. Between Labour and Conservative there was therefore cross-party support in favor of apathy. Rushdie got more reliable aid from Paddy Ashdown, the leader of the Liberal Democrats, whose seats tend to be in the whiter extremities of the country.

A second alternative narrative is to imagine the affair taking place in another country. When I put this hypothesis to Rushdie, he replied that in another country he might very well be dead by now. Still, it's revealing to compare British and French attitudes. There is no close parallel to the Rushdie case, but we could remember the time when de Gaulle got Régis Debray out of a South American jail. Despite a profound political antipathy between the two men, the Presidential view was that their shared Frenchness remained the overriding consideration. The French tend on the one hand to refer to basic humanitarian principles, and on the other to be practically effective in obtaining the release of hostages and pseudohostages. (French nationals were the first to be released from Baghdad during the Gulf War, with Paris characteristically claiming that no sort of deal had been done.) The British stiffly view this as hypocrisy; but it came as a bracing relief when an Air France spokesman, asked about the British

Airways ban, simply replied, "We respect the French custom regarding the rights of man, which means that we transport passengers without discrimination. If Mr. Rushdie wished to travel with Air France he would not be refused."

Similarly, in early 1989, when British and French Muslims were demonstrating on the streets of London and Paris, the French Prime Minister, Michel Rocard, put a straightforward limit on the nature of protest: "Any further calls for violence or murder will lead to immediate criminal prosecution." In Britain, the police, the Director of Public Prosecutions, and the Cabinet apparently didn't notice that there was open incitement to murder in several major cities. This meant ignoring tape of Muslim leaders, footage and stills of street demonstrators. Here, for instance, are two British Muslims in Derby holding a banner saying "Rushdie Must Die"; here is a protester in Slough with an unconvincing effigy garnished with the words "Dog Must Lose Life"; here is a cheerful fellow in collar and tie, beneath Churchill's statue in Parliament Square, with a "Death to Rushdie" placard. (An extra tinkle of irony here lies in the fact that Churchill was awarded the Nobel Prize—for literature.) Imagine if one of these slogans had said "Death to Thatcher" and had been waved by an Irishman: some slight action might have been taken. So what was going on? Torpid pragmatism laced with a little upside-down racism: let Britons of subcontinental origin have a burn of street democracy, let "them" run around in "their" excitable way and get it off their chests. Anyway, we shouldn't provoke them at home—we've seen how touchy they can get abroad.

White Britons' attitudes to nonwhite Britons are, at best, fluid (fine if you're an Olympic champion, less good if you're stopped by police and aren't carrying your gold medal). This inconstancy has certainly applied to Rushdie in some quarters. When an issue is complicated and seemingly insoluble, the urge to simplify is alluring. What could be more simplifying, therefore, than to return Rushdie to "his people"? The story beneath the story can be made to run like this: clever Indian boy, English public school (hated it, but so do we all; character-building anyway), Cambridge, advertising, scribbling, Booker Prize, fame, money: one of us. Then, public figure with opinions (hostile, God damn it) about the Government, ungrateful for the privileges we gave him, stirrer not just with us but with his own people, went too far this time, should have known better, can't understand the book anyway: one of them. Got to protect him from hotheads, murderers, and fuzzy-wuzzies generally, but Islam, after all, that's not really our bag, is it? Anyway, didn't he prove our point for us, first by converting to Islam and then by calling the whole affair "a family quarrel"? In this line of "thinking," Rushdie, already condemned in the East as a racist colonialist CIA provocateur corrupted by Western values, is flung back by the West in a game of pass-the-parcel. He has been, in two senses, blackened.

One way of making this point in a slimily indirect manner has been to complain about the cost of protecting the writer. Sir Philip Goodhart, MP, of the Tory right, had the dishonorable distinction of raising this matter less than a month after the *fatwa*, though right-wing commentators such as Auberon Waugh had anticipated him. Not: a million a year (or whatever), that's a pretty cheap price to pay for showing the country's proud belief in individual liberty and freedom of expression. But: this chappie must have a few quid squirreled away, why not make him stump up—after all, he started the rumpus, didn't he? In fact, Rushdie does help foot the bill, having paid out an estimated £500,000 so far. The same question—how much money is his life worth?—is not, it must be said, asked about minor royals and dud ex–Northern Ireland ministers, let alone more illustrious protectees. Last October, for instance, Lady Thatcher did a signing session in Chester to promote her memoirs. There was the usual protection from the Cheshire police, backed up by officers from North Wales and Manchester, plus a helicopter overhead. A tenacious Labour MP winkled out the information that this hour or so of promo, which hardly constituted state business, cost the taxpayers £26,398, not a pfennig of which was being paid by author or publisher. If such expenditure was typical, then the price to the nation of her twelve-day book tour was around £300,000. Right-wing columnists have not made much noise about this so far.

Torpor, active indifference; but there has also been worse. "Quite often," Rushdie told me, "the place where there has been the most hostility has been in my own country." Of course, since freedom of expression is the central issue in the Rushdie case, it might seem artless to complain about people saying and writing what they believe. Even so, you might think there would, or should, be a level of decorum when sounding off about someone who is incarcerated under threat of death. You might think so for the very good reason that in a parallel case there was. Terry Waite, routinely described as "the Archbishop of Canterbury's special envoy," though later evidence suggests that the Archbishop may have had doubts about letting this loose cannon roll around the eastern Mediterranean, was held captive in Beirut for five years. While he was away, awkward questions about what exactly he was doing there, about how closely he was involved with Oliver North, whose patsy he might be, about whether vanity, self-delusion, and a love of headlines were part of his makeup, and whether all these factors made him partly complicit in his own fate, were, quite rightly, avoided. When he came out, they were, cautiously, addressed.

No such decorum has applied with Rushdie, whose motives were questioned and whose supposed character was imaginatively trashed even before the *fatwa* had been analyzed. Here are some of the ranker items: Roald Dahl called his fellow writer a "dangerous opportunist." Former Tory Party Chairman Norman Tebbit dubbed him "an outstanding villain" before musing on the inadequacy of that description: "Is villain a strong enough word for one who has insulted the country that protects him and betrayed and reviled those to whom he owes his wealth, his culture, his religion and now his very life? Happily, villains such as Rushdie are rare. What a pity it is our country in which he chose to live." Germaine Greer oddly denounced him as "a megalomaniac, an Englishman with dark skin" (are these two conditions related, or did she mean melanomic?) before observing, "Jail is a good place for writers; they write." (But what about execution? They don't write much after that.) The plain-man tendency was exemplified by the tabloid thinker Richard Littlejohn: "I couldn't care less if the Iranians top Salmoon Rushdie tomorrow. . . . But I'd rather they didn't do it here." The posh, windy, high-table version of this same line came from the historian Hugh Trevor-Roper, who asserted, after giving the matter four months' academic reflection, that Rushdie's "offence is one of manners, not a crime, and the law cannot notice it. That being so, I would not shed a tear if some British Muslims, deploring his manners, should waylay him in a dark street and seek to improve them. If that should cause him thereafter to control his pen, society would benefit and literature would not suffer. If caught, his correctors might, of course, be found guilty of assault; but they could then plead gross provocation and might merely, if juvenile, be bound over. Our prisons are, after all, overcrowded."

Still, the most distasteful item in this local *trahison des clercs* came from Marianne Wiggins, Rushdie's second wife, who had initially gone into hiding with him. She talked expansively to the *Sunday Times* about his character flaws, and explained how wrong we would be to consider him any sort of hero. Even allowing for the bitterness of a soon-to-be-ex-spouse, this seemed especially repugnant. It also had its ironic side for those who had come across Ms. Wiggins in pre-*fatwa* days. I remember, for instance, how she once winsomely declared to me that she wanted, as a writer, to be no more than a mere foothill beside the mighty mountain that was Salman. Alas, when Muhammad came to the mountain the foothill hightailed it over the horizon.

Two years ago, faced with "the absence of any real political enthusiasm here," Rushdie and his Defence Committee decided to go on the road. Despite the aloofness of British Airways, he traveled to Europe and North America, usually finding access to government ministers easier than in his own country. "Basically, in those two years we did rather better than I'd hoped," he told me. Germany, being not just the most powerful country in Europe but also the largest trader with Iran, was a key target, and in December 1992 the Bundestag passed an all-party resolution holding the Iranian government legally responsible for Rushdie's safety. (Whether such a motion would get through the House of Commons as currently constituted is doubtful.) The Nordic countries, traditionally strong on human rights, offered active support; and in January 1993 the Irish President, Mary Robinson, became the first head of state to meet Rushdie and his committee.

All this high-profile activity shifted the pack ice at home a little. The Foreign Office, being reactive, reacted. Their change of heart after four years wasn't so much a belated recognition of principle as a pragmatic admission that being supine and smarmy wasn't getting anywhere with the Iranians. Statements became stronger: Douglas Hogg, No. 2 in the Foreign Office, addressing the United Nations Commission for Human Rights in February 1993, called the *fatwa* "infamous and outrageous," a visible upping of the adjectives. The Foreign Secretary himself, Douglas Hurd, told the Council of Europe, in Strasbourg, that he remained "greatly concerned at the continuing failure of the Iranian authorities to repudiate the incitement to murder." This may not sound especially severe, but it made a change from Hurd's ritual pronouncements of "deep respect" for Islam; and it should not be forgotten that earlier in the affair Hurd, when asked by a journalist what his most unpleasant experience in politics had been, jauntily replied, "Reading *The Satanic Verses*." When Hogg met Rushdie on February 4, 1993, it was the first time since the affair began that the writer had been publicly received at the Foreign Office. In a Commons explanation, Hogg stated, "It was right to demonstrate our support," while A. Spokesman, that reliable anonymity, pronounced as follows: "You have a policy and you pursue it until you reach a solution. Salman Rushdie is now being more visible and if you ask, 'Are you angry about that?' the answer is no. He enjoys the same rights to free speech and travel as everyone else." This may seem a tortuous, almost Carrollian piece of bureaucratese, but it's good to have it on record. The Foreign Office is not angry that Mr. Rushdie is more visible. And he has the same travel rights as everyone else. As long as he doesn't try booking on the nation's flagship airline.

And then, at last, in May 1993, Rushdie was allowed to meet John Major, who promised him twenty minutes and gave him forty-five. The *Daily Mail*, which tends to articulate the middle area of the

Conservative brain, thought the encounter "astoundingly ill-advised." Former Conservative Prime Minister Edward Heath objected on the ground that Britain was losing "masses of trade" because of "that wretched book"; while Peter Temple-Morris, Tory chairman of the all-party Britain-Iran Parliamentary Group, said, "I think whoever is advising the Prime Minister needs their heads reading." (Strange that he said "reading" rather than the normal "examining," but a pertinent lapsus in the present case.) None of these objectors thought it odd, or scandalous, or humiliating, that a law-abiding British citizen, in order to meet a peacetime Prime Minister at the desire of both parties, should have to be smuggled into the House of Commons.

There is no photographic record of Rushdie meeting Major (or meeting Hogg, Hurd, or Clinton). The Defence Committee, aware that the encounter was more symbolic than productive, pushed for one, but without success. This rare shrinkingness of British politicians before the camera is a minor yet interesting aspect of the Rushdie affair. The novelist has in his two years of shuttle diplomacy been photographed with Václav Havel, Klaus Kinkel, Mário Soares, Jack Lang, Jean Chrétien, and most leading Scandinavian politicians. In Britain, only the Labour leader John Smith has so far agreed not to treat Rushdie as an infectious case.

Still, the statements from Hogg and Hurd, plus the meeting with Major–whom Rushdie found "well briefed, sympathetic, and engaged with the issues"–have left Britain in a comparatively less inactive position; indeed, we have practically hauled ourselves into line with the rest of Europe. Whether, as Rushdie suggested after meeting the Prime Minister, the British government is now "leading from the front" remains very much to be seen; one rather imagines the British government preferring to lead from somewhere in the middle on this issue. One other side benefit of John Major's public gesture of support might be the tacit reinclusion of Rushdie, a handing back of his symbolic passport: one of us, not one of them.

When I asked Rushdie what hopes he has for Year Six, he replied, "That the promises made in Year Five will be fulfilled." He himself is giving up his traveling campaign–"It can't go on with me being this endless ambassador for myself"—and applying himself to fiction. The Defence Committee (and its half-dozen associate bodies in Europe and the States) will keep up the pressure on national governments. The problem, of course, is turning the fine words into effective deeds. As Rushdie observes, strong verbal stances are a good beginning, but "in terms of economic muscle nobody wants to take any action, and unless they do Iran isn't going to mind. . . . The United States talks most emphatically about economic pressure, but they are the country which has most increased their trade with Iran over the last twelve months, despite the embargo." A nation spouting high principle looks over its shoulder to see its neighbor taking low economic gain. Can the Western alliance afford to apply serious economic pressure? On the other hand, can it afford not to? The Belgian Foreign Minister, Willy Claes, told Rushdie that any continuing desire among Western governments to placate Iran would be "a great historical mistake."

Over the last five years, we have learned new things about the speed and communicability of international outrage. When the House of Chanel recently apologized to Muslims for the Koran-embroidered bustier worn by Claudia Schiffer in its latest summer collection, the protest had come not from some street march in the Rue de Rivoli but from the Muslim community in Jakarta. The affair of the Satanic Breasts, as it became known in France, could be seen as a comic analogue of the Rushdie case were it not for the chilling presence of fire, as promised by Chanel's chief executive: "The three dresses and the texts will be destroyed by incineration." We have also learned that *The Satanic Verses* is not a one-off blasphemy but, rather, one among various categories of thought which fundamentalists seek to eradicate. The English newspapers may not have got a shot of the Rushdie-Major encounter, but there were pictures enough of the five thousand or so Muslim fundamentalists who met in Dacca last December to demand the death of the thirty-one-year-old poet and feminist Taslima Nasreen. Two months previously, a group of clerics had pronounced a *fatwa* on her and offered the paltry fee of £850. Nasreen had, inter alia, denounced Bangladeshi men for keeping women "veiled, illiterate, and in the kitchen"; and the women certainly don't seem to have enough status to take part in this heavily bearded protest. Then there is the recent misfortune of the Muslim actress from Bombay, Shabana Azmi: she was threatened with a campaign of "severe action" for the "un-Islamic and un-Indian act" of kissing Nelson Mandela on the cheek while presenting him with the Newsmaker of the Year award in South Africa.

Rushdie argues strongly that his own case, while the most publicized, is not egregious; it exists in a specific intellectual and political context. In the West, we tend to be picky about individual cases, and unwilling to countenance the idea of a general punitive movement. According to Rushdie, most journalists were not interested in the deaths of seventeen writers and journalists in Algeria between March and December of last year: "It happened in Arabic." He points out that when the Western nations pooled their intelligence about Iran a couple of years ago, every expert agreed that Iran now has an extensive terrorist network in place across Europe. And the assassins-in-waiting are not, we can be sure, all there in case Rushdie does a signing session in the nearest town. This generality of threat is, apart from anything else, one answer to the sneery little charge against Rushdie that he "knew what he was doing." Did the others—the Algerian writers, for example? What is it that suddenly, worldwide, makes Iranian dissidents, antifundamentalists, novelists, and journalists of various ideological stripes decide that they simply must throw themselves upon the enemy's sword? Or could it be the sword that is moving?

Toward the end of the Oxford fund-raiser, Rushdie read the scene from *Midnight's Children* in which the ten-year-old Saleem, pursued by school bullies, loses the top third of his middle finger by having it shut in a door. Then the evening closed with a Brahms violin sonata, and we all trooped back to the greenroom. The litterateurs offered congratulations to the musicians, but they weren't having any. "The Brahms was *not* good," said the pianist self-reproachingly. "I've *never* before failed to play two whole notes of the opening chord." The violinist admitted that she had also had problems. They did not like to imply blame, but one minute they were listening to Rushdie read a line about "the top third of my middle finger lying there like a lump of well-chewed bubble-gum," and the next they were applying digits to ivory and gut while trying to ignore the whistling afterlife of the novelist's image. It seemed a local but appropriate reminder of the basic truth: words count.

February 1994

The rest of 1994 passed without any visible sign that the British government was "leading from the front." There were more signs of life from Mr. Rushdie, who published a new collection of stories. In July 1994 I interviewed Tony Blair, the new Labour leader, and asked where he stood on Rushdie. "Fully supportive of him. . . . I absolutely one hundred percent support him." When I pointed out that the Labour Party had had its problems with the case, he replied, "There were some people who had problems with it. But you can't muck around with something like this at all. I mean, you can't have someone having a death sentence passed on them because they happen to have written a book people don't like. I mean, that was supposed to have gone out many centuries ago in this country."

■ 14 ■

Froggy! Froggy! Froggy!

In Flaubert's *Bouvard et Pécuchet,* there is a scene in which Pécuchet, who has temporarily turned geology student, explains to his friend Bouvard what would happen if there were an earthquake beneath the English Channel. The water, he maintains, would all rush out into the Atlantic, the coastlines would begin to totter, and then slowly the two landmasses would shuffle across and reunite. On hearing this prophecy, Bouvard runs away in terror—a reaction, we are invited to conclude, not so much to the idea of cataclysm as to that of the British coming any nearer.

On Friday, May 6, 1994, after more than a century of dreaming, fantastical planning, botched beginnings, enthusiasm, and paranoia, the Channel Tunnel was officially opened, creating a fixed link between Britain and France for the first time since the Ice Age and fulfilling Bouvard's worst nightmare. Yet few ran away in terror as the Queen and President Mitterrand inaugurated the Tunnel—twice, as if to make doubly sure after all this time. They opened it first at the Coquelles terminal outside Calais, where low cloud choked off the flypast; and then, after a refreshing fish lunch, at the Cheriton terminal near Folkestone. At Coquelles there was a pleasant symbolic moment when two enormous Eurotrains, each carrying a head of state, approached, one from London and one from Paris, on the same line of track, and drew slowly to a halt close enough to kiss cheeks. Then President Mitterrand, as host, hopped from his carriage first and waited on the platform for the various high British dignitaries to disembark: Her Majesty in a vivid fuchsia ensemble (clashing horribly with the sodden red carpet underfoot), John Major (clashing horribly with current electoral opinion), and Baroness Thatcher (clashing horribly with the whole idea of European fraternity).

At both Calais and Folkestone, there were the traditional salutings and stiff-necked language, accompanied by Lord Lieutenants and bechained mayors. But the Queen and M. Mitterrand were in fact presiding over a fairly untraditional—indeed, postmodern—inauguration. For no sooner was the Tunnel "opened" than it was closed again, and it won't reopen for business until various safety tests have been passed and operating certificates obtained. The last months saw a blur of constant rescheduling in which the only things not to be derailed were the regal and presidential diaries. Still, Her Majesty did the decent democratic thing and tried out for the rest of us the two different transport systems that in due course will operate through the Tunnel. For her outward journey, from Waterloo Station to Calais, she used the swanky new Eurostar passenger train. For her return journey, like any other Francophile punter back from the Dordogne, she put the old Rolls-Royce Phantom VI on the car transporter, known under the nasty macaronic of Le Shuttle. This drive-on, drive-off service, which targets the cross-Channel ferries, may not enter its full turn-up-and-go glory until next spring, but will be available before then to those described as "opinion-formers." These consist of travel operators, piqued Eurotunnel shareholders who must by now be wondering when they'll ever see a return on their money, and those bold optimists who back in January actually laid out some cash for a booking on this temporarily notional service. It is indicative of the public mood that, although the proposed timetables were widely advertised and plausibly detailed, although first-day fever strikes here as elsewhere, and the nation seethes with transport buffs and train spotters, a mere hundred tickets for Le Shuttle were presold.

Such wariness was typical of the response on the Tunnel's northern shore. The British attitude was one of phlegm and skepticism. The French, meanwhile, were much more openly celebratory, with Calais voting itself nine days of heavily subsidized festivity (bands, midnight dances, the traditional carnival giants of northern France, the National Orchestra of Lille playing a hymn of peace). You might have expected things to be the other way round, since in statistical terms Britain seeks Europe much more than Europe seeks Britain: figures from the ferry companies show that eight out of ten Channel crossings currently originate in Britain, while a profile of Tunnel-users-to-be indicates that only a measly 7 percent of them are expected to be French. But this rare joint venture (the first major Franco-British collaboration since the Concorde) has accentuated one of the profounder differences between the two countries. The French have a taste for and commitment to what they call *grands projets*: large public endeavors, backed by government money, that revel in the latest technology and add luster to the nation. Recent examples include the TGV express-rail network, the Louvre Pyramid, the Grande Bibliothèque, the Beaubourg, and the Ariane rocket. The British are temperamentally more suspicious, or shy, about expressing the national spirit through such means; in addition, they have had for the last decade and a half a government ideologically opposed to large capital projects except when funded by the private sector. Our spirit of muscular self-deprecation also seems to ensure that the running news about such few projects as exist is usually depressing: underfunding, overspending, delays, and cock-ups. One of the last British *grands projets*, the Humber Bridge, was opened by the Queen in 1981. It cut fifty miles off the journey from Grimsby to Hull, replaced an ancient ferry system, and was designed to bring prosperity to a moribund region. But the bridge itself has now become a symbol of failure: the fifteen thousand vehicles that cross it each day pay off only 25 percent of the interest charges on the bridge's debt, which is currently £439 million and rising at the rate of £1.42 a second. Similarly, there has been scarcely a single upbeat report on the new British Library over the last decades. In 1993, the proposed shelving, all 186 miles, was found not to work for the dismal and basic reason that the books fell off the end of it.

Of course, French *grands projets* have their cock-ups, too. In its initial design, the Grande Bibliothèque audaciously overthrew the hackneyed old concept of storing the books underground and putting the readers on top of them; instead, the readers were to be placed at ground level and half the books in four eighteen-story towers above. Too late was it pointed out that the last thing valuable books want is to be exposed to heat and light; and so–to the accompaniment of much Parisian mockery–the sky-high library had to be protected by a whole additional system of internal insulation paneling. But even so, the French bring more self-belief and political will to such projects, plus an intellectual chutzpah that the British tend to dismiss as pretension. Dominique Jamet, appointed by President Mitterrand to establish the Grande Bibliothèque, remarked, naturally enough, that "the primacy of the book resides in the spirit of each of us." It is hard to imagine a library official in Britain making a comparable remark without being packed off into early retirement.

The British affect to believe that they are stern pragmatists while the French are airy dreamers. This could not be less true than in the case of the Channel Tunnel. Honors and deadlines may have been shared in the digging and boring; but aboveground the difference is instructive. The French have their high-speed rail link to Paris already in place, the TGV Nord network having been built from scratch in only three years. They also have a chain of new stations and a glittering terminal at Lille for transfers to the rest of Europe. On the British side, there is at least a fine new extension to Waterloo Station, built within budget and opened on time in May of 1993. But there is no high-speed rail link between Waterloo and Folkestone, only a low-speed one over tracks clogged with commuter traffic; and when the high-speed link is finally in place (its cloud-cuckoo-land completion date has just been pushed back from 2002 to a probable 2005) it won't run directly into Waterloo anyway but into St. Pancras in

North London. John Prescott, as Opposition transport spokesman, declared that the Channel Tunnel was joining a twenty-first-century rail network to a nineteenth-century one; and the Eurobusinessman looking for national metaphors might unhappily find one as his Paris-to-London train gradually decelerates from 180 miles per hour in *Germinal* territory to a third of that in the Kentish hop fields. President Mitterrand, himself the son of a stationmaster, could not resist a lofty professional tease: future passengers, he said as he opened another gleaming section of TGV Nord, would "race at great pace across the plains of northern France, hurtle through the Tunnel on a fast track, and then be able to daydream at very low speed, admiring the landscape." There is a particular irony about this, given that 150 years ago it was British engineers and British navvies who laid out the first elements of the French rail network.

It was appropriate that the first of the Tunnel's two inaugurations took place on the French side, since historically the French have shown more consistent zeal for the subaqueous link. In 1751 the Amiens Academy held a competition to explore new ways of crossing the Channel, while the first serious tunnel proposal came from the French engineer Albert Mathieu in 1802, a project favored by Napoleon. Throughout the rest of the century, an inventor's fun pack of ideas was put forward: bridges of various sorts, iron tubes laid along the seabed, tunnels surfacing at halfway islands for a change of horses, monster ferries capable of devouring whole trains. Though exploratory borings were made on both sides of the Channel in the 1880s, lack of money and lack of plausibility scuppered most of these schemes. Just as important on the British side, however, was a toxic nationalistic mix of military caution, political snootiness, and intellectual skepticism. When the Channel Tunnel (Experimental Works) Bill was under discussion, Lord Randolph Churchill, in one of those primped declarations which easily pass for wit in political life, claimed that "the reputation of England has hitherto depended upon her being, as it were, *virgo intacta*." In 1882, there was a petition from 1,070 members of the Great and the Good urging that lascivious Continental hands be kept off the chaste body of Britannia. Signatories ranged from Queen Victoria's gynecologist to the Archbishop of Canterbury and Cardinal Newman, via Tennyson, Browning, Herbert Spencer, and T. H. Huxley.

The *virgo intacta* claim of Lord Randolph Churchill (who himself died of syphilis, while we're about it) was a direct descendant of that famous piece of realtor's spiel uttered by John of Gaunt in *Richard II*: this sceptered isle, this other Eden, demiparadise, this fortress against infection and the hand of war, this precious stone set in the silver sea, which acts as a moat defensive to a house against the envy of less happier lands, and so on. The hand of war has always been one of the principal British objections to tunneling: Field Marshal Wolseley turned Queen Victoria against the notion (Prince Albert had been in favor) by asserting that the British Army would have to be doubled in size to cope with the consequent threat. There have been fears of enemy borings, too: recently released documents in the Public Record Office show that in the early years of the Second World War the government had an active anxiety about a possible German tunnel. It was calculated that a speed-dig might take the enemy as little as twenty months, and at one time the Royal Navy instructed its ships in the Channel to keep a lookout for giveaway muddy water. Fear of invasion is nowadays a diminishing factor, though last-ditch advocates of the moat defensive might point to the events of May 1991. Shortly after British and French engineers had shaken triumphant hands, a hundred Parisian printers slipped surreptitiously into the Tunnel and marched on London to protest against their maltreatment by Robert Maxwell. They managed thirteen miles beneath the waves before coming up against a locked chamber, which at that time was all that protected Britain from France.

A fortress against infection? Very much so. It has been one of this country's justifiable boasts that rabies has been virtually extinct here since 1902. Over the last few years, however, paranoid amateur pathographers have been able to watch the disease patter northward across Europe, almost in anticipation of the Channel Tunnel's opening. It was as if, lining up behind Mitterrand and the Queen as they cut the tricolor ribbons at Calais were packs of swivel-eyed dogs, fizzing foxes, and slavering squirrels, all waiting to jump on the first boxcar to Folkestone and sink their teeth into some Kentish flesh. Decent publicity was therefore given to a system of defenses, ranging from stalag fencing to "stun mats," which will protect the Tunnel entrance. (And here there was another anxiety to calm, that of the animal lover. So: no, the "stun mats" would only immobilize the rogue animal, rather than fricassee it on the spot.) Nor was this all: what about those carriers of *la rage* who are not so obligingly pedestrian? Well, that had been thought of, too, and it was solemnly reported that "Eurotunnel officials will mount patrols for signs of bats."

Even though the main risk of rabies will continue to be (as it is now) from the smuggled family pet, the chihuahua in the hatbox, Eurotunnel was quite right to treat this question gravely. A survey by the Automobile Association's magazine of those who found the Tunnel "a bad or very bad idea" showed that, while 32 percent objected because they "liked being an island" or didn't want to "lose the security of being an island," 40 percent disapproved because the Tunnel would make it "easy to bring rabies into this country." Quite why a rabid beast might find the cuttings at Coquelles particularly inviting is another matter: as Tony Stevens, of the British Veterinary Association, put it, "There's no incentive for any animal to enter the tunnel, let alone traverse its thirty-five miles." A psychiatric interpretation of this British obsession with rabies (which strangely seems to bite so few British tourists as they travel through Europe on their holidays) might see it as a transference: no longer permitted by social and political norms openly to hate and fear the foreigner, the frustrated islanders turn their feelings instead against the Continental animal.

The Channel Tunnel is being declared open in a year that ought to lead the British and French to celebrate the warmer, more constructive side of their relationship: 1994, after all, marks both the ninetieth anniversary of the Entente Cordiale and the fiftieth anniversary of D day. But few remember what the former was—something to do with Edward VII and Parisian actresses?—while no one quite knows what to do about the latter. At first, the British government wanted to ignore it, preferring to wait for the anniversary of the war's end in 1995; then they rushed off in the opposite direction and miscalculated the public mood by scheduling street parties and "light-hearted" civilian events such as Spam-fritter-cooking competitions. Not only did they offend veterans by emphasizing "celebration" rather than "commemoration"; they offended Dame Vera Lynn, the wartime warbler who is as much a national monument as Rodin's *Burghers of Calais*. Dame Vera, whose mere name sets off the words "There'll be bluebirds over/The white cliffs of Dover" in the skull of anyone over the age of about twelve, even threatened to boycott the main jamboree in Hyde Park unless and until the government sorted its act out.

As for the wider matter of Franco-British relations, it can't be said that they are noticeably in better shape now than at any other point since D day. Churchill used to quip that the heaviest cross he had to bear was the Cross of Lorraine; later, de Gaulle took his revenge with a policy of committed Anglophobia. Since then, British Prime Ministers have repeatedly disappointed the French by being such lukewarm Europeans, while French Presidents have in return always seemed keener on smooching with their German counterparts than with their British ones. When François Mitterrand arrived in Canterbury for the official signing with Mrs. Thatcher of the Channel Tunnel deal in 1986, his Rolls-Royce was hit by an egg and the crowd chanted, "Froggy! Froggy! Froggy! Out! Out! Out!" For her part, Mrs. Thatcher became the first British Prime Minister to be booed on the streets of Paris in modern times.

The bickering legacy of history is exacerbated on the British side by the poverty of geography. Britain has only France as its obvious neighbor, while France may divert itself with three other major cultures—Spain, Italy, and Germany. Beyond France's southern shore lies Africa; beyond Britain's northern shore lie the Faeroe Islands and many seals. France is what we first mean by Abroad; it is our primary exotic. Small wonder, then, that we think about the French much more than they think about us (they can even get their Anglo-Saxon culture elsewhere—from across the Atlantic if they prefer). The British are obsessed by the French, whereas the French are only intrigued by the British. When we love them, they accept it as their due; when we hate them, they are puzzled and irritated but regard it rightly as our problem not theirs.

For instance, they can make some sense of our unfraternal posturing in matters of high politics, but not in matters of low journalism. As an English Francophile, I find myself frequently asked to explain the chauvinism, aggression, and contempt of our popular press. This Rottweiler tendency found its most complete recent expression on *The Sun*'s front page of November 1, 1990, exactly a month before the Tunnel breakthrough. Under the headline UP YOURS DELORS and the subhead "At midday tomorrow *Sun* readers are urged to tell the French fool where to stuff his ECU," the lead news story was a sort of atavistic fart: "*The Sun* today calls on its patriotic family of readers to tell the feelthy French to FROG off! They INSULT us, BURN our lambs, FLOOD our country with dodgy food and PLOT to abolish the dear old pound. Now it's your turn to kick them in the GAULS." This crisp political analysis, under the amusing byline of the "*Sun* Diplomatic Staff," was backed by a special collection of xenophobic jokes—"What do you call a Frenchman with an I.Q. of 150? A village"; "What do you call a Frenchman with twenty girlfriends? A shepherd"—all of which could be safely reapplied to any other hated nation. *The Sun* urged its readers to assemble the next day in public squares up and down the country and, as twelve o'clock struck, to turn toward Paris and shout "Up Yours Delors!" in order "to make sure the French feel the full blast of your anti-Frog feelings."

Neanderthal? Despicable? Pathetic? Certainly. And the fact that this rabble-rousing didn't translate into street action—when the posh papers sent their journalists down to Trafalgar Square the next day they found only half a dozen *Sun*-inspired protesters—doesn't make this sort of story "just a bit of harmless fun" or whatever. Such peddlings of coarse national myth and beery racial demonizing are base and self-damaging stuff. They are also culturally baffling to the French. Their own tabloid press has traditionally had quite different preoccupations. The last time I took the Dover–Calais ferry, in mid-April, I picked up in Péronne the roughest equivalents to *The Sun*—

Infos du Monde, Spéciale Dernière, and *France Dimanche.* Their lead stories were, respectively, about an eighty-four-year-old female Canadian bodybuilder who had just been elected Miss Muscle 1994, the supposedly "tragic" close to Mitterrand's rule, and the news that Princess Caroline of Monaco had ordered her wedding dress. Other matters of top concern were a group of American schoolchildren with hair sprouting from their tongues, an Italian woman who eats spaghetti through her nose, the "tragic" life of actress Martine Carol, the newly discovered Camus novel, the haunting of Robert Wagner by the shade of Natalie Wood, the alleged pregnancy of Claudia Schiffer, and the possible remarriage of the singer Johnny Hallyday to one of his various previous wives. Each paper had one important item about Britain: a write-it-in-your-sleep rerun of Wallis Simpson and Edward VIII, a tale about the annual dinner of the Her Royal Majesty Dog Society (pooches dress up to eat a candlelit supper: menu attached, of course), and a bit of Kitty Kelley about the Duke of Edinburgh's whispered mistresses. This latter story, needless to say, concentrated on the Duke's erotic powers and the Queen's silent heartbreak rather than on, say, any cultural or institutional hypocrisy. Gossip, snobbery, and sentimentality continue to rule this journalistic domain as ever before.

Moreover, when the French do attempt to answer atavistic fart and lunkhead gibe with its equivalent, things never quite work out. Earlier this year, a French professor writing under the nationalistic pseudonym Chanteclair published a satirical English grammar called *Pour en Finir avec l'Anglais.* Its robust jocosity is well displayed in the list of Useful Phrases you might require in a British hotel ("Is the chambermaid included?" "There is a rat under the sheets. Is it normal?") or at the grocer's ("Your eggs are rotten," "Your bananas are too green," "Stick them up your ass," "Look, my dog doesn't want it"). But it is the sections on our national character which hold the attention and seek to justify the publisher's wraparound claim for "The Book Which Is Scandalizing England!" We are, according to Chanteclair, "the most dirty, hypocritical and bestial of races," a "brutal and drunken people" ruled by "puritan inhibitions." We are taciturn to the point of mutism; our celebrated love of animals exists only because we "feel ourselves to be on the same level as them"; while our schooling gives us an enthusiasm for corporal punishment and sodomy. This is pretty much the usual charge sheet (former French Prime Minister Édith Cresson also publicly accused us of not sufficiently endorsing heterosexuality), though Chanteclair fails to add the popular French complaint that the British are shabbily dressed and have miserable underwear. Nor is stinginess mentioned. (This is a universal objection. Australians have joined our mythic avarice and unwashedness into a cute double insult: the British, they say, "keep their money under the soap.")

But the professor, while doing his best at mockery, lacks any real taste for trans-Channel eye gouging. Look, for instance, at the way his book begins: "I have always been an Anglophile and an Americanophile, to the point where those around me have often reproached me for it. But he who loves well also chastises well." Hopeless: absolutely no viciousness in the fellow at all. Furthermore, he is constantly let down by a very French preference for the elaborate and elegant tease over the gross insult. Faced with the mystery of how the English manage to reproduce, the professor comes up with the following logical—indeed, Cartesian—solution. Yes, they are puritanical, and, yes, they are sodomites; however, they are also drunkards. Therefore, the answer must be as follows: drink helps them get over their puritanism about sex; yet drink also makes them woozy about aiming at the correct target, with the result that fecundation mistakenly ensues and the race continues to stagger on. QED. How could a sensible English person possibly take offense at this?

The Channel Tunnel contains the world's longest subaqueous stretch (twenty-four miles) and is an astounding piece of engineering. The rail link will spare us the harassments and mayhem of the airport and offer an attractively seamless transfer from London to the center of Paris or Brussels. And if we are in our car, Le Shuttle will gain us thirty or forty minutes in time over the Pride of Calais. But both will, I think, finally lose us something much more important: a sense of crossing the Channel. Since the day thirty-five years ago when the family Triumph Mayflower was hoisted from the Newhaven dockside into the depths of the Dieppe ferry, I have done this trip scores of times, but I still remember the sense of quiet awe instilled by that first occasion. After the laborious business of loading came the wide-eyed scamper around the deck, the anxious examination of lifeboat cradles whose key joints seemed encrusted with fifty-four layers of paint, the bass saxophone growls as the boat pulled out, the cross-shock as you eased beyond the protection of the breakwater, the opening whoosh of spray in the face, the discovery of those extra handles in the lavatories to stop you falling over or in, the silhouette of honking gulls against the receding Sussex coast. Next came the middle passage, when land was out of sight and the sea more serious, when the light began to change (looking north from the French side is more dramatic than looking south from the English), and when you waved at the rare passing ships as violently as if you were on the Raft of the Medusa. Finally came the slow approach of the French coast, a twist of apprehension in the stomach, a strip of unpopulated sand, a clifftop church no doubt dedicated to the trawlerman's protectress, anglers on the breakwater looking up as your swell annoyingly disturbed their floats, then the creak of damp ropes pulling tight, and the sudden anticipation of your first French smell—which turned out to be a mixture of coffee and floor disinfectant.

This sense of transition, of a psychological gear change, a necessary pause, survived until quite recently, when a new generation of ferries actively undermined the experience. They were much larger for a start, yet paradoxically, the more passengers they carried, the smaller the deck space became: just a couple of thin strips as a walkway for claustrophobes. So your sense of the sea now came double-glazed. Second, these big boats were much more stable, which reduced the amount of vomiting. No doubt this helped ticket sales, but vomiting (and the sight of others doing it) was an important endorser of transition. Third, the ferries became entertainment centers and emporia: things nowadays are not so much shipshape as shopshape. The modern cross-Channel passenger no more voyages to enjoy the sea than the illegal gambler goes to an offshore casino to

admire coral growth. Ferry companies routinely offer one-pound return tickets to standby foot passengers, and as Hoverspeed spokesman Nick Stevens put it, "The crossing of the Channel becomes
immaterial. It is an alternative to the High Street." The boats have
turned into thrumming bazaars crammed with bustling, whooping
discount seekers: put the concept of the bargain next to the concept
of booze and the British (as Chanteclair would understand) become
overexcited.

So the experience of transition has deteriorated in recent years.
You do not have to be anti-European or xenophobic to like the idea
of the frontier. On the contrary: it seems to me that the more Europe
becomes integrated commercially and politically, the more each nation should confirm its cultural separateness. (The French were quite
right in the recent GATT negotiations to hold out for the "cultural
exception" in the matter of government subsidies: that is why they
have a film industry, and we have only a collection of cinematic individuals.) Frontiers are therefore useful. It is good to be reminded that
over here is the place you are leaving, where you come from, while
over there is the place you are going to, where you don't come from,
and where things are done differently. It's one thing to know this, another to be made to feel it. There wasn't much to be enjoyed about
border crossing in the old Eastern Europe, but one thing they always
did well was make you feel alien. You do not come from here, the
men in strange uniforms implied, and because of that we view you
with suspicion: you are guilty until proved innocent, and here you
will not find that variety of warm beer you like to drink at home. I remember crossing from Poland into Russia with a vanload of fellow
students in the midsixties, and being compelled by the Russian border guards to destroy the tiny quantity of fresh fruit and vegetables
that we had with us: in other words, our dinner. It seemed pointless
and bullying at the time, but in retrospect had a grim usefulness: no, it
said, this is no longer Poland, the rules are different here. At about
this time, a friend of mine took a holiday in Albania. Puritanical by
nature and not unsympathetic to the Tiranë regime, he deliberately
had his hair cut before departure so that he would not be judged a

decadent hippie. I had never seen his hair so short; but at the entry point from Yugoslavia they took my friend off the coach, sat him in a wooden chair by the customs post, shaved off what crinal remnants they could find, and charged him a few farthings for the put-down.

There is not much chance of getting a cheap haircut out of Euro-tunnel. Indeed, from now on your passage from England to France will be sweetly unpunctuated unless, say, you are a Rastafarian smoking a joint the size of a baguette and driving a car with Colombian number plates. Otherwise, your journey will go like this: you turn up at the Cheriton terminal whenever you like, buy a ticket at the toll booth, pass through British and French customs with a couple of flaps of your passport, and drive onto one of the double-decker shuttle carriages. Your thirty-five-minute translation to France will be an austere experience: no smoking, no bar, no shops, no duty-free, though you will be allowed to leave your car and visit one of the lavatories, which are placed in every third carriage. It will also be an austere experience spiritually: first reports indicate that your ears may not even pop to remind you of where you are. You will not see the White Cliffs of Dover as you leave or the Bassin du Paradis in Calais Harbor as you arrive; indeed, you will not spot water at any time. Then you will emerge into a French marshaling yard and roar off, unhindered by any authority, toward the *autoroute* and that rented holiday cottage.

In 1981, when the Humber Bridge was opened, a cantata was performed with words by the poet Philip Larkin. In his closing stanza he described the bridge as

> Reaching for the world, as our lives do,
> As all lives do, reaching that we may give
> The best of what we are and hold as true:
> Always it is by bridges that we live.

This is what most people feel, or would like to feel. A *grand projet* should inspire, should stun us into reassessing our place and purpose in the world. But perhaps the Channel Tunnel has come too late to do this. Imagine if it had been built a century or more ago, before

Blériot flew the Channel, before radio and television. Then it would have been a marvel: it might even have changed history, instead of merely adjusting it. What we have now, though, is the ultimate nineteenth-century project completed just before we enter the twenty-first century. So it is a convenience, something to be thankful for, as impressive as a fine new sweep of motorway. And it will still be there on that distant, perhaps apocryphal, day when the British finally get over their complicated and self-destructive feelings about the French, when they decide that difference does not logically entail inferiority, and when Little Englanders, tabloid journalists, and John-of-Gaunters line up at Folkestone with a *chanson* in their hearts to bellow invitingly down the Tunnel's mouth, "Froggy! Froggy! Froggy! In! In! In!"

June 1994

■ 15 ■

Left, Right, Left, Right:
The Arrival of Tony Blair

On July 14, the country's public elite gathered at Westminster Abbey for the memorial service of the Labour leader John Smith. Foreign ambassadors, church leaders, an ex–Prime Minister or two, and the nomenklatura of all major parties: an IRA wet dream. It was a sweltering day: paramedics and the British Red Cross were deployed in force, on red alert for the toppling of elderly pols. But the Abbey was cool inside, and made somehow cooler by the playing of the Grimethorpe Colliery Band. There is something about an English brass band, when not in jolly-oompah mode, that induces a powerful and rather stately melancholy. It is the sonic equivalent of damp hillsides, mill chimneys, and the smell of soot. As Mrs. Smith and her three daughters were led beneath the crossing to their seats, the band was playing "Nimrod" from Elgar's *Enigma Variations*. There was an added political poignancy about the music: the Conservatives, during their pit-closure program, finished off the Grimethorpe Colliery, and all that remains of it now is the after-echo of its band.

Smith's death, at fifty-five, had been signaled by a heart attack five years earlier, but even so it took people by surprise. Party leaders, like orchestra conductors, tend to live a long time, the proximity to power seeming to act like royal jelly. When Smith died last May, no fewer than four previous Labour leaders, including two Prime Ministers from the Jurassic sixties and seventies, were still alive. The active mourning even extended to the Tory press, whose praise for a man it had greedily reviled at the last election was quite extravagant. This wasn't just hypocrisy, or good manners, or political canniness (raise up your dead opponent the better to diminish your living ones). The death of a politician before he can come into his expected power has a particular emotional effect. The leader-in-waiting who never becomes leader is the man who never disabuses us of our expectations, as all the others did; his death gives us a permit for idealism, which we transfer back onto him.

The tributes hailed Smith as a warm and passionate man of blazing wit, a fellow of infinite jest who was always first to the bar on the train back to Scotland after a hard Parliamentary week. This was a deep surprise to most of the nation, since he had always come across as an owlish, lawyerly figure whose main strategy seemed to be to keep the Labour Party from squabbling and wait for the Tories to disembowel themselves. He seemed cleverer than John Major but not fundamentally more thrilling: you might not be surprised to find Mr. Major behind the grille at your suburban bank dishing out the tenners, and Mr. Smith in the paneled back office frowning about your overdraft. This public dourness was apparently deliberate. A Labour MP's wife, known for her reluctance to humor bores, assured me, "John was very, *very* funny. If you went to dinner, you knew you were going to have a good time." So why, I asked her, when most politicians try to make themselves seem more exciting than they are, rather than the reverse, had Smith gone in for this peculiar and chameleonic behavior? "He decided not to be witty in public," she replied, "because of Kinnock and seeming frivolous." There was probably some sense in this: wit and spontaneity are tolerated here among effete backbenchers whose chance of real power has gone, but among the higher echelons everything must sound as if it had been triple-drafted by civil servants, spin doctors, and ideological minders. Neil Kinnock,

John Smith's predecessor as leader, once ran into trouble over the Falklands War. He was appearing as a TV panelist, and a member of the audience put it to him that Mrs. Thatcher had displayed "guts" as a politician. He responded, "It is a pity that other people have to leave theirs on the ground in Goose Green in order to prove it." In the circumstances, this was an excellent reply—sharp, angry, and appropriate—yet Mr. Kinnock discovered that it was not deemed politically acceptable, and shortly thereafter was dispatching letters of explanation and regret to Falklands widows. John Smith was unlikely to make mistakes of this order: a Scottish Presbyterian lawyer who scared neither middle England nor the City, he was par excellence a safe pair of hands.

The catcher's mitt has now passed to the youngest-ever leader of the Labour Party. Tony Blair is forty-one, has been a Member of Parliament only since 1983, and is still young enough (or well enough briefed) to be able, when interviewed by a Radio 1 disc jockey, to cite numerous different rock groups whose music he fancies. He grew up in Durham, went to Fettes public school in Edinburgh, and then to St. John's College, Oxford. Here he sang and played guitar in a band called Ugly Rumours; more significantly, he converted to both Christianity and socialism. In London, he joined the Labour Party and became a barrister; he met his barrister wife in the same set of chambers. In 1982, he fought the parodically unwinnable Tory seat of Beaconsfield in a by-election; then, thanks to a mixture of good fortune and personal persuasiveness, landed the safe Labour constituency of Sedgefield, in County Durham. His career so far has featured luck and timing as well as good judgment. But he was also singled out early as a rising talent by the Labour hierarchs, and as a rising danger by the Conservatives. Most people I spoke to about Tony Blair—even a sleepy House of Commons porter—assured me that they had picked him as a future leader from the beginning.

It was frequently asserted during the leadership election (in which Mr. Blair defeated two rivals with just about the right degree of emphasis—handsome but not humiliating) that one of his key political virtues is his appeal to the Southeast. By "the Southeast" we are to understand those key voters, from the skilled working class and middle management, who defected to Mrs. Thatcher and stayed with Mr. Major. This assessment is probably correct, though the new leader is hardly repugnant to the North: a Durham childhood, a Scottish schooling, a Durham constituency, and, as a clincher, the fact that his wife was the stepdaughter of the actress Pat Phoenix, who for many years played the regal role of Elsie Tanner in *Coronation Street,* the long-running TV soap about Northern working-class life. This is indirect yet unarguable pedigree, rather like the Royal Family being related to Barbara Cartland.

Another part of his pedigree is equally interesting, and had been unknown even to Mr. Blair himself until the journos started trampling over his life. *The Daily Mail,* acting no doubt in the public interest, and surely without any hope that it might turn up an embarrassing secret, commissioned genealogical research into the Blair family. It had frequently been reported that the new leader's paternal grandfather was a rigger in the Govan shipyard by the name of William Blair. This added useful proletarian authenticity, given that Tony's father, Leo, was not only an academic but a lifelong Conservative and convinced Thatcherite. The investigation discovered, however, that Leo's true parents were not the Blairs but a pair of music-hall performers named Charles Parsons and Cecilia Ridgeway; they had been on a Northern tour at the time of Leo's birth, and put him out to board with a Mr. and Mrs. Blair. The distant tang of illegitimacy is scarcely scandalous; more to the point is the extraordinary coincidence that both the present Prime Minister (son of the artiste Tom Ball) and the present Leader of the Opposition have music-hall blood in their veins. That they should end up heading their parties in the House of Commons seems Lamarckian: positive proof of the inheritance of acquired characteristics.

Most echelons of the press also went on the trawl for the personal stuff. In this they have so far been disappointed: Ugly Rumours has proved no more than the name of a band. For instance, Mr. Blair must be the only student rocker in the entire 1970s who never took drugs. What's wrong with the University of Oxford? President Clinton went there and failed to inhale; Tony Blair didn't even touch his fingers to the smoldering sin. As one of his Oxford contemporaries put it, "Listen, I would know, and the answer is definitely no. Unlike most of us, the guy hardly ever drank." *Whaaat?* And then there is the other thing, the thing that people, especially young people, tend to do when left alone in pairs; but even here it seems that the state troopers will not be called in evidence. At Oxford, according to *The Independent on Sunday*, the consensus was that Tony did not "get laid." Unbelievable: you'd think the fellow was running for the See of Canterbury. On the other hand, this is probably just as well, since the insertion of overt ethical content into British politics—such as Mr. Blair has done in recent weeks—normally leads to self-slaughter. No sooner had the Tories launched their "Back to Basics" campaign last year than it emerged that numerous Tory MPs had been getting back, or up, to some pretty basic things themselves. Does Mr. Blair have any sinister, or even ordinary, peculiarities? Well, I can add one speck to the dunghill of data currently accumulating, which may or may not be indicative. Anthony Howard, the seasoned political observer and former editor of *The New Statesman*, reported to me in awed tones this action-man detail: "He is the fastest eater I've ever come across. I mean, I'm a quick eater, but I was only halfway through my liver and he'd cleaned his plate!"

Mr. Blair's victory was a success for those in the Labour Party currently called "modernizers." Political struggles are in part struggles of nomenclature: pin the best label on your own chest, and slap the worst on your opponent's back, preferably at a place where the knife goes in the most easily. In the Tory Party there was the enduring scuffle between "wets" and "dries" (which has elided into one between "consolidators" and "radicals"). In the Labour Party for a long time it was "moderates" versus "militants" (which some arrant compromisers tried to solve linguistically, by calling themselves "militant moderates"). More recently, it has been "modernizers" versus "traditionalists." The modernizers sought, apart from anything else, to make Labour electable again: this involved smartening the Party up, democratizing its electoral systems, reducing the influence of the trade unions, and accepting a certain amount of market reality. Such activities are regarded by some as classic right-wing middle-class treachery. During the leadership election the far left in the constituencies wittily dubbed Blair "the liquidationist candidate," and the depths of suspicion with which the modernizers are viewed can be judged by this recent remark from the veteran *gauchiste* Tony Benn: "If you look at apartheid in South Africa, it didn't end because Nelson Mandela had a pink rose, a new suit, a policy review, and Saatchi & Saatchi." However, the modernizers have not only the ascendancy but also the better label. "The traditionalists *hate* being called traditionalists," I was told by one Westminster correspondent. And they won't even be allowed to call themselves left-wing for much longer if the nameplate stealing continues. Here is Tony Blair during the run-up to the election: "Many of those that call themselves left aren't on the left at all if left means radical. They simply represent a kind of conservatism."

Thus is the old left neutered with words. For the modernizers, musty, prelapsarian socialism is dead. And such is their confidence that they are now even reclaiming the very word *socialism*. It used to be a bogey term, and failed to appear in the 1992 Labour manifesto, presumably on the ground that it was deemed to induce projectile vomiting among the Don't-Knows. It is now coming back into shy usage again, purged of its old associations like a paint-thickened door plunged into an acid bath and coming out all shiny new pine. In Tony Blair's words, from a campaign speech in Cardiff: "The essential belief is that a strong united society is necessary to individual achievement. That is why we call it social-ism." Mr. Blair even published a Fabian Society pamphlet, timed to coincide with his election, boldly entitled "Socialism." His socialism, or, to insert its occasional and diluting hyphen, social-ism, is not that of the command economy, class warfare, and public ownership, but rather that of state partnership and gentle interventionism, fostered by those "notions associated with the left— social justice, cohesion, equality of opportunity, and community."

Tony Blair's acceptance speech was not one of those occasions on which you announce policy; rather, it was a time for showing yourself to the people and playing your theme song. Mr. Blair did this very well. He is not a great orator, though in opposing Mr. Major he does not need to be: he is already Demosthenes to a speak-your-weight machine. And, in any case, orating simultaneously to a crowded hall and a television camera is probably an impossible job; like being a stage and TV actor at the same time. But he seemed seriously pleased, sufficiently moved to leave a tremor in his voice, and he spoke with the sort of zeal that makes average viewers slightly embarrassed if they do not feel quite the same zeal themselves. (This is no bad thing, since not every benefit brought into the world comes through virtue and probity; guilt and hypocrisy also get things done.) Mr. Blair's theme song, like all theme songs, consists not so much of sound bites as word bites, and his speech would not be greatly betrayed by simply playing the highlighted words in the order he used them: "Responsibility/trust/trust/service/dedication/dignity/pride/ trust/mission/renewal/mission/hope/change/responsibility/mission/spirit/community/community/pride/pride/socialism/change/wrong/right/wrong/right/wrong/right/communities/passion/reason/change/change/change/solidarity/community/anew/afresh/inspire/crusade/change/progress/faith/serve/serve/serve."

A few days later, I found myself in the Shadow Cabinet room at the House of Commons awaiting an audience with the new leader. It is a high-ceilinged, rather gloomy office overlooking the north end of Westminster Bridge, and it was in end-of-term disarray: the conference table snapped apart at its join, the heavy green-leather chairs stacked higgledy-piggledy. Two things stood out in this somber space: the elegant brass door hinges by Pugin, and a volume bound in bright scarlet leather lying next to Mr. Blair's abandoned jacket. Aha, I thought, let's check out the browsing material he keeps for those quiet moments between interviews. It was a copy of the New Testament. A sea mist of agnostic dismay descended on me; I mean, I knew the fellow was a serious Christian and all that, but this was taking it a bit far. He'll be turning the money changers out of Westminster next. . . . Then my thumb loosed the title page to disclose a pasted-in presentation slip, dated and signed by Tony Newton, Leader of the House of Commons. Mr. Blair, it appeared, had been to see the

Queen that afternoon, and this was his school prize for having been made a member of the Privy Council. I confess to a certain relief at this point.

"You'll find him very charming," people had said beforehand; and, yes, this was the case. During the campaign he had been stuck with the pretty-boy tag by various ill-wishers; he is not as good-looking as this suggests, though of course in the context of the House of Commons he is incredibly good-looking. There is a relaxed thoughtfulness about him, plus at times the wary air of one who has just had to cram for examinations in subjects he didn't know he was going to be tested on for years to come. But then Smith's death and his own sudden apotheosis had come in a dizzying rush.

Given that Mr. Blair is fluent, telegenic, and young, the first line of attack is to accuse him of lacking ideas. Anthony Howard once watched him address a meeting of the political pressure group Charter 88: "He absolutely charmed them, but he didn't say a chipolata sausage." Of course, it's not essential for politicians to have ideas, and sometimes they may be liked specifically for not having any. This was certainly the case with John Major when he took over from Mrs. Thatcher: he was seen as a decent, middling chap whose decency would do service for positive thought. This is probably still part of Mr. Major's dwindling allure, since on the only two occasions that he has visibly lapsed into having an idea, or a powerful belief, or at least a personal view that doesn't come with the official limo, he has made himself look ridiculous. Early in his Premiership, he made an impassioned plea for more motorway toilets; for this cross-legged moan he was treated with wry compassion. More recently, however, Mr. Major came up with a second idea: that vagrancy should be denounced. Begging, he told a Bristol newspaper in May, was an "eyesore," and maximum legal penalties should be enforced against those who extended the cupped paw: "It is an offensive thing to beg. It is unnecessary. So I think people should be very rigorous with it." Even if Mr. Major was at the time trying to woo the Tory right for the European elections, this was a doubly inept piece of politics. First, because everyone who lives in a city knows that begging has greatly increased during the lifetime of the present administration. Second, because Mr. Major's sudden expertise in the matter of down-and-outs left him wide open to the obvious riposte: that it takes one to know one.

But in a wider context a Conservative attack on Mr. Blair for lacking ideas would have its ironic side. The Conservatives are still eking out the brainpan that they came in with fifteen years ago. And as the Thatcherite impetus dribbles away, Thatcherite "ideas" become ever wackier. In April, for instance, the Adam Smith Institute, a think tank of the Conservative right, produced its vision of Britain in the year 2020 (a vision predicated, it goes without saying, on the continuation of Tory rule until then). The institute has been going since 1977, and as its director, Dr. Madsen Pirie, said a few years ago, "We propose things which people regard as on the edge of lunacy. The next thing you know, they're on the edge of policy." Dr. Pirie has himself invented the Pirie knot, a cure for men whose bow ties humiliatingly detumesce to a level below the horizontal. "With the conventional knot," he explains, "you don't know until you've finished tying it how it's going to come out. I tie a layered knot, constructed systematically so that you get it right every time."

20-20 Vision: Targets for Britain's Future is the published attempt of Dr. Pirie and twenty-five co-thinkers to do for Britain what the director has already done for the bow tie. By the end of the next quarter century, a reknotted nation would, if all went well, be able to gaze out upon the following things: a basic rate of income tax at 10 percent, with a top rate at 20 percent; a growth rate which doubles the standard of living every twenty years ("this is very high by the standards of the Twentieth Century, but it was a century which taught us many mistakes to avoid"); elimination of most major illnesses; legitimation of the "black" economy; renovation of all housing stock; privatized motorways with electronic pricing, guided buses with regenerative braking systems, and the extinction of auto crime (a felony in which Britain is currently the European leader); nursery education for all at three, and foreign-language learning for all at five; an end to homelessness ("We should bear in mind the image which Britain presents to foreign visitors when they see people sleeping in shop doorways and begging on the streets"—so that's where John Major got his "idea"); life expectancy of a hundred; the restoration of English wild-flower meadows and the fresh glory of "prairie acres covered by exotic crops of lupins"; the reforestation of Britain, raising its wooded proportion from 5 percent to 65 percent; and finally, the reintroduction into this cheap, safe, healthy, newly fronded environment of bears, wolves, and beavers.

One of the key moments for those who endured, rather than enjoyed, the Thatcher years came when the Prime Minister, late in her reign, explained to a women's magazine that "there is no such thing as society." It was like being in one of those dragging dreams of irrational persecution, from which you seem unable to wake, when your tormentor finally turns to you and says, "But can't you see, it's because you're wearing a white shirt and carrying a newspaper." Oh, *now* I understand, you reflect to yourself in your new unconscious wisdom. I thought you were persecuting me because you were mad, and of course you are still mad, indeed even madder than I thought before, but at least I can follow what it is you thought you might have been up to.

Most people, of course, tend to believe that there is such a thing as society, and Blairism is in part a direct riposte to that Thatcherian negative. His is an ethical socialism, out of R. H. Tawney and Archbishop Temple, based on the necessity of communal action if the individual life is to have its best chance of fulfillment. "The power of all . . . used for the good of each," as Blair put it in his acceptance speech. "That is what socialism means to me." It still, of course, means something different to the traditionalists in his party. As one left-wing MP privately put it, "If you tried supporting the 1945 Labour manifesto today, you'd be thrown out of the Party as a Trotskyist."

Blairism, or Labour modernity, stands for, or believes in, or hopes to get elected on, the following: a dynamic market economy with a greater wealth-creating base; a strong and cohesive society that protects the individual from the vagaries and cruelties of the market; improved education, higher skills, better training; a rethought welfare system, aimed at ending long-term dependency and getting people back to work; pro-Europeanism; a Bill of Rights, a Freedom of Information Act, and an elected second chamber; a Welsh Assembly and a Scottish Parliament.

Blairism also believes in keeping the trade unions at a distance. To Party modernizers, the folk memory of union barons turning up at No. 10 to discuss economic policy over beer and sandwiches is an embarrassment. Blair was Shadow Employment Secretary under Neil Kinnock, from 1989 to 1992. There, according to his fellow modernizer and fellow Durhamite MP Giles Radice, "he made the unions face up to a modernized system of individual rights for workers on the Continental model rather than collectivist rights. He also persuaded the trade unions that it was coercive and no longer appropriate to support the closed shop." On top of this, Blair was a key supporter of a new system of electing the Labour leader by the individual votes of MPs, Party members, and unionists, thereby cutting out the traditional union bloc vote. For Anthony Howard, "the union bosses had their industrial strength destroyed by Mrs. Thatcher and their political strength destroyed by John Smith and Tony Blair." Now Blair says things like "It is not the function of a Labour Government to come in and do particular favors for the trade union movement." This may sound reasonable, even right, but it is historically heretical. Imagine a Tory leader promising that when his Government came in there would be no special favors for those who contribute to Conservative Party funds; for employers, businessmen, and the City; for big landowners, rich people, and posh people.

Blairism also accepts that the long postwar battle about public versus private ownership of industries and utilities is over—and lost. The program of "privatization" (or the selling off of national assets) was opposed with varying amounts of doggedness, resignation, and ferocity by Labour; now it is grudgingly accepted as economic force majeure. For instance, Labour supporters of varying ideological hues feel strongly about the sale in 1989 of the water industry. There is something almost totemic about water (this stuff that comes out of the ground, that falls from the sky, and which somehow ought to belong to those upon whom it falls) and therefore something particularly offensive about the privatized industry's quick lesson in monopoly capitalism: greatly increased prices, large profits, and highly paid executives enriching one another with nice rights issues. When I put all this to Blair, he replied, "Do I believe the water industry should be privatized? No, I don't. Do I think that any serious Labour Government, certainly in the immediate term, is going to be sitting round the Cabinet table, and, let us say there is two billion pounds to be spent, that the hands are going to go up for it to be spent repurchasing the share capital in the water industry—well, it won't happen, so you may as well not mislead people into thinking that it will." Besides, "there is very little you can't do by control and that you can only do by ownership."

This is an honest reply, if dismaying to some. But then government is about not being able to do as much as you want to, or as much as you believe in; it is about the curdling of idealism. Even so, there are times when Mr. Blair seems to be pitching it a bit high. Take this lofty sentence from his election manifesto: "An education system which serves an elite and neglects the majority is an affront to our morality and a drain on our economy." At any time in my political awareness, and on any normal constructions of the words, this ought to indicate an intention to abolish the public schools. But the words don't mean that, do they? "No." Why not? Isn't it "an affront to morality" that the hazard of parental wealth dictates a child's education? "It is an affront," he agrees cautiously, "that the quality of your education is determined by the amount of wealth that you have. But the question is how you deal with it. Do you deal with it by abolishing the ability of people to educate their children privately, or do you concentrate on raising the standards of state education?" Why not do both at the same time? "I think not, either as a matter of principle or as a matter of political reality." It seems almost unfair to press Mr. Blair on this, since he is committed to educating his own children in the public sector, and abolitionism hasn't been on the Labour agenda for some while, but he in a way brought it up. "You've got to decide in politics where you want the dividing line to be," he concludes.

Abolishing the public schools, he judges, "would be perceived as in principle wrong, and vindictive. . . . It would inevitably place the dividing line between ourselves and the Conservatives in the wrong place."

Mr. Blair is already, and will continue to be, a most practical politician. The scrap, he knows, is over the middle ground (that is why his party elected him), and there is no point fighting over that distant hill, even if it does have a fine view. Someone once said that there was only half an inch of difference between Labour and the Conservatives, yet it was the half inch within which we all live. Mr. Blair is idealistic without being ideological, which naturally makes him an object of suspicion to his left wing. Anthony Howard, who is still awaiting delivery of chipolata sausages, saucily refers to Blair as "Little Boy Blue," for his rightist leanings. On the other hand, Howard acknowledges the atypical strength of the current leader's position. He has arrived at his present eminence carrying little baggage and few debts. He owes the unions nothing. He is less of a machine politician than his two predecessors, Kinnock and Smith. "That's his asset," says Howard. "He can cut the painter with the past."

Certainly Mr. Blair offers the Labour Party its likeliest chance since 1979 of a return to power. (And, as a further modernizing footnote, his success would put the first working wife into No. 10.) You would have to be cruel–or Conservative–not to wish him well: few countries benefit from extended periods of single-party rule. Labour is at present comparatively united, the electorate comparatively pissed off with the Tories, and the Tories themselves comparatively rattled. As one unnamed Tory minister brazenly said of Blair, "We still don't know whether to argue that he has no policies or to argue his policies are bad ones." For the moment, it is Labour who is setting the agenda and the Tories who are fretfully responding. Thus, no sooner had the words *full employment* been bandied around for the few weeks of the Labour election campaign than the Employment Secretary, David Hunt, addressed a Trades Union Congress meeting and committed the Government to such a policy as well. This was an incredibly conciliatory, or wet, thing for a Tory Minister to do, and suggested seismic rumblings of panic. It is unlikely to have been a coincidence that a mere fortnight later, in Mr. Major's Cabinet reshuffle, Mr. Hunt found himself suddenly without employment at Employment.

Blair sees the main danger between now and the general election (which may not come until 1996 or 1997) as "a sense of complacency on the part of the Party." There are others: that he has longer to run than is ideal, that his face might not seem quite so fresh in a couple of years, that his evangelical language might begin to sound preachy, his talk of crusades and missions a bit too happy-clappy for our jaundiced times. There is also the danger that Labour's long-term strategy–actively modeled on Mrs. Thatcher's 1979 game plan–of enunciating principles and general themes rather than detailed, price-able policy may come to seem evasive. And what is there to fear from the Tories? "Their election strategy is no great mystery," he replies. "They will go for some large-scale tax cut. They will probably back themselves into a fairly anti-European position. And they will throw as much at the Labour Party as it is humanly possible or inhumanly possible to dredge up."

At Westminster Abbey, the Grimethorpe Colliery Band's plain-tive presence had made a fitting prelude to a service that, like Tony Blair's manifesto, might have been titled "Change and National Re-newal." There was the reading from the Book of Isaiah ("And they shall build the old wastes, they shall raise up the former desolations, and they shall repair the waste cities, the desolations of many genera-tions"). There was the hymn by R. B. Y. Scott which seemed full of Blairist principles ("Bring justice to our land,/that all may dwell se-cure,/and finely build for days to come/foundations that endure") and aptly short on policy specifics. There was even the Archbishop of Canterbury quoting Václav Havel: "I am deeply convinced that poli-tics is not essentially a disreputable business, and in so far as it is, it is politicians who have made it so."

The Archbishop also quoted John Smith's belief that "politics ought to be a moral activity." As the Tory Party seems increasingly weary at the center and increasingly sleazy at the edges, as its thinkers and dreamers go yelping off into the reforested landscape babbling over the return of bears, income tax at 10 percent, and prairie acres covered with exotic crops of lupins, it's not surprising that Labour is currently in the political and moral ascendancy. Now one publicly avowed Christian has replaced another as leader of the Party. "Cleanse the body of this nation through the glory of the Lord," sang many if not all of the congregation at Westminster Abbey.

Tony Blair won the leadership with uplifting rhetoric which starred the word *radical;* like his rival candidates, he deliberately invoked the famous year of 1945, when Clement Attlee's Labour Government instituted a fundamental shift in the national structure. I asked Giles Radice about Mr. Blair's hot selling line. He replied, "He said something rather clever. He said, 'I'm not a revisionist, I'm a radical.' That's balls, actually. He's trying to be Harold Wilson. And he needs to be a mixture of Gaitskell and Wilson." One of the constant fascinations—and rhythmical deceptions—of politics lies in the disparity between the Onward Christian Soldiers rhetoric and the subsequent announcement that, sorry, folks, we can't afford the lance and the breastplate, and by the way, the horse has been downsized to a mule. The name of Hugh Gaitskell (John Smith's predecessor as official lost leader and recipient of transferred hope) is safe enough to invoke; that of Harold Wilson—remembered now less for the libertarian legislation of his first years in office than for the pragmatic divagations of his later ones—does not lift the heart. Tony Blair releases optimism in many for his youth, his intelligence, his expressions of idealism, his promise to cleanse, and his electability. He may very well be the British Prime Minister as the century turns. But millenarians would be premature in renting space on mountaintops.

August 1994

Index

Addams, Charles, 172
Agincourt: fake spur, 26; Maastricht compared to, 98
Akhmatova, Anna: abused by Zhdanov, 25
Alcohol: Liebfraumilch and Ron Brown MP, 18–21; champagne and Ron Brown MP, 20; sparkling wine and Ron Brown MP, 20; "Johnnie Hawker" whisky, 26; unspecified liquor and Patrick Nicholls MP, 43–44; Nicholas Ridley's "smallest glass of wine," 46; Glenda Jackson's champagne, 126; none allowed in Camden Council chamber, 128; Queen Mother's gin-and-tonic, 132; bought by Norman Lamont, 145–150; sold by Lloyd's Names, 181; collapse of port market, 181; sales on cross-Channel ferries, 294; Tony Blair, 301
Ambrosia creamed rice: bought by Americans, 35
Amis, Kingsley: devotion to Mrs Thatcher, 223–224
Angerstein, John Julius, 216
Animals: dream about hamsters, xvi;

Mrs. Thatcher as she-elephant, 7; Sir Anthony Meyer, 6–7; Rector of Stiffkey's lion, 21; fur-bearing trout, 24; Nicholas Ridley as lizard, 33; Geoffrey Howe as rabbit, 47–49; Geoffrey Howe as Rottweiler in drag, 50; Geoffrey Howe as bee, 51; Michael Heseltine as hornet, 52; rats and Hampton Court Maze, 76; Churchill's British lion, 97; Labour policy on animals in transit, 102; Labour policy on blood sports, 121; Mister Major (horse), 123; Andrew Neil, 136–137; Old English rabbit in Deptford, 179; bird designs for £1 coins 168–172; cat-mortgaging, 176; West Country pug dog, 190; Nigel Short as bunny rabbit, 245; Britain as sleeping hog, 269; rabies and the Channel Tunnel, 287–288; seals, 289; why the British love animals, 291–292; return of bears, wolves, beavers, 306; horse becomes mule, 311
Anne, Princess: only Royal with rising popularity, 140; remarries, 153; lack of commemorative mugs produced, 153